C

An Introduction with
Advanced Applications

C
An Introduction with Advanced Applications

David Masters

Department of Computer Science,
American University of Paris

Prentice Hall

New York   London   Toronto   Sydney   Tokyo   Singapore

First published in 1991 by
Prentice Hall International (UK) Ltd,
66 Wood Lane End, Hemel Hempstead,
Hertfordshire, HP2 4RG
A division of
Simon & Schuster International Group

Printed and bound in Great Britain at
Page Bros, Norwich

Library of Congress Cataloging-in-Publication Data

Masters, David, 1945–
    C: An Introduction with advanced applications /
David Masters.
      p. cm.
    Includes bibliographical references and index.
    ISBN 0–13–480781–2 (paperback)
      1. C (Computer program language)   I. Title.
QA76.73.C15M365   1990
005.26′2–dc20   90–45281
                                        CIP

British Library Cataloguing in Publication Data

Masters, David
    C: An Introduction with advanced applications.
    1. Computer systems. Programming languages
    I. Title
    005.13

    ISBN 0–13–480781–2

Contents

Preface

The growth in the use of the C language since its early days, when it was a semi-private language in use within a small part of one organization, has been remarkable. Its importance and central role in application development have now been recognized by its being 'blessed' with an ANSI standard.

The success of the language comes from its combination of high-level language constructs suitable for writing well structured programs with facilities for manipulating 'low-level' objects such as bits or addresses in ways which usually require assembler language.

A programming language is not just a way of instructing a machine, it is a tool for thinking about the solution of problems. C provides many facilities (such as bit manipulation operations, unions and pointers to values, structures, functions and other pointers) which, while not being unique to C, are nevertheless not widely understood. An understanding of programming techniques based on these facilities can lead to novel, elegant and efficient solutions to many common problems. It is important that programmers study many programming languages, even those who only write in one language. For example, the more modern languages introduce concepts such as abstract data types, generic data structures, modularity, encapsulation and object-oriented programming. It is a remarkable tribute to the flexibility of the C language that although thinking about these topics has changed and advanced considerably since C was first invented, a C programmer can apply all of them, and enjoy the benefits they bring.

It is to this end that the present book describes some of these more advanced ways of using C. The reader will need some experience of programming, preferably in a structured language such as Pascal. Apart from the first three chapters, which are a concise introduction to the basics of the language and constitute a sort of 'conversion course' for a Pascal (or whatever) programmer, most of the book is devoted to data structures, algorithms to manipulate them and ways of using them to solve problems.

There is an emphasis on interesting and useful algorithms; topics covered include Boyer and Moore's string searching algorithm, evaluating algebraic expressions, constructing Huffman codes, finite state automata and using bit-strings to implement sets. It is intended that as many as possible of the example programs or functions should be useful either directly or with slight modification. In effort to make them all as portable as possible they are all in ANSI C and do not assume ranges of values greater than the minimum requirements stipulated in the standard. There is also no use of facilities (such as graphics libraries) which are specific to particular machines or operating systems.

It is a great pleasure to to be able to thank the people who have assisted me by reading and commenting on the material during preparation, by correcting errors and by making invaluable suggestions for improvement. Their help has improved the book greatly and is much appreciated, but all remaining flaws are, of course, my own. Apart from my students, who have often had material inflicted upon them in draft form, I should like to thank the critical contribution of Barbara Raither and the particular help of John Hughes and John Brazier and the patience of my editor Helen Martin.

David Masters

1

Introduction to C
Programming

1.1. Background to the C Language

C was designed originally for writing the Unix^{TM} operating system by Dennis M.
Ritchie in the 1970s and is a descendant of B which was itself derived from BCPL, a
typeless 'system-oriented' language. The language has evolved since its earliest days
and many versions have come into existence. In order to resolve the conflicts that this
situation has inevitably caused, ANSI (American National Standards Institute) has been
working on a standard for the language and it is this version of the language that will be
described in this book. The standard accepted the language as described by Kernighan
and Ritchie [KER 78] but also added new facilities, many of which had already become
widely accepted in various implementations. Although this book uses standard C, any
facility that is unlikely to be provided by an older, pre-standard compiler will be noted
and the old method will also be described. Although a standard exists, the language
continues to evolve, and another important version is C++ [STRO 86] which adds
many new facilities, including object-oriented constructs (the suitability of the name
will become clear later). However, discussion of C++ is outside the scope of this book.

C has facilities for writing well structured programs but allows low-level operations
to be performed when necessary. That is, one can use machine addresses directly,
explicitly request that hardware registers be used for storage, manipulate individual
machine bits, abuse type rules and commit all the other depravities so beloved of bit-
twiddlers. Most C compilers generate fairly efficient code, and a good optimizing
compiler generates programs which approach the efficiency of hand-written assembler
code.

When C is chosen as the language for a project, it is often because of its low-level
facilities, its efficiency or the means it provides for splitting large programs into
separate modules. However, many programmers enjoy using it because of the freedom

of expression it allows compared with languages such as Pascal or Ada and also because of the techniques which can be used in C which are difficult or impossible in most other languages, for instance pointers to functions, unions or pointers to pointers. Thus a C programmer has more ways of expressing the solution of a problem than, say, a COBOL programmer.

The language tends to be criticized on three counts: unreadability, lack of enforced programming discipline and poor error checking.

Unreadability arises from the language's conciseness and can be countered by careful layout and commenting. The lack of discipline arises from the 'freedom of expression' mentioned above, which is so attractive to certain types of programmer, but which can lead to 'cleverness' at the expense of clarity or maintainability. It can also lead to confusing variations in style when several programmers work together on the same project. Overcoming it requires adherence to standards both of language and style and a disciplined program development methodology. The criticism concerning weak error checking is valid compared with languages such as Pascal, which demand that a system provide very strict checking at both compile and execution time. C puts a greater burden on the programmer to be careful, but there are tools (the best known of which is Lint) and techniques which, if applied consistently, can reduce the problem. Some of these techniques will be described later in this book as will areas where special care is needed.

C is widely used for developing personal computer applications, operating systems, compilers and communications software, as well as day-to-day application programming. It offers two particular challenges to its users: firstly to master its power and secondly to curb this mastery in the interest of good taste (otherwise known as sound software engineering practice).

1.2.   Two Simple Programs

Kernighan and Ritchie posit that the first program that one should attempt in any language should produce the text:

Hello, World.

Since it is impossible to improve on their proposition a (slightly modified) version of their solution is shown below:

```
/*  With acknowledgments to Kernighan and Ritchie   */
#include <stdio.h>
main( ) {
    printf("Hello, world\n");
}
```

The following points should clarify this program:

- Every complete C program contains one function called **main**. (A function corresponds to what other languages call a procedure or subprogram.)

- The ( ) after **main** are used for parameters (described in Chapter 4) and must always be present, even if they are empty.

- The { and } serve the same purpose as **begin** and **end** in Ada or Pascal; they enclose a block, in this case the main program block.

- **printf** is a general purpose output function.

- Strings of characters are enclosed in " ".

- \n stands for newline. The \ notation is called an *escape sequence* and is used for denoting *control* characters, i.e. characters with no printed form (glyph) which are used to control terminal devices. Other escape sequences are:

\t	tab	\b	backspace
\"	double quote	\f	form feed
\\	back slash (\)	\'	single quote
\r	carriage return	\0	the null character

- In C, the semicolon is used to terminate statements, unlike some other languages in which the semicolon is a statement separator. This means that a ; cannot be omitted before }.

- The **#include** introduces a directive to the C preprocessor (see Chapter 13) causing it to include the contents of the file whose name immediately follows.

- **stdio.h** is a file containing the definitions of input/output functions and is provided by all C systems. The pointed brackets indicate that this is a system file rather than a user's file. User file names are enclosed in double quotes.

- /* and */ enclose comments; these have no effect on the program but (one hopes) explain it to humans. A comment starts with /* and continues until */. Comments cannot be nested within one another and forgetting a */ can be catastrophic.

To illustrate a more advanced program, the example below will accept as input a date in the form **day/month/year** and will print the day of the week on which that date falls by using Zeller's congruence:

```
/*  Calculate the day on which any date falls using Zeller's congruence */
#include <stdio.h>
main() {
    int Day, Month, Year, YearInCentury, Century,
        AdjustedMonth, DayOfWeek;
    char ch;

    printf("Write a date in the form day/month/year\n");
    scanf("%d%c%d%c%d", &Day, &ch, &Month, &ch, &Year);

    do {            /*  start of loop  */
        YearInCentury = Year % 100;   Century = Year / 100;

        /*  Adjust the month so that March is month 1 and February 12 */
        AdjustedMonth = Month - 2;
        if (AdjustedMonth <= 0) {
            AdjustedMonth += 12;
            --YearInCentury;
        }

        /*  Calculate the day of the week with Sunday = 0, Monday = 1 etc.*/
        DayOfWeek = ((13 * AdjustedMonth - 1) / 5 + Day + YearInCentury +
                    YearInCentury / 4 + Century / 4 - 2 * Century) % 7;

        /*  Print the result  */
        printf("\n%d/%d/%d is a ", Day, Month, Year);
        switch(DayOfWeek) {
            case 0: printf("Sunday\n");        break;
            case 1: printf("Monday\n");        break;
            case 2: printf("Tuesday\n");       break;
            case 3: printf("Wednesday\n");     break;
            case 4: printf("Thursday\n");      break;
            case 5: printf("Friday\n");        break;
            case 6: printf("Saturday\n");      break;
        }
        printf("Write another date: (0/0/0 will stop the program)\n");
        scanf("%d%c%d%c%d", &Day, &ch, &Month, &ch, &Year);
    } while (Year > 0);  /*  end of loop  */
}
```

While this program does not use C in the way that an experienced programmer necessarily would regard as the 'best way' (the **scanf** function is called twice and the **switch** statement is not a good way of printing the names of the days), it uses many of the facilities of the language, in particular:

- The program declares *variables* at the start of the main program block; **Day**, **Month**, **Year**, etc., are declared to hold integers whilst **ch** can hold a single character.

- Most of the program is contained within a single loop which takes the form:

```
do {
    . . .
} while (Year > 0);
```

  The effect of this statement is to repeat the statements between **{** and **}** until the condition after **while** becomes false. The program repeatedly calculates the day until the user types a value for **Year** that is no longer greater than zero.

- The first parameter of **printf** (the part enclosed in double quotes) is the *control string* which contains any text to be printed directly plus the *conversion specifications* for any values which are also to be printed. A conversion specification is preceded by a percent sign %; %**d** represents a place where a decimal number is to be printed and %**c** a character (they are described in more detail in Chapter 2). After the control string come parameters separated by commas; these are expressions which give values to be printed, and each one corresponds to a conversion specification in the control string.

- **scanf** is a general purpose function for reading values from a file of input data or some terminal device; the significance of the ampersand (**&**) is described in detail in Chapter 4, but let it suffice for now that it indicate that the value of the accompanying variable will be changed by a call to the **scanf** function. As with **printf**, the first parameter is a format but this time it describes the layout and types of the input data.

- There are two conditional statements in C, both of which are used in this program. The first is the **if** statement illustrated by:

```
if (AdjustedMonth <= 0) {
    AdjustedMonth += 12;
    --YearInCentury;
}
```

  which will obey the two statements between **{** and **}** only if the condition in parentheses (**AdjustedMonth <= 0**) is true.

- The second conditional statement used is:

```
switch(DayOfWeek) {
    case 0: printf("Sunday\n");
            break;
    case 1: printf("Monday\n");
            break;

    . . .

}
```

which compares the integer value **DayOfWeek** with each of the constants 0, 1, 2 etc. If a match is found, the statements between the **case** label (the number before the colon) and the **break** statement are obeyed. If no match is found then no action is taken.

• This program uses many operators, most of which have obvious meanings, but a few need a little explanation:

=   is the assignment operator; the value of its right-hand operand is copied into its left operand. A series of = can be used to assign a value to several variables at the same time, e.g.

        a = b = c = 3;

The assignment operator = is easily confused with ==, the comparison operator and care should be taken with this.

%   is the modulus operator. It gives the remainder when the value of its left-hand operand is divided by the value of its right-hand operand.

/   is the division operator.

--   causes its operand to be decremented by one. For example, if **x** holds the value 27 then --**x** will leave **x** holding the value 26.

+=   adds the value of the expression on its right to the variable on its left. Thus, **AdjustedMonth += 12** is an abbreviation for:

        AdjustedMonth = AdjustedMonth + 12.

There is a whole group of such operators. The other arithmetic ones are -=, *=, /= and %= and are discussed in Chapter 2.

1.3.   Lexical Requirements and Program Layout

An identifier is a name chosen by a programmer to represent a variable, type, function, etc. An identifier can contain letters, digits and the underscore character _ but must start with a letter. The underscore character is treated as a letter. C distinguishes the case of letters in identifiers; in other words **Capital** and **CAPITAL** are regarded as distinct, although it is bad practice to use two identifiers which are distinguished only by the case of some of their component characters. An identifier can be any length but some older compilers only treat the first eight characters as being significant. Such a compiler would regard **PiecesOfEight** and **PiecesOfCheese** as equivalent. Also, some systems have linkers which have strong restrictions on acceptable names. The linker is the system program which is responsible for joining together as one unit the different parts of a program which has been compiled as separate modules. Some old linkers are not sensitive to case of letters and some accept only fairly short name.

It is a common practice to type variable names in lower case and constants in capitals; for example, **don_juan** might be used for a variable, **PENELOPE** for a constant. In this book we shall not use underscores in variable names as we prefer to write names such as the above in the style: **DonJuan**. This offers an advantage on compilers which only recognize a limited number of characters in an identifier.

Words which have special significance in the language such as **while**, **int**, **do**, **for** etc. must be written in lower case and may not be used as identifiers. The reserved words are:

auto	extern	sizeof
break	float	static
case	for	struct
char	goto	switch
continue	if	typedef
default	int	union
do	long	unsigned
double	register	void
else	return	while
enum	short	

Some compilers may add other reserved words to this list and some non-ANSI compilers may not include **enum** or **void**.

All professional programmers claim that programs should be clear and readable (and of course claim that theirs always are); that C permits programs to be obscure, tricky and arcane is, unfortunately, also true. However, by adopting a disciplined approach to layout, style, commenting and choice of programming constructs, it is possible to write C programs that are as readable as programs in any other language. The following points may help indicate approaches to good style:

White space, meaning use of spaces, tabs and blank lines, improves readability. For example

```
(sum+=term/=2)<=epsilon
```

is a little less readable than:

```
(sum += term /= 2) <= epsilon
```

In general, it is a good idea to surround assigning operators by space characters. Blank lines should be used to separate functions and logically distinct sections of a program.

Indentation and statement separation can be used to show the scope of a control statement. Thus the following program fragment, which prints Fibonacci numbers,

```
fib1 = fib2 = 1;
printf("%d, %d", fib1, fib2);
do {
    fib = fib1 + fib2;
    fib1 = fib2;
    fib2 = fib;
    printf(", %d", fib);
} while (fib < 1000);
```

is more readable than:

```
fib1=fib2=1;printf("%d, %d", fib1, fib2);
do {fib=fib1+fib2;fib1=fib2;fib2=fib;
printf(", %d", fib);} while (fib<1000);
```

The first version uses indentation to show which statements belong inside the **do ... while** loop, there is only one statement per line, and space characters separate the components of a statement.

In general it is a good idea to use only one statement per line, but this rule can be broken if the statements are very simple and related, such as assignments initializing a few variables. For example, instead of:

```
i = 2;
j = 4;
k = 6;
```

it can be just as clear to use:

```
i = 2;   j = 4;   k = 6;
```

where the statements are separated by several spaces rather than a new line.

Part of the purpose of indentation is to distinguish statement blocks and to show which symbols are intended to match. Two styles are commonly used for this. The first is illustrated by:

```
if (ch == '\n')
{
    ++Lines;
    CharPosition = 0;
}
else
{
    ++CharPosition;
    if (CharPosition > MaxLength)
    {
        printf("Line too long\n");
        exit();
    }
}
```

where each { and } is on a separate line and each } is directly beneath its matching {. The second method would write this fragment as:

```
if (ch == '\n') {
    ++Lines;
    CharPosition = 0;
}
else {
    ++CharPosition;
    if (CharPosition > MaxLength) {
        printf("Line too long\n");
        exit();
    }
}
```

where each } is below the reserved word introducing a section of a control statement. The examples in this book use the second form because it is more concise.

Meaningful identifier names help comprehension enormously: **LineNumber** is better than **L**, or even **LinNo**. Programmers should not be unduly deterred by length when choosing a good name although over-zealous application of this principle can look a little ridiculous. For example,

LineNumberOfTheSourceCodeOfTheTestProgram

has a well explained purpose but it would be confusing if it were to appear in a complicated expression.

Comments should be used at the start of a function to describe its parameters and purpose and at the start of each logically separate section of a program. Comments should also be used to clarify code which may not be immediately transparent, as in the case:

```
if ((n / 2) * 2 == n)   /* test for even n */
```

Some inexperienced programmers find it difficult not to over-comment or give trivial comments; the following style of comment is often produced by well-meaning beginners:

```
i = 1;   /*   assign 1 to i    */
```

However, this is not helpful and its perpetrators should be excluded from polite society.

2

Elements of C Programs

2.1. Data Types

All variables in C have a type which defines the operations that can be applied to them, the effects of those operations and how they are stored in a computer. Every variable must be declared, the style of a declaration being illustrated by:

```
float Velocity, Acceleration;
int NumberOfBodies;
char Initial, Terminator;
```

This declares various variables of types **float** (floating point number), **int** (a whole number) and **char** (a character). A variable can be given an initial value in its declaration, as in:

```
float Velocity = 0;
```

When an identifier is initialized in a declaration it can be qualified by the symbol **const**. For example

```
const float pi = 3.14159265;
```

The action which a compiler will take if an attempt is made to change a constant depends on the implementation, but a good system will give an error message. In some circumstances the qualifier may also enable a compiler to generate better code.

C provides the basic types **int, char, float** and **double** and a set of qualifiers **short, long, signed** and **unsigned** so that other possible declarations could be:

```
long int Overdraft;
unsigned char Alpha, Beta;
```

11

long can be used with **int** or **double**; **short** can be used with **int** or **signed**; **unsigned** can be used with **int**, **long int**, **short int** or **char**. If **long**, **short**, **signed** or **unsigned** are used with **int**, the symbol **int** can be omitted so that

short int Income;

is equivalent to

short Income;

All sizes of integers will be assumed to be signed unless **unsigned** is specified, but the default for **char** is implementation-dependent.

The sizes of these types varies from machine to machine and it is often necessary to know the maximum and minimum possible values for them in a particular implementation. In systems complying with the ANSI standard there are two standard header files called **<limits.h>** and **<float.h>** which contain definitions of appropriate constants, the full set of which is given in Appendix 3, but the most important ones are mentioned below.

int A signed integer in some implementation-defined range. It should correspond to the most natural size of an integer on a particular machine. Numbers can be written in the number bases 10 (decimal), 8 (octal) and 16 (hexadecimal) as shown in the examples below. (The terms octal, hexadecimal or decimal are explained in Appendix 1.)

Examples of integer values:

37	the decimal number 37.
-37	the decimal number -37.
037	37 base 8. The leading 0 (zero) implies octal. This number is 31 in decimal.
0x37	37 base 16. The leading 0x implies hexadecimal. This number is 55 in decimal. A capital X can be used.

On a machine with 16-bit integers the range is -32,768 to 32,767 and for 32-bit integers is -2,147,483,648 to 2,147,483,647. However, the number of bits a computer uses for an integer varies widely; values used on quite common machines are 24, 40, 48, 60 and 64 bits.

<limits.h> contains definitions of the constants **INT_MAX** and **INT_MIN** which are the largest and smallest plain (that is, not short or long) integers available in a particular implementation and which are at least +32,767 and -32,767 respectively.

short   A signed integer in some implementation-defined range which *may* be less than that for integers. Many implementations will provide short integers of the same length as normal integers but it is guaranteed that at least 16 bits will be used. Short integers are provided in order to allow programmers to attempt to save space in certain circumstances or to provide a convenient mapping onto some hardware feature; significant space savings are only possible if a compiler implements short types fully and a program uses large arrays of them. Short integer values can be written in all the same ways as normal integers.

   <limits.h> contains definitions of the constants **SHRT_MAX** and **SHRT_MIN**, the largest and smallest short integers available on a particular implementation and like plain integers, have values of at least +32,767 and -32,767.

long   A signed integer in some implementation-defined range which *may* be larger than that for integers. Again, an implementation may make long integers the same as normal integers but it is guaranteed that at least 32 bits will be used; typical micro-computer implementations of C use 16 bits to represent an integer and 32 bits to represent a long integer, although this is not universal; many large machines use 32 bits for both. Values written in programs (but not values read by a program from input data) which are larger than the maximum integer are automatically converted to long integer, so that often it is unnecessary to do anything special to write long integer values. Sometimes, however, it is necessary to store a small value as a long integer, for example when passing a small constant as a parameter to a function that expects a long integer. This can be done by following the constant with an **L** (or **l**, although a small **l** is inadvisable as it looks too much like the digit one). For example, 37L represents the number 37 in long integer form. Octal and hexadecimal forms can also be used in long values, for example 0x42L, 077L.

   <limits.h> contains definitions of the constants **LONG_MAX** and **LONG_MIN** which are the largest and smallest long integers available on a particular implementation and which should have values of at least +2,147,483,647 and –2,147,483,647.

unsigned short, int or **long**   An unsigned integer in the range 0 to some implementation-defined maximum (which is usually double the range of the appropriate integer type). It is are natural to use unsigned numbers for variables such as counters which can never be negative. Unsigned, constant values are written with a **u** or **U** at the end (e.g. 37U). They can be long and can also be written in octal or hexadecimal; 077LU, 0x3FLU and 63LU are all equivalent.

   <limits.h> contains definitions of the constants **USHRT_MAX, UINT_MAX** and **ULONG_MAX** which are the largest short, plain and long integers available on a particular implementation and which are at least 65,535, 65,535 and 4,294,967,295 respectively. The minimum for each of these types is, of course, zero.

char, **signed char** and **unsigned char**   A single character. C regards characters and integers as interchangeable, but the integer corresponding to a particular character will depend upon the character set of a machine. Most machines use 8 bits to store a character and on such a machine a signed character would be in the range -128 to 127 and an unsigned character in the range 0 to 255. Whether or not a plain character is signed or unsigned depends upon the implementation. Character values are written in single quotes.

Examples of character values:

'A'   the representation of the character 'A'.

'\101'   another representation of the character 'A'. The digits (up to three of them) are in octal, even though they are not preceded by a zero, and are the internal code for the character. There is, in fact, no need to represent printable characters in this way and it is bad practice to use the form except for characters that cannot be represented by printable glyphs. For example, '\012' is line feed in the ASCII character set. The leading zero is not necessary but is included to emphasize that the digits are in octal.

'\n'   the newline character. Even though it looks like two characters, this is an escape sequence to represent a single non-printable character. Other escape sequences can be found on page 3.

<limits.h> contains definitions of the constants **CHAR_MAX**, **UCHAR_MAX** and **SCHAR_MAX** which are the largest values of plain characters, unsigned characters and signed characters. **CHAR_MIN** and **SCHAR_MIN** are the smallest plain character and signed character values available on a particular implementation. There is also a constant **CHAR_BIT** which is the number of bits in one character and is at least 8.

float   A floating point number. The value is represented as a mantissa with a decimal point and an exponent in the style 123.4e15 or 123.4E15 where the symbol **E** or **e** indicates 'times ten to the power of'.   Thus the value above is 123.4×10^{15}. Either the decimal point or the exponent part can be omitted as in 1.23 or 2e5. The exponent can be negative so that 1e-3 is equivalent to 0.001. Floating point numbers have a limited accuracy which can be as small as six decimal places on some machines and as large as twenty on others and the range of permitted values also varies. In order to provide information about the environment in which a program is running, the header file **<float.h>** provides a number of constants, among them **FLT_DIG**, the precision as a number of decimal digits (at least 6), **FLT_MAX**, the largest floating point value (at least 1e37) and **FLT_MIN**, the minimum value (at least 1e-37).

double A double precision floating point number. On some machines the precision of **double** values will be no different from that of **float** but on others it will be larger (although there will not necessarily be twice as many decimal digits). Floating point constants are **double** unless followed by an **F** or **f** and they are shortened when necessary. For example, if **x** is a **float** variable, then in the statement **x** = **3.1415927e3** the constant on the right-hand side is **double** and is automatically narrowed to **float**, but in **x** = **3.1415927e3F** the right-hand side is **float** and does not need narrowing. In **<float.h>** there are the constants **DBL_DIG**, the precision as a number of decimal digits (at least 10), **DBL_MAX**, the largest double value (at least 1e37) and **DBL_MIN**, the minimum value (at least 1e-37). Since most of the standard mathematical functions use **double** for their arguments it can be slower to use **float** variables because of the time for conversion.

long double An extended-precision floating point number which may be more precise than a **double**. **long double** constants are written with a suffix **L** or **l**, e.g. 1.602e-19L.

The types described above have different *widths* and the order, from the narrowest to the widest, is: **char**, **short**, **int**, **long**, **float**, **double**, **long double**. An **unsigned** type is wider than the corresponding signed type. The type of a value will be automatically *widened* if the context demands. For example, given the declarations:

```
char     Cvar;
short    Svar;
int      Ivar;
long     Lvar;
float    Fvar;
double   Dvar;
```

then:

Lvar + Ivar	converts **Ivar** to **long** before the addition.
Fvar = Ivar	converts **Ivar** to **float** before assignment.
Dvar * Svar	widens **Svar** three times (first to **int**, then to **float** and finally to **double**) before multiplying.
Cvar + Svar + Ivar	widens **Cvar** to **short**, performs the first addition, then widens the result to **int** and performs the second addition.

Type conversion from a wider to narrower type is trickier because information must be discarded, and it is essential to understand how this will occur. **float** to **int** will cause loss of the fractional part; for example, 3.7 is converted to 3. If an **int** is converted to a **short int** then part of the integer value (the bits at the left-hand end of the representation) will be lost and you should be very careful to be sure you know what is happening. In general, such operations are dangerous and machine dependent.

In some circumstances it is necessary to specify that a type is to be converted; this is done with a *cast* which is illustrated by **(int) x** where **x** is a floating point variable which will be converted to **int**. The cast in this case is **(int)**, and in fact a cast is simply a type enclosed in parentheses which precedes a value or expression. In some circumstances, even when a cast is not required, it can be a good idea to use one to emphasize to a human reader that a conversion is taking place.

If an attempt is made to give a whole number (**char**, **int**, **long** or **short**) a value outside its permitted range, a condition called *overflow* is created. However, most implementations of C will not detect this error. Hence if the largest integer on your machine is 32767, you are likely to find that after the statements:

```
i = 32767;
i++;
```

the value of **i** is -32768. If you do not understand why, read Appendix 1.

Note particularly that **char** and **int** the same type. A compiler will allow you to calculate the square of '?' with no qualms but the result may not be very useful.

Most languages have a *boolean* or *logical* data type which is used to represent the truth values TRUE and FALSE. There is no explicit boolean type in C, but in all places where such a value is needed, the value zero represents FALSE and anything else represents TRUE. As integers must serve the purpose of boolean values, a **#define** statement is often used in the way shown below to make a programmer's intentions more explicit.

#define, like **#include**, is a preprocessor directive and is described in detail in Chapter 13. In its simplest form, it is used to create symbols which act as *aliases* for other objects, such as types, constants or variables. The example below shows how it could be used to create the effect of a boolean data type in C:

```
#define     bool      int
#define     FALSE     0
#define     TRUE      1
```

If these statements were included at the beginning of a program, it would then be possible to write statements such as:

```
bool Offended;
float Speed;

Offended = FALSE;
...
if (Speed > 30)
    Offended = TRUE;
...
if (Offended)
    printf("You have exceeded the speed limit, Sir. \n");
```

An alternative way of achieving the same effect is to use an *enumeration*. The three **#define** statements above can be replaced by:

```
enum bool {FALSE, TRUE};
```

where **FALSE** and **TRUE** are called *enumeration constants*. When an enumeration list is given in this way, the first item has the value 0, the second 1, and so on. If different values are needed they can be specified explicitly as illustrated by:

```
enum flora {Tulip, Daffodil = 5, Narcissus}
```

This gives **Tulip** the value 0, **Daffodil** 5 and **Narcissus** 6. Note that **Narcissus**, because it is not given an explicit value, continues the sequence started by the value specified for **Daffodil**.

2.2. Operators

Operators in C are used to calculate, select or assign values. As an example, consider the statement:

```
x = (-b + sqrt(b*b - 4*a*c))/(2*a);
```

This contains the operators +, -, *, / and =. The - occurs in two forms which are regarded as distinct; in **-b** it is *monadic* (has one operand) and gives a result that is the negative of the current value of **b**, but in **b*b - 4*a*c** it is *diadic* (has two operands) and gives a result that is the difference between the value of **b*b** and the value of **4*a*c**. Here the multiplying operator * and the dividing operator / are also diadic.

Almost all operators yield a result; thus in **5 + 5** the operator + yields the value 10. The assigning operator = is no exception and yields a result as well as assigning a value. It takes the value of the expression on its right-hand side and copies it to the variable on its left-hand side but it also yields, as a result, the value copied. For example: z = 5*(y = 2*x + 3);   calculates the value of **2*x + 3** and copies it into **y**. This is not, however, all that happens because the value of **y** is also delivered as the result of the inner = . The value of **y** is multiplied by 5 in order to produce the value ultimately assigned to **z**. If **x** were 3 before the statement, then afterwards **x** would still contain 3, **y** would contain 9 and **z** would contain 45.

All operators have a *priority* (or precedence) and an *associativity* which, between them, decide the order in which operations are performed. Operators with a higher priority will be performed before operators of a lower priority, and operators of equal priority will be performed according to whether they associate left-right or right-left. The expression **24/6*2** contains the operators / and * which have equal priority and associate from left to right so that the result of the expression is 8.

The normal priority and associativity can be overcome by use of parentheses; thus **24/(6*2)** yields the value 2. Because there are so many levels of priority in C it is a good idea, when in doubt, or when writing complicated expressions, to use parentheses to make your intention explicit. Most operators associate left-right but there are some, in particular the assigning operators (=, +=, -=, *=, /= and a few others), which associate right-left:

a = b = c = 4;

puts the value 4 into **c**, then into **b** then into **a**.

Operators are classed as *postfix* (used after an operand, e.g. **p++**), *prefix* (used before an operand, e.g. **++p**), diadic (used between two operands e.g. **p + q**) or *triadic* (used with three operands. There is only one triadic operator, :?. It is used in expressions of the form **(a > 0) ? a : -a** where the first operand is **(a > 0)**, the second is **a** and the third is **-a**).

The operators below represent only a part of the full list, which can be found in Appendix 4. In the descriptions **l** represents a left operand, **r** a right operand and **m** a middle operand.

The simple diadic arithmetic operators are +, -, *, / and %; addition, subtraction, multiplication, division and modulus respectively. If both operands of / are integer, then the division will be integer division but if either operand is of type **float** then floating point division is used. For example **7/2** gives the result 3 but **7.0 / 2** gives the result 3.5. The operator % can only be used between integer operands and gives the remainder. For example, **27 % 6** gives 3.

Because expressions such as **l = l + r** are very common, a special set of operators is available which provide a shorthand. Thus the example above can be written **l +=** **r**. This shorthand version, apart from being easier to write, is more explicit and will often be be faster, especially if **l** is a complicated expression. Analogous to += there are the operators -=, *=, /= and %=, each with the obvious meanings. These are examples of the assignment operators, the most important of which is =. They all change the value of the left operand. The others can be found in Appendix 4.

When adding to, or subtracting from a value it is most common to need to add or subtract unity (one). In these cases it is convenient to use the increment and decrement operators, ++ and --. These can be used as prefix or postfix operators, the difference between lies is in the value delivered by the operator, not in the effect on the left operand.

Use of the post-increment operator is illustrated by l++. l is incremented by one, but because it is the post-increment version of ++ the value delivered by the operator is the original value of l; the incrementing takes place after the value has been delivered. Thus, after **b = 27; a = b++;** the value of **b** would be 28 and **a** would be 27.

The pre-increment version of the same operator takes the form **++r**. With this operator incrementing takes place before the value is delivered. Thus after the statements **b = 27; a = ++b;** **a** and **b** will both equal 28.

The decrement operators are similar, for instance **b = 27; a = --b;** leaves **b** equal to 26 and **a** equal to 26 and **b = 27; a = b--;** leaves **b** equal to 26 and **a** to 27.

Comparison of values is done with the relational operators <, <=, >, >= (less than, less than or equal, greater than and greater than or equal respectively), and the lower priority operators == and != (equal and not equal). A typical example of the use of one of these operators might be:

```
if (age == 21) printf("eligible");
```

A very common error is to write:

```
if (age = 21) printf("eligible");
```

which is legal C because **age = 21** changes the value of **age** and delivers a result which is taken to represent TRUE.

More complicated relationships can be formed by combining relational operators with logical operators. These are logical AND **&&** and logical OR **||**. Given these operators one can create expressions such as

```
if (age >= 21 && height > 1.8)
```

Notice that the logical operators have a lower priority than the relational ones. The relational operators in turn have lower priority than all the arithmetic operators so that expressions such as **b*b - 4*a*c < 0** have the meaning that one would probably expect, i.e. **(b*b - 4*a*c) < 0**.

It is a characteristic of the C language that logical expressions are 'short-circuited'. This means that in an expression such as

```
if (i >= 0 && sqrt(i) < 10) . . .
```

offers no danger of taking the square root of a negative number because if **i** should be negative the right operand of **&&** will not be evaluated. The general principle is that when the left operand of **&&** is false, or of **||** is true, the right operand will not be evaluated (because the result is a foregone conclusion).

There is an unusual, but important, operator which takes three operands. It is **? :** and takes three operands in the form **left ? mid : right**. If **left** is non-zero (representing TRUE) then the operator delivers the value of **mid** and otherwise it delivers **right**. The left operand is a logical expression. For example:

```
Rate = (Income > CutOff) ? HighRate : StandardRate;
```

is equivalent to:

```
if (Income > CutOff)
      Rate = HighRate;
else
      Rate = StandardRate;
```

The sequence operator **,** (comma), which has the lowest priority of any operator, can also be regarded as a part of the control structures. Its purpose is to ensure that the left operand will be evaluated before the right operand. The result it yields is the value of its right-hand operand. For example,

```
p = (total = 1 + 2 + 3,   square = total*total)*2;
```

leaves 6 in **total**, 36 in **square** and 72 in **p**. It has the same effect as

```
total = 1 + 2 + 3;
square = total * total;
p = square * 2;
```

Examples of its use will be seen shortly in the description of **for** loops.

2.3.   Control Statements

The control statements of a language are those statements which allow choices to be made or which express repetition. C has two statements for making choices: the **if** and **switch** statements. Repetition is provided by the **while, do - while** and **for** statements. Most of the descriptions of syntax below indicate where a statement can occur. In these places this may be a simple statement terminated with a semicolon but often one wishes to include several statements. A sequence of statements can be made into a *compound* statement or *block* by enclosing them in curly brackets { }. For example

```
{   printf("Please give the name of your disc.\n");
    scanf("%s\n", DiscName);
}
```

The part enclosed in curly brackets above can appear anywhere where a statement is required.

The 'if' statement

This takes either the form:

if (*expression*) *statement*

or

if (*expression*) *statement*
else *statement*

In the first case *statement* will only be executed if the expression yields a non-zero value (true). If it yields zero (false) then *statement* is skipped. In the second case, if the expression is false then the statement after the **else** will be executed. For example,

```
if (Discriminant < 0)
    printf("There are no real roots for this equation.\n");
else {
    CalculateRoots();
    PrintRoots();
}
```

if statements with **else** parts can be chained together to provide multiple choices in statements of the form

if (exp$_1$)
    statement$_1$
else if (exp$_2$)
    statement$_2$

For example:

```
if (ch >= 'a' && ch <= 'z')
    ch -= ('a' - 'A');
else if (ch < ' ')
    ch = ' ';
```

The above statement could be used to change lower case letters to upper case and to change all control characters to space (assuming that the character set of the computer is ASCII). Programmers used to other languages should note that the parentheses around the condition which follows **if** are mandatory, there is no reserved word **then**, and there is a semicolon between the statement in the first part and the **else** section. In C semicolons act as statement terminators and must be included even before **else** or }.

The next fragment could be used to print a new line automatically after 80 characters have been printed:

```
if (chars == 80) {
    printf('\n');
    chars = 0;
}
else
    chars++;
```

Notice here how { and } are used to group statements. All the parts in the first section of the **if** statement can be treated as one statement, but notice also that the } is not followed by a semicolon.

There is a trap for the unwary in the so called 'dangling **else**'. Look carefully at the statement below:

```
b = 2;
if (a < 0)
    if (a == -1)
        b = 3;
else
    b = 4;
```

After this statement, what would be the value in **b** if **a** contained 1? The indentation implies that the fragment is intended to set **b** to 4 but in fact it will leave it unchanged. The **else** associates with the **if** immediately before it and the indentation should be:

```
b = 2;
if (a < 0)
    if (a == -1)
        b = 3;
    else
        b = 4;
```

If the true intention is to assign 4 to **b**, the fragment should be rewritten:

```
b = 2;
if (a < 0) {
    if (a == -1)
        b = 3;
}
else
    b = 4;
```

It is important to use semicolons correctly. A compound statement (i.e. statements enclosed in { and }) should not be followed by a semicolon, but all other statements should be. Common errors are:

```
if (a == 37);        /* WRONG.   The ; ends the if statement so that */
    b += 1;          /* b += 1 is obeyed irrespective of the value of a */
if (a == 37) {
    b += 1;
};                   /* WRONG.   No ; after } */
else
    b += 2;
```

The 'switch' statement

The **switch** statement is used when it is necessary to check an integer value against a list of possible values and to take different actions in each case. As an example:

```
switch (ch) {
    case 'y':
    case 'Y':
        printf("Yes\n");
        break;
    case 'n':
    case 'N':
        printf("No\n");
        break;
    default:
        printf("Please reply Y, y, N or n\n");
        break;
}
```

Here the value in the variable **ch** is compared with each of the constant values after the reserved word **case** (remember that a **char** is just an integer). If a match is found then execution switches to the start of the section marked by the matching **case** from where execution continues until either the } at the end of the **switch** statement, or a **break** statement is reached. If no match is found in one of the **case**s then the section labelled **default** is taken. The effect of the above statement is thus equivalent to:

```
if (ch == 'y' || ch == 'Y' )
    printf("Yes\n");
else if (ch == 'n' || ch == 'N')
    printf("No\n");
else
    printf("Please reply Y, y, N or n\n");
```

The following points should be noted:

1. Usually each section ends with a **break** statement, but this is not always so. If **break** is omitted on any section, then after execution of that section control will flow into the next case. For example, if the **break** after **case'Y'** were omitted, the output, if **ch** were 'y' or 'Y', would be:

    ```
    Yes
    No
    ```

    This effect can sometimes be useful, as it is above for **'n'** and **'y'**, but should be treated cautiously; it should be carefully commented because the intended action may be obscure to an unwary reader of the program.

2. The **default** section is optional; if it is omitted and no **case** matches the expression following **switch** then no action will be taken. In the example the **break** in the default section is not necessary because it is the last section, but it has been included because it helps prevent mistakes if new sections are added later.

3. **case** must be followed by a constant or constant expression. The rules for what constitutes a valid constant expression are complicated, but for our purposes will be treated as expressions containing only constants, simple operators and parentheses e.g. **(CHAR_MAX - 1)**. Assigning operators, the sequence operator, increment and decrement operators and function calls are not allowed, either because they would not make sense, or because they would make the life of a compiler writer too difficult. All the constant expressions in a **switch** statement must have different values.

A more practical example of the use of **switch** statements can be found in the Zeller's congruence program in section 1.2.

The 'while' loop

The pre-condition loop (i.e. the loop which tests its condition before execution) is the **while** loop. The general form is: **while** (*expression*) *statement*.

The effect is to execute the statement part repeatedly for as long as the expression is true (non-zero). As an example, the following complete program calculates the sum 1 + 1/2 + 1/4 + 1/8 ... accurately to six decimal places (the result should be close to 2.0):

```
#include <stdio.h>
main() {
    float sum = 0.0, term = 1.0;

    while (term > 1e-6){
        sum += term;
        term /= 2;
    }
    printf("\n The sum is %8.7f \n", sum);
}
```

The 'for' loop

The **for** loop takes the form:

> **for** (*initial statement* ; *condition* ; *update statement*) *statement*

where: *initial statement* will be obeyed only once before the loop begins.
                condition is tested before each trip through the loop.
                update statement is obeyed after each trip through the loop.

For example, the following program prints the squares of the numbers from 1 to 10:

```
#include <stdio.h>
main()
{
    int i;
    for (i = 1;  i <= 10;  ++i)
        printf("%d   %d\n", i, i*i);
    /*  At this point i will have the value 11   */
}
```

The loop above could be written as a **while** loop:

```
i = 1;
while (i <= 10) {
    printf("%d   %d\n", i, i*i);
    ++i;
}
```

These loops are identical in effect; in particular notice that the variable **i** has a defined value, in this case 11, at the end of both loops. In fact a **for** loop is just a shorthand notation for a **while** loop. It is good to bear this in mind because the conditional expression in a **for** loop, as in a **while** loop, gives the condition under which the loop should keep running. This is the opposite of the behavior of **for** loops in most other languages.

The initial and update statements (more strictly they are expressions) can consist of more than one statement if the constituent statements are separated by the sequence (comma) operator. The loop below would print a table of powers of two up to the sixteenth.

```
for ( i = 1, j = 2;  i <= 16;  i++, j *= 2)
    printf("%d   %d\n", i, j)
```

Here the initial and update parts each comprise two statements, separated by commas. In general, these parts can contain any number of statements, with commas in between, or even none at all since any of the three parts can be omitted. Omitted initial or update statements are ignored. Omitted condition parts are treated as being always true. As an example of the effect of leaving out all three sections, the endless loop

```
for ( ; ; )
    print("$\n");
```

will print more dollars than anyone could need.

The do ... while loop

The post-condition loop takes the form:

> **do** *statement* **while** (*expression*);

statement is executed first and then *expression* is evaluated; if *expression* yields a non-zero (true) value then *statement* is repeated, and this sequence continues until *expression* yields zero (false). For example, assuming two variables **x** and **sqrtx** of type **float**, the program fragment:

```
sqrtx = 1.0;
do {
    sqrtx = 0.5 * (sqrtx + x/sqrtx);
} while (fabs((sqrtx * sqrtx - x)) > 1e-6);
```

will calculate the square root of **x** accurately to six decimal places by using Newton's method. The function **fabs** is a standard function which calculates the absolute value of a **float** or **double** value; to use it, the header file **<math.h>** should be included in the program. Of course, the standard function **sqrt**, also declared in **<math.h>**, would be a much more practical way of calculating square roots. (A warning to the unwary: on a machine which uses 32 bits to represent a floating point number, the loop above could fail to terminate for even a fairly small **x** because of round-off error in the terminating condition. Declaring **x** and **sqrtx** as **double** would correct the situation but further discussion of this type of problem is not within the scope of this book.)

The 'break' and 'continue' statements

Sometimes it is necessary to terminate a loop before reaching the end of the statements within it. This can be achieved by using the **break** statement, causing the loop to terminate immediately:

```
count = 0;
while ((ch = getchar()) != '.') {
    if (ch == EOF) break;
    count ++;
}
```

The function **getchar** used in this example is a standard input function which returns one character from the default input stream known as **stdin**. **ch** is an integer variable and **EOF** indicates that an end of a file has been read. (These are discussed in more detail in section 2.5.) The loop above will count characters up to a period (full-stop) but terminate if the end of file is reached before a period has been read.

   continue is used similarly to **break**, but instead of terminating the loop it merely terminates the current trip round the loop and execution continues with the next iteration. As an example, the loop below reads characters up to the end of a file and prints only those which are digits:

```
while ((ch = getchar()) != EOF) {
    if (ch < '0' || ch > '9') continue;
    print("%c", ch);
}
```

In this particular case the use of **continue** is not very helpful, but in a larger, more complicated loop it could prevent having deeply nested **if** statements.

2.4.   Arrays

An array is a collection of elements of the same type. The declaration

        float DailyIncome[365];

defines **DailyIncome** to be an array with 365 elements numbered 0 to 364, each element being a floating point number. All arrays in C have a lower bound of zero. The first element is **DailyIncome[0]**, the last is **DailyIncome[364]** and a general element could be **DailyIncome[i]**. The size specified in an array declaration must be a constant, but section 4.5 shows a technique for circumventing this restriction when necessary.

It is an error to use an index to an array that is less than zero or greater than the index of the top element. Since this error is unlikely to be detected by a C system, its effect may be catastrophic and its cause can be difficult to trace. It is a common error to forget that the index of the last element of the array is one less than its size. For example

        DailyIncome[365] = 0;

will probably change some location of computer memory that does not belong to **DailyIncome**, possibly another variable. Such problems can take many tears to find. This problem can be compounded because arrays in C are intimately related to pointers, but this will be discussed further in section 4.1.

Arrays and **for** loops tend to go together, as in:

        for (i = 0; i < 10; ++i)
            a[i] = b[i];

Multi-dimensional arrays are declared as 'arrays of arrays'. For example:

        int table[10][10];

declares a two-dimensional array with ten rows and ten columns with **table[0][0]** being the first element and **table [9][9]** the last. The statement

        table[1][2] = 99;

will put the value 99 into the array element at row one, column two.

To illustrate the use of arrays, consider the problem of how to print Pascal's triangle (shown below). The particular property of this triangle is that each number is the sum of the two numbers above it. The values are important in probability calculations and are known in mathematics as the binomial coefficients. Writing this program involves two problems: calculating the numbers on each row and formatting the triangle nicely in the output.

```
                        1
                      1   1
                    1   2   1
                  1   3   3   1
                1   4   6   4   1
              1   5  10  10   5   1
            1   6  15  20  15   6   1
          1   7  21  35  35  21   7   1
        1   8  28  56  70  56  28   8   1
      1   9  36  84 126 126  84  36   9   1
```

At first sight it seems to be necessary to build a table (two-dimensional array) to hold the whole triangle, but this is not so; in order to calculate the numbers of one row, it is only necessary to know the contents of the previous row, not all the previous rows. A single, one-dimensional array can be used to store a row as it is being calculated, the row can be printed, and then the next row calculated from the current row. A suitable array can be declared:

```
int Row[MaxRow];
```

where **MaxRow** is an appropriate constant (10 for the diagram above).

Since it is possible to use a single array, a way has to be found to update it at each step. To illustrate what needs to be done, at step five the array is:

Row

1	4	6	4	1	0	0	0	0	0
0	1	2	3	4	5	6	7	8	9

and at step six it contains:

Row

1	5	10	10	5	1	0	0	0	0
0	1	2	3	4	5	6	7	8	9

Row[0] never changes and **Row[1]** can be calculated from **Row[0]** + **Row[1]** but if the next step were

    Row[1] = Row[0] + Row[1];

there would be a problem; the following step should be

    Row[2] = Row[1] + Row[2];

but the value needed from **Row[1]** here should be 4, the original value, and not 5, which it now holds. Thus it is impossible to go up the array replacing each value by itself plus the number on its left. The answer is to come *down* the array. The first step, for the above example, is

    Row[5] = Row[5] + Row[4];

then

    Row[4] = Row[4] + Row[3];

and so on.

The triangular format is easily obtained by printing a diminishing number of spaces before each row; in the program below the number of spaces diminishes by two per row.

```
/* Print Pascal's triangle  */
#include <stdio.h>
#define    MaxRow   10

main() {
    int LeadingSpaces = 2*MaxRow,  RowNo, n, s;
    int Row[MaxRow];

    /* Set the first element of Row to 1 and all the others to 0  */
    Row[0] = 1;
    for (n = 1;  n < MaxRow;  n++)
        Row[n] = 0;

    for (RowNo = 1;  /* will escape using break */ ; ++RowNo){
        /* Print the leading spaces  */
        for (s = 1;  s <= LeadingSpaces;  s++)
            printf(" ");

        /* Print the numbers on one line  */
        for (n = 0;  n < RowNo;  n++)
            printf("%4d", Row[n]);    /* %4d means 4 characters wide */
```

```
                printf("\n");
                LeadingSpaces -= 2;

                /*  Terminate the loop if the last row has been printed   */
                if (RowNo == MaxRow)
                    break;

                /*  Calculate the next row from right to left excluding element 0 */
                for (n = RowNo;  n >= 1;  --n)
                    Row[n] += Row[n-1];
            }
        }
```

It is possible to avoid the loop which gives **Row** its initial set of values by giving them when it is declared, but this requires a knowledge of storage classes which are discussed in section 4.6.

The **for** loop above is an example of what is known as an 'n-and-a-half times loop'; the part of the loop before the **break** statement is obeyed once more than the part after it. This is one of the most common uses of **break**.

2.5.   Input/Output Operations on stdin and stdout

stdin and **stdout** (declared in the header file **<stdio.h>**) are standard input and output files which are automatically opened and closed by the C system. The way in which they are associated with physical files or devices varies from one operating system to another, but a common approach is to assign **stdin** directly to a keyboard and **stdout** to a screen. A third file, **stderr** is also opened automatically and is used for error messages. It also is commonly assigned to a screen.

stdin can be thought of as a sequence of characters organized in lines; each line ends with the newline character '**\n**' and the whole sequence is terminated with a special value to mark the end of file. This is not necessarily how the operating system organizes the file, but the C system will automatically make any changes needed to present the file in this way. It is automatically opened so that the reading position, when a program starts to run, is at the first character of the file. Characters are then read in sequence up to the end of the file. If **stdin** is automatically associated with a keyboard then it is necessary to consult system documentation to find how an end of file can be typed; a common approach is to use a control character (often control-D).

stdout is organized similarly; it is empty when it is opened and writing to it adds characters to the end of the sequence of characters which it contains.

To read or write single characters from these standard files, it is simplest to use the function **getchar**() which reads one character from **stdin** and returns the value of the character as its result, and **putchar()** which writes one character to **stdout**. The result of the function **getchar** is not, in fact, of type character but integer, the reason being that when it reaches the end of a file it will return a value that is not a valid character. This 'invalid' value is usually -1 and is represented by the symbolic constant **EOF** (defined in the header file **stdio.h**).

The following program will read text from **stdin** and write it to **stdout** putting separate words on separate lines. Words are assumed to be separated by one space, one period or one comma.

```
/* Print a text with separate words on separate lines   */
#include <stdio.h>
main()
{
    int ch;
    while ((ch = getchar()) != EOF) {
        if (ch == ' ' || ch == '.' || ch == ',' )
            putchar('\n');
        else
            putchar(ch);
    }
}
```

Notice that the condition at the start of this **while** loop involves an assignment, **ch = getchar()**, the result of which is compared with **EOF**. This is a common idiom and avoids constructions of the form:

```
ch = getchar();
while (ch != EOF) {
    . . .
    ch = getchar();
}
```

This is, in fact, another way of implementing an 'n-and-a-half times' loop. In the above example, **ch = getchar()** is performed for every character read, but the body of the loop is not obeyed for the last character.

3

Functions

3.1. Declaring and Calling Functions

C programs consist of one or more functions, but all complete programs contain one function called **main** where execution begins. A function can take parameters, declare variables which belong only to itself, contain executable statements and deliver a result. Many other languages allow functions to be declared inside other functions, but this is not possible in C.   Below is a program to read two numbers and calculate their sum by using a function with two parameters. Of course, this would be a bad way of writing such a simple program.

```
#include <stdio.h>

int Sum(int i, int j) {
    return(i + j);
}

main() {
    int a, b, Total;

    printf("Give two numbers\n");
    scanf("%d%d", &a, &b);
    Total = Sum(a, b);
    printf("The sum of %d and %d is %d\n", a, b, Total);
}
```

The function **Sum** starts with the type of its result, then its name and finally a list of parameters in parentheses. i and j are called *formal* parameters and the type of each is specified in the formal parameter list. In the **main** function is a call to **Sum** with the parameters **a** and **b**. **a** and **b** are called *actual parameters*. The effect of this call is to copy the values of the actual parameters into the corresponding formal parameters,

33

execute the body of the function and then return the value provided by the **return** statement in **Sum**. It is important to realize that formal parameters contain copies of the corresponding actual parameters; consequently any change to formal parameters inside a function has no effect on the actual parameters given in the call. In other languages this mechanism is usually known as *call-by-value* but as it is the only mechanism in C it is not normally graced with a name in C manuals.

Since **Sum** returns a value it can be used in expressions in the same way as variables or constants. The above program can therefore be simplified by changing the **printf** statement to:

```
printf("The sum of %d and %d is %d\n", a, b, Sum(a, b));
```

Sum is simpler than most functions; its parameters are only integers and are not changed by a call of the function, it contains no local variables and it gives a result of type integer. More complicated (and useful) examples can be found in the following sections.

A second style of function declaration is permitted, illustrated by:

```
Sum( i, j)
    int i, j;
{
    return(i + j);
}
```

The version of **Sum** declared in this way has the same meaning as the earlier form. Because the type of the result is not specified, it is taken to be integer by default. The parameters are specified in a different way, which allows the actual arguments (those of the call) to vary in type and number from the declaration. This is the original form of function declaration and it generally provides less secure type checking. The new form was introduced into the language with the ANSI standard. The new style is strongly to be recommended since the old one is retained only so that older programs will continue to work. The ANSI standard warns that future versions of the language may drop the old form entirely.

Function arguments can be preceded by the qualifier **const** described in section 2.1. For example,

```
int PrintLines(const int n) { . . . }
```

This qualifier may enable a compiler to detect an inadvertent attempt by the function **PrintLines** to change the value of **n** and it may also allow more efficient code to be generated as a compiler will be able to assume that the value of **n** is the same after the call as before it.

3.2.   The Result of a Function

A function can give a result of any type except an array or a function (although some non-ANSI compilers forbid structures or unions). The function **NextNonSpace** shown below takes no parameters but delivers a result of type integer.

The first line, **int NextNonSpace(void)** declares a function that delivers a result of type **int** but which has no parameters. The reserved symbol **void** in the place of the parameter list indicates that the function has no parameters. In pre-ANSI C the function would be declared as **NextNonSpace()**, but this does not mean a function with no parameters but a function with unspecified parameters. In other words it fails to provide information about the parameters, and the compiler will assume that whatever parameters are given are correct. The old form is still available but its use is not recommended.

NextNonSpace reads characters from the default input channel **stdin** until it finds a character that is not 'white space' (space, tab or newline). It delivers this character as its result.

The variable **ch** is *local* to **NextNonSpace** (in C jargon it said to have storage class **auto**, but this will be discussed later in section 4.6), which means that it exists only inside this function. It is created when the function is called, destroyed when the function ends, and is not visible outside the function.

```
int NextNonSpace(void) {
    int ch;

    do {
        ch = getchar();
    } while (ch == ' ' || ch == '\t' || ch == '\n');
    return(ch);
}
```

The execution of a function ceases when either the final **}** or a **return** statement is reached. If **return** is followed by an expression, then the value of that expression (the value of **ch** in the above case) is the value yielded by the function. If no expression follows **return** then the value yielded by the function is undefined. Returning from a function by reaching the final **}** is equivalent to a **return** statement with no expression. A function can contain many **return** statements although they do not all have to return a value. The parentheses around **ch** in the **return** statement are not mandatory (**return ch** is also valid) but are included for clarity.

A call to this function might be:

```
a = NextNonSpace();
```

which would put the value of the next significant character in **a**. Notice that there are parentheses after the function name even though there are no parameters; these are necessary whenever a function is called. Forgetting the parentheses will probably not produce a syntax error from your compiler because, as so often in C, the resulting statement is valid but has a different meaning. In fact

```
a = NextNonSpace;
```

means put the *address* of **NextNonSpace** into **a**.

It is allowed to discard the result of a function. For example, the simple statement

```
NextNonSpace();
```

would read the next non-space character but do nothing with it; the effect would be to set the reading position to the character after the next non-space character. It is possible to emphasize that a result is being discarded by explicitly casting it to **void**:

```
(void) NextNonSpace();
```

If the result type of a function is not specified in the function declaration, then it is taken to be **int** by default; the function above could have been declared:

```
NextNonSpace(void) {
    . . .
}
```

with the same effect, but it is good practice always to specify the result type for the sake of clarity. If a function is not intended to deliver any result then it can be declared to be of type **void.** For example,

```
void Initialize(void) {
    ...
}
```

declares **Initialize** to be a function with no parameters and delivering no result. (Some old C compilers do not provide **void.**)

3.3.   The Order of Function Declarations

In the examples given up to now, a function has always been declared before it is used. It is sometimes convenient, however, to call a function before it has been declared or to declare the function in a different file than that from which it called. In this case the result type and the parameter types of the function can be specified before the call. This is demonstrated in the modified version of the addition program shown below.

The *function prototype* before **main** tells the compiler the result type and the parameter types of the function **Sum** which will be defined later in the same file or, possibly, in a different file. The compiler can then check that the call is correct and will further check that **Sum**, when it is finally defined, matches the prototype. If a function is called without a preceding definition or prototype, it is assumed to return an integer and its parameter list is assumed to match the call; it is a dangerous practice to make use of this as many common errors cannot then be detected by a compiler.

```
int Sum(int i, int j) ;

main() {
    int a, b;
    printf("Give two numbers\n");
    scanf("%d%d", &a, &b);
    printf("The sum of %d and %d is %d\n", a, b, Sum(a, b));
}

int Sum(int i, int j) {
    return(i + j);
}
```

3.4. Array Parameters to Functions

Arrays can be passed to functions as parameters as is shown by the next function which finds the index of the smallest element of an array of **float**s and deliver it as a result:

```
int SmallestElement(float a[ ], int Size) {
    /*  'a' is an array of floating point numbers.
        'Size' is the number of elements in 'a'.
        'SmallestElement' returns the index of the smallest element of 'a'   */

    int i, SmallestSoFar = 0,       /*  The index of the smallest element
                                        found so far, initially the first element
                                        of the array */

    for (i = 1;  i < Size;  i++)
        if (a[i] < a[SmallestSoFar])
            SmallestSoFar = i;
    return(SmallestSoFar);
}
```

Notice that the size of **a** is not specified in its declaration as a parameter but must be given as an extra parameter, in this case called **Size**. A call to this function could be:

```
n = SmallestElement(list, 10);
```

if **list** is a **float** array with ten elements.

Strings are arrays of characters which terminate with the null character '\0'. The next function accepts two parameters, a character and a string, and returns the index of the character in the string, or -1 if the character is not present:

```
int Index(char ch, char s[ ]) {
    /* 'ch' is a character.
       's' is an array of characters (a string).
       'Index' returns the index of the first occurrence of 'ch' in 's'
       or -1 if 'ch' does not occur in 's' */

    int i;

    for (i = 0; ; i++)
        if (s[i] == ch)
            return(i);
        else if (s[i] == '\0')
            return(-1);
}
```

A call to this function might be:

```
printf("  %d\n", Index('e', "abcdefghijklmnopqrstuvwxyz"))
```

which will print 4. Because the second parameter to **Index** is a string constant, the null character ' \0 ' is provided automatically by the C system. It is more likely that this parameter would be a variable, the value of which has been built up through several previous program steps. This creates the possibility that the final null might be inadvertently omitted and thus cause the function to fail to produce the correct result; programmers should take great care to ensure that strings always have the terminating null character.

The **for** loop in the **Index** function has no condition part and so is potentially an infinite loop; it will, in fact, terminate when either of the **return** statements inside it is obeyed.

The functions above do not use the most efficient way of referring to successive elements of arrays, but it will be necessary to discuss pointers in more depth before they can be improved upon.

3.5. Global or External Variables

Variables can be declared to be global (external) to several functions by declaring them before the functions that use them. Variables declared in this way exist throughout the life of the program but are only visible from the point of declaration to the end of the file in which they are declared (although this behavior can be modified by using the **extern** specification discussed in section 4.6). Functions cannot refer to variables declared after them in a file.

The program below searches a file for control characters (non-printable characters) other than newline, assuming the ASCII character set. The variables **CharNumber**, **LineNumber** and **ch** are external to the functions **NextCh**, **Initialize** and **main** and so can be used in all of them.

```
#include <stdio.h>
int CharNumber, LineNumber, ch;

void NextCh(void) {
    /*  Read the next character and leave it in 'ch'.
        Update 'LineNumber' and 'CharNumber'.  */

    if ((ch = getchar()) == '\n') {
        LineNumber++;
        CharNumber = 1;
    }
    else
        CharNumber++;
}

void Initialize(void) {
    /*  Initialize global variables  */

    CharNumber = 0;
    LineNumber = 1;
    NextCh();
}

main() {
    initialize();
    while (ch != EOF) {
        if ((ch < ' ' || ch > '~')  && ch != '\n')
            printf("Non-printable character at line %d, character %d\n",
                    LineNumber, CharNumber);
        NextCh();
    }
}
```

3.6.   Block Structure

Recall that variables declared inside a function are local to that function and cease to exist when execution of the function stops (a way of modifying this behavior will be shown later when storage class is discussed). This property of local variables provides a valuable mechanism for saving storage space as the locations released can be reused by other functions for their own variables. The concept of locality can be taken beyond the function level and can be applied to any block inside a function (a block is a piece of program enclosed between { and }). This is illustrated by the fragment below:

```
if (SpaceAvailable) {
    double Matrix[100][100];
    Matrix[50][50] = 10;
    . . .
}
else {
    float SmallModel[10][10];
    SmallModel[5][5] = 10;
    . . .
}
```

Here, if **SpaceAvailable** is true (non-zero) then the first section of the **if** statement will be obeyed and **Matrix** will be created. However it will only exist between its enclosing { and }; at } the space occupied by **Matrix** is released. If the **else** section is executed, only the space for **SmallModel** will be used and it will be released at the appropriate }. A block can contain declarations but they must occur before any executable statements and objects so declared will not exist outside the block. If an identifier declared in an inner block has the same name as an identifier declared in an enclosing block, the variable in the outer block becomes hidden until the end of the inner block as is shown by:

```
{ float Blackbird, Lark, Swallow;
    /* Swallow has type float */
    Swallow = 3.7;
    . . .
    { int Gulp, Gobble, Swallow;
        /* Swallow is a new variable of type int  */
        Swallow = 4;
        . . .
    }
    /*  Swallow is the original float variable again.  Gulp, Gobble and the int
        version of Swallow no longer exist */
    printf("%f\n", Swallow);  /* prints 3.7  */
    . . .
}
```

3.7. Recursion

Functions can call themselves either directly or indirectly; such calls are said to be *recursive* and can be used to obtain powerful effects, some of which are shown later. The example below declares a function **Power** which calculates the value of a floating point number raised to an integer power (C does not have an exponentiation operator, although there is a standard function **pow** described in the next section). **Power** is much more efficient than simple repeated multiplication; it makes use of the relationships $x^{2n} = (x^n)^2$ and $x^{2n+1} = x(x^{2n})$ to minimize the number of multiplications. It does not check whether **x** is zero. This function could be written without recursion but the recursive solution is particularly transparent:

```
float Power(float x, int n)   /* Raise x to power n recursively */ {
    if (n < 0)
        return(1.0/Power(x, -n));
    else if (n == 0)
        return(1.0);
    else {  /* n is positive */
        int nBy2 = n/2;
        if ((nBy2 * 2) == n) {  /* n is even */
            float Factor = Power(x, nBy2);
            return(Factor*Factor);
        }
        else  /* n is odd */
            return(x*Power(x, n-1));
    }
}
```

Much more powerful examples of recursion can be found in Chapter 8 (to manipulate trees) and in section 11.5 (to evaluate algebraic expressions).

3.8. Functions with a Variable Number of Arguments

(This section is included in this chapter for the sake of completeness. It shows techniques which require an understanding of macros and pointers. It can be omitted until after Chapters 7 and 12 have been read.)

Standard functions such as **printf** and **scanf** have a variable number of arguments each of which can be from a wide variety of types. One call of **printf** could be

```
printf("%s, %c", Surname, Initial);
```

and another

> printf("%d   %d   %d   %d", a, b, c, d);

where the first call has three parameters (the format string being the first) while the second has five. Not only does the number of parameters vary but so do the types; **printf** is able to deduce the number and types of the parameters from the format string. There is a special notation for declaring such functions; **printf** could be declared:

> int printf(char format[ ], ...);

The ellipsis (...), which must be the last item in the list, indicates that there can be other parameters, but their types and number are not specified.

In order for these parameters to be referenced, since they do not have names C systems provide a header file called **<stdarg.h>** which contains the definitions of three macros and a type. The three macros are called **va_start**, **va_arg** and **va_end**, and the type is called **va_list.**

To illustrate how to use them a function **Max** will be defined which finds the largest value of any of a number of **double** values presented as arguments. Calls to **Max** could be:

> printf("The largest is %f\n", Max(3, 4.4, 55.5, 6.6));

which would print 55.5 and

> printf("The largest is %f\n", Max(5, 4.4, 5.5, 6.6, 44.3, -1.8));

which would print 44.3. The first parameter to **Max** is an integer which gives the number of unnamed parameters; all such functions must have at least one named parameter although it need not be an integer. It is up to the programmer writing the function to provide one or more named parameters from which the function can deduce the types (if necessary, **Max** assumes **double**) and number of the remaining parameters. A possible version of **Max** is shown overleaf.

The first line

> double Max(int NoOfArgs, ...)

declares the function to have one named argument, **NoOfArgs**, and then a list of unnamed arguments. Next it is necessary to declare a variable of type **va_list**

> va_list ArgPointer;

ArgPointer will be used to run through the arguments in the parameter list. The two variables **Largest** and **Arg** which are declared next will hold respectively the largest value found up to the current point in scanning the list and the current value referred to by **ArgPointer**. The local variable **ArgPointer** must now be made to point to the first unnamed parameter by the statement:

```
va_start(ArgPointer, NoOfArgs);
```

va_start must be given a variable of type **va_list** (**ArgPointer** in this case) and the name of the last of the named parameters. Successive unnamed parameters are then accessed by repeated calls of **va_arg**. For instance, the statement

```
Largest = va_arg(ArgPointer, double);
```

puts the value of the first unnamed parameter (specified to be of type **double**) into **Largest,** and then moves **ArgPointer** to refer to the next parameter. The subsequent loop uses repeated calls to **va_arg** to take in the remaining parameters and to find the value of the largest.

Finally it is necessary to make a call to **va_end**, with **ArgPointer** as a parameter, to perform any tidying-up that the system requires. The whole function is

```
#include <stdarg.h>

double Max(int NoOfArgs, ...) {
    va_list ArgPointer;
    int ArgNumber;
    double Largest, Arg;

    va_start(ArgPointer, NoOfArgs);
    Largest = va_arg(ArgPointer, double);
    for (ArgNumber = 2;  ArgNumber <= NoOfArgs;  ++ArgNumber) {
        Arg = va_arg(ArgPointer, double);
        if (Arg > Largest)
            Largest = Arg;
    }
    va_end(ArgPointer);
    return(Largest);
}
```

Great care must be taken when using functions such as **Max** because an error in the parameter list cannot be detected by the compiler and will have strange effects. For instance, if you gave a value of five as **NoOfArgs** but only provided four arguments then the extra call of **va_arg** would fetch a value from some unknown part of the computer's memory. The effect of this is highly unpredictable. Such errors can be very difficult to trace because they can cause variables or other data to be corrupted.

This may cause a program to crash at a later stage or may even allow it to run to an apparantly successful conclusion, but producing invalid output.

3.9.   Standard Functions

There are many standard functions provided by all C systems. The full list required by the ANSI standard is given in Appendix 3 and includes trigonometric, hyperbolic and other mathematical functions as well as functions for input/output, file operations, string manipulation, interrupt handling and date and time calculations.

4

Elementary Data Structures

4.1. The Relationship between Arrays and Pointers

A pointer is a variable which holds the *address* of another location and is therefore said to point to it. Its declaration is similar to the declaration of any other variable but the symbol ***** is used to indicate a pointer. For example:

        float x, y, z, *CurrentAxis, *p;

declares three **float** variables **x**, **y** and **z** and two pointer variables **CurrentAxis** and **p** which can hold the address of **float** variables. The address of a variable can be obtained by using the **&** operator so that the statement:

        CurrentAxis = &y;

makes **CurrentAxis** point to **y**; that is, the address of the variable **y** is stored in **CurrentAxis**. To obtain the value of the variable to which **CurrentAddress** points it is necessary to use the ***** (dereference) operator. Thus:

        z = *CurrentAxis;

puts into **z** the value currently in **y**.

The effect of using pointers is made clear by the example below which also shows one of the dangers of using pointers. The fourth statement changes the value of **y** even though the statement does not explicitly refer to it; the variable **y** is said to have an *alias*, in this case **CurrentAxis**. Indiscriminate use of pointers can lead to programs which are very difficult to read or test, but proper use allows the creation of dynamic data structures (see Chapter 7) as well as improvement in the efficiency of many operations.

```
CurrentAxis = &y;                  /*  Sets CurrentAxis to point to y  */
y = 3.7;
printf("%f", *CurrentAxis);        /*  Prints 3.7  */
*CurrentAxis = 4.2;                /*  Puts 4.2 into y, the variable to
                                       which CurrentAxis points  */
printf("%f", y);                   /*  Prints 4.2  */
p = CurrentAxis;                   /*  p now points to the same place as
                                       CurrentAxis, i.e. y  */
printf("%f", *p);                  /*  Prints 4.2 */
```

Unlike most other languages, arrays and pointers are intimately related in C. This is because an array declaration such as: **float Values[5]** actually creates an array of five **float** locations and **Values** points to (is the address of) the first element. It should be emphasized that **Values** is a constant pointer and so cannot be changed to point to anything else. This is a special property of the pointers associated with array names.

Since an array name is a pointer, ***Values** is synonymous with **Values[0]**. The addition operator + can be used with pointers so that **Values + 3** is a pointer to the fourth element of the array, i.e. **Values[3]**. Notice that the addition in this case is in terms of **float** locations, not machine locations; the addition and subtraction operations automatically adjust themselves to the size of the object to which the pointer refers. As an example, if a computer uses four machine locations to hold a single floating point value, then **Value + 1** will actually add four to the address referred to by **Value**. This allows address arithmetic to be carried out in a machine independent way.

As an extension of the principle explained above, it follows that a construction such as **Values[j]** is equivalent to ***(Values + j)** or ***(j + Values)** or **j[Values]**. Although these are all logically equivalent and are equally efficient, it is normal to use only the first form for the sake of clarity. [ ] is, in fact, a monadic operator and can be applied to any operator.

4.2.   Using Pointers to Avoid Indexing

Array indexing can be a slow operation on a computer and pointers are often used to avoid it for the sake of program speed. As an example, given the declarations:

```
int a[Size], i, j, *pai, *paj, Temp;
```

The following code represents the obvious way to swap the ith and j^{th} elements:

```
Temp = a[i];  a[i] = a[j];  a[j] = Temp;
```

This method indexes each element twice. The version below achieves the same effect but only indexes each element once:

```
pai = &a[i];  paj = &a[j];
Temp = *pai;  *pai = *paj;  *paj = Temp;
```

This example is intended only to illustrate the technique and in this case the advantage in speed would be slight or even non-existent in such a small fragment of code. However, it can become important when successive elements of an array are referred to within a loop, as is shown in the example below. It should be borne in mind, when using pointers in this way, that the second version is less clear and that advantages of speed should always be weighed against readability.

The function below is an improved version of the **Index** function that was given in section 3.4 It delivers as its result the index of the character **ch** in the string s or -1 if **ch** does not occur in s. It makes use of the ++ operator on a pointer s. If s points to an element of an array, the statement ++s moves s to point to the next element of the array. This works no matter what the size of an element.

```
int Index(char ch, char *s)  {
    int i;

    for (i = 0;  ; ++s, ++i) {  /* Move s to the next array element  */
        if (*s == ch)          /* *s is the character to which s points  */
            return(i);
        else if (*s == '\0')
            return(-1);
    }
}
```

This version of **Index** avoids indexing altogether. It makes use of the fact that the parameter s is, like all formal parameters in C, a *copy* of the actual parameter and so can be changed (in this case made to point to successive elements of the string by the expression ++s) without affecting the corresponding actual parameter. Array parameters are different from array variables; it was pointed out on the previous page that array names are constant pointers and cannot be changed, but this restriction does not apply to array parameters.

4.3.   Pointers as Function Parameters

As has been explained, when a parameter is passed to a function it is the value of the parameter that is passed; there is no direct equivalent of the mechanisms of call by name or call by reference of other languages. However, a similar effect can be achieved by passing the address of an actual parameter to a function and declaring the corresponding formal parameter as a pointer. Consider the function below which searches an array of **float**s for its largest and smallest elements.

```
void FindLimits(float a[ ], int Size, float *Low, float *High) {

    /*  'a' is an array of floating point numbers.
        'Size' is the number of elements in 'a'.
        'Low' and 'High' are the addresses of variables where the values
        of the lowest and highest elements of 'a' will be returned.
    */
    int i;

    *Low = *High = a[0];
    for (i = 1;  i < Size;  ++i)
        if (a[i] < *Low)
            *Low = a[i];
        else if (a[i] > *High)
            *High = a[i];
}
```

This function accepts four parameters: an array, an integer giving the size of the array and two pointers to) addresses of variables which will receive the values of the smallest and largest elements of the array. Given a declaration

```
float Min, Max, List[10];
```

a possible call to this function could be:

```
FindLimits(list, 10, &Min, &Max);
```

The addresses of **Min** and **Max** will be passed to **Low** and **High** respectively so that ***Low** refers to the contents of **Min**. The statement

```
*Low = a[i];
```

then puts the value of **a[i]** into **Min.** The effect of the call would be to find the largest and smallest values of a ten element array called **List** and put the results in **Min** and **Max**. It is very important to remember to precede **Min** and **Max** by **&**, because it is their addresses which must be passed to **FindLimits**. It is a common error to forget this, as it is also common to omit the ***** in front of pointer variables such as **Low**. These errors may be undetected by compilers.

Exercise 4.1 Rewrite the function **FindLimits** so that indexing is replaced by use of pointers.

4.4.   The Heap: malloc, calloc and free

All programs manipulate information of some form, and a large part of the art of programming involves finding ways to represent information (data structures) that facilitate the kind of operations that are needed. Often data structures need to be able to grow and shrink, or are of a size which cannot be known when the program is being written; in these cases they are said to be *dynamic*. Dynamic data structures require a different approach to allocating computer memory from what has been seen up to now.

A C program, when it is running, divides its data space into three parts: the *static* area, the *stack* and the *heap*. A program chooses which of these areas is appropriate by selecting a suitable *storage class* for each of its variables. Storage classes are discussed in detail in section 4.6, but some basic notions are needed here. The static area contains global variables (known as **extern** variables) and all variables of the **static** data class (described later), the *stack*, which is used to hold variables local to a function (known as **auto** variables) and the *heap*, which holds dynamic data. Strictly speaking, the heap is not part of the C system itself but is provided by standard library functions, but it is easier to regard it as an integral part of the whole system.

The *static area* is simplest since it never changes its size. The compiler can reserve a fixed section of memory for this area, and all objects in it will exist throughout the lifetime of the program.

The *stack* consists of a set of blocks of memory, one for each active function, i.e. each function that is still executing. Each block, called an *activation record*, is created on top of the stack whenever a function is called and holds all local variables plus some 'housekeeping' information. When the execution of a function is complete its corresponding activation record is removed from the stack top and the variables allocated to that record will no longer exist. The record to be released is always the one most recently allocated. This process is fast and orderly and makes efficient use of memory.

As its name suggests, a *heap* is a more anarchically structured part of the memory allotted to a program. Space on the heap can be claimed or released in chunks of any size and in any order. Special functions are provided in order to keep track of which chunks are available and to allocate and free them as the program demands. If a function calls for space to be created on the heap, the objects allocated that space can continue to exist after the execution of the function has finished. Because heap space is not freed automatically this imposes greater demands on the programmer who must ensure that objects created on the heap can be accessed throughout their useful life and are not freed too early; errors of this type can be very hard to trace.

There are four functions which manipulate the space on the heap: **malloc, calloc, realloc** and **free**. They are defined in the standard header file **<stdlib.h>**, which should be included, using **#include**, in any program which uses them. The first three are of type **void *** which means that they deliver a pointer to a space which has no particular data type. **free** is of type **void** since it delivers no result.

malloc(size) claims an area of storage of **size** number of bytes (**size** being integer) and returns a pointer to the first element. The area of storage will not be set to any particular value. The following statements would leave **p** pointing to a ten byte block of data on the heap:

```
char *p;
p = (char *)malloc(10);
```

The cast **(char *)** is used because **malloc** delivers a *generic* pointer (**void ***), that is, one which points to an object of no particular type. Pointers to **void** have the unique property that they are coerced to (i.e. forced to match the type of) any other type of pointer when necessary, and any other type of pointer can be coerced to **void ***. Strictly speaking, the cast could be omitted above, but it is included for emphasis. Prior to the ANSI standard the generic pointer was **char ***, which had to be explicitly cast to the required type; adopting the habit of always casting **malloc** and **calloc** will never do any harm and will make programs more likely to work with older compilers.

calloc(Number, Size) generates space for **Number** items each of **Size** bytes and returns a pointer to the first byte. The total space allocated by the function will be **Number * Size** bytes. A use could be:

```
int *ip;
ip = (int *)calloc(10, sizeof(int));
```

which allocates space on the heap for ten **int** locations and leave **ip** pointing to the first byte of it. **sizeof** is a standard operator which gives, as its result, the number of bytes needed to store a variable of the specified type. **calloc** also automatically sets the space created to zeros, which can be expensive if the space is large. If this initialization is unnecessary the statement above could be replaced by:

```
ip = (int *)malloc(10*sizeof(int));
```

realloc(OldBlock, Size) reallocates the space pointed to by the pointer variable **OldBlock** with a new size. **Size** is the number of bytes to be allocated for the new block. It can be used to enlarge an object such as an array because it copies the contents of the old block into the new block, but it should not be used to make frequent, small increases because it is a slow operation. As an example, the space pointed to by **ip** in the example above could be doubled by a call:

```
ip = (int *)realloc(ip, 20 * sizeof(int));
```

The extra space created in this way is not set to any particular value.

malloc, calloc and **realloc** could all fail because there may be no more space available, in which case they deliver the value **NULL**. **NULL** is a constant pointer which has the value zero and which can be assigned to any pointer value or compared with any pointer value. It is defined in the header file **<stdio.h>**.

free(BlockPointer) will free the space pointed to by the pointer variable **BlockPointer** so that it can be used again. The space *must* have been allocated by **malloc**, **calloc** or **realloc**. The space pointed to by **ip** in the example above could be released by the call:

```
free(ip);
```

4.5.   'Dynamic' Arrays

As was mentioned earlier, when an array is declared it must be given a size and the size must be a constant. This can be restrictive since sometimes the size needed for an array can only be determined as a program runs, so called *dynamic arrays*. **malloc** or **calloc** can be used to achieve the effect of a dynamic array. For example:

```
float *vec;
int Size;

scanf("%d", Size);                      /*  Read the array size  */
vec = (float *) calloc(Size, sizeof(float));   /*  Generate space and set
                                            vec to point to it  */
vec[Size-1] = 4.3;                      /*  Set the last element  */
```

vec can be indexed in the usual way, e.g. **vec[4]**, but care should be taken to ensure that any index used has a value in the range 0 to **Size-1**. If an index were outside this range, it is unlikely that the error would be detected by the system and the effect is likely to be the corruption of the some other item of data. For instance, in the above program fragment, assume that **n** is 10 so that the largest legal index is 9. If a programmer were to write

```
vec[10] = 3.1415927;
```

the value assigned will probably be moved into the memory locations immediately after the end of **vec**. This may be part of another data structure stored on the heap or it may be unallocated memory. In the first case the other data structure would appear to have been mysteriously altered, although the effect may not show up until much later in the program. In the second case there may be no harmful effect and the program may seem to work perfectly. Such errors are often very difficult to trace and the best way to avoid them is by taking extreme care with array indices. Mistakes with pointer arithmetic can also produce similar effects.

4.6.   Storage Classes

In C all variables have a type and a storage class. The type (**int, float** etc.) determines
the amount of space needed to store a variable and the storage class determines how the
variable will be stored. There are five storage class specifiers: **auto, extern, static,
register** and **typedef. typedef** will be dealt with in Chapter 6 and the others are
discussed below.

auto is the default storage class for all objects defined inside functions. **auto** variables
are local to the function or block which contains them; in other words they are created
when the function or block starts to execute and are destroyed when the function or
block is finished. For example:

```
void sink(void)  {
    auto float Titanic;
    float Hesperus;
    . . .
}
```

Both **Titanic** and **Hesperus** are strictly local to the function. The **auto** declaration
for **Titanic** is optional and is sometimes used for emphasis.
External variables are those defined outside the functions that use them. As an
example consider a program with the structure illustrated below:

```
float Density;

float func1(void) {
    Density = 1;
    ...
}

int AtomicNumber;

float func2(void) {
    AtomicNumber = 2;
    ...
}
```

In this program fragment the variables **Density** and **AtomicNumber** are external
because they are not declared inside a function. **Density** can be used in both **func1** and
func2 but **AtomicNumber** can only be used in **func2**. Suppose now that it is
necessary that **func1** be able to use **AtomicNumber** but the programmer does not
wish to move the definition (this is unlikely, but a less contrived example would be
more complicated). A compiler needs a mechanism to signal that some variable or

function that is defined elsewhere is going to be used at this point. This can be done by modifying **func1** in the following way:

```
float func1(void) {
    extern int AtomicNumber;
    Density = 3.3;
    AtomicNumber = 34
    ...
}
```

This now declares **AtomicNumber** as an integer but the compiler will not reserve space for it at this point because its definition will come either later in the same file or from a completely different file (the way in which this other file is to be linked to a program will depend upon the computer system). The keyword **extern** is only used when it is necessary to *refer to* an object defined elsewhere.

Up to now, a clear distinction has not been made between the terms definition and declaration. In fact, C uses the term *definition* to refer to the place in a program where the space for a variable is created and a *declaration* merely gives information about a variable without making space. In the functions above, the statement

```
int AtomicNumber;
```

before **func2** is the definition of **AtomicNumber**. The statement

```
extern int AtomicNumber;
```

in the revised version of **func1** is a declaration; it creates no space but informs the compiler that **AtomicNumber**, defined elsewhere, is an **int**. All variables must have only one definition but can have many declarations.

The keyword **static** before a local variable is used to create variables which are visible only in the function where they are defined, but which exist throughout the lifetime of the program rather than being destroyed when their function ceases executing. A **static** variable retains its value between separate calls of a function. For example:

```
void memo(void) {
    static int value = 1;
    printf("%d\n", value++);
}
```

Repeated calls of **memo** will print 1, 2, 3 ... Because **value** has been declared **static** its initialization to 1 is only done once, and not each time **memo** is called. The same effect could be achieved by making **value** global:

```
int value = 1;
void  memo(void) {
    printf("%d\n", value++);
}
```

but now **memo** is not self-contained. Another function could change **value** inadvertently and so prevent **memo** from working properly.

Global variables and functions are external and consequently can be referred to by other parts of the program in different files, provided that they are declared **extern** in those files. This is undesirable if these variables or functions should be private to the file containing them. By declaring an external object to be **static** its visibility is restricted to the file in which it is declared. As an example, suppose **file1** contains the following definitions:

```
char Roof;
static int Wall;

int Window(void) {
. . .
}

static char Cellar(void) {
. . .
}

float Door(void) {
. . .
}
```

If another part of the program in **file2** contains the declarations:

```
extern char Roof;
extern int Window(void) ;
extern float Door(void) ;
```

Roof, Window and **Door** can now be used in **file2**, but **Wall** and **Cellar** cannot because of the **static** definition in **file1**. This is an example of *information hiding*; external **static** objects correspond to what other languages often call 'private' objects. Section 11.5 shows a more realistic example of how to split a program into modules held in separate files.

register variables may, if a compiler and hardware are accommodating, be stored in machine registers. Using **register** in a declaration is a suggestion to a compiler that it may be a good idea to store the nominated variables in hardware registers (an optimizing compiler may do this automatically). However, the compiler is permitted to ignore this suggestion, in which case the variables will default to **auto**. Only local variables and function parameters (which are treated as **auto**) can be of class **register**. To illustrate the style, the function **Index**, declared in section 4.2, could be changed to:

```
int Index(register ch, register *s) {
    register int i;

    for (i = 0;  ; ++s, ++i) { /* Move s to the next array element  */
        if (*s == ch)          /* *s is the character to which s points  */
            return(i);
        else if (*s == '\0')
            return(-1);
    }
}
```

In this case the variables **ch**, **s**, and **i** may be stored not in memory, but in hardware registers. As access to registers is often about two or three times faster than access to memory and as these variables are heavily used inside the loop, storing these variables in registers may make a program faster, although it will have no effect on its results. As the number of registers in a computer is small, and the number of types which can fit into them is possibly even smaller, **register** declarations should only be used for a few, simple variables which are heavily used. Register variables cannot be used with the **&** (address) operator. The use of **register** variables to improve performance will be further discussed in Chapter 15.

Below is a possible implementation of the standard function **strcmp** showing a typical use of **register** variables. **strcmp** compares two strings **s1** and **s2**, and returns a negative number if **s1** is lexically before **s2**, zero if the strings are equal and a positive number if **s1** is lexically after **s2**:

```
strcmp(register char *s1, register char *s2) {
    /*  While the corresponding characters of s1 and s2 differ
        and the end has not been reached move one element along
        each string  */

    for ( ;  *s1 == *s2  && *s1 != '\0';  s1++, s2++)
        ;  /*  There is no loop body because all the work is in the
                condition and update parts  */
    return (*s1 - *s2);
}
```

The loop, in this case, seems a little complicated at first; it steps through the elements of the arrays **s1** and **s2** until a character is found where they differ or a null character '\0'. The result of the function is the difference between the character values pointed to by **s1** and **s2** when the loop stops. If the strings are equal then these will both be '\0', and the difference is zero, but otherwise the difference indicates the order of the strings.

Exercise 4.2 Why does the condition on the loop above not read

```
*s1 == *s2 && *s1 != '\0' && *s2 != '\0' ?
```

4.7.   Initializing Arrays

Whole arrays can be initialized at the point where they are defined as is illustrated by:

```
static int powers[7] = { 1, 2, 4, 8, 16, 128, 256};
```

Here **powers** has 7 elements (0...6) and all are initialized. If one were to write:

```
static int powers[7] = {1, 2, 4, 8};
```

then the last three elements would be zero, but

```
static int powers[4] = { 1, 2, 4, 8, 16, 32}
```

would cause a compilation error. To avoid such errors it is better to use the form:

```
static int powers[ ] = { 1, 2, 4, 8, 16, 128, 256};
```

which sets the correct size of **powers** automatically. The values used in the initializer must be constants or constant expressions.

The effect of initializing an array depends upon its storage class; static and external arrays are effectively given their values only once, before the program begins to execute. For automatic arrays the effect is different; the array is initialized at each entry of the function in which the array is declared. As an illustration, consider the function

```
void TopGod(void) {
    int Jupiter[ ] = {0};

    static int Jove[ ] = {0};
    printf("%d   %d\n", Jupiter[0], Jove[0]);
    ++Jupiter[0];
    ++Jove[0];
}
```

which will, on successive calls, print:

```
0 0
0 1
0 2
etc.
```

since **Jupiter** is always reset to zero but **Jove** 'remembers' its previous value.

The ability to initialize automatic arrays was introduced into the language with the ANSI standard and is not available on many older compilers which only permit external and static arrays to be initialized. When initializing automatic arrays it should be borne in mind that the initialization takes place at each call of the function which holds the array. This can be a costly operation, especially if the array is large, and you should always consider whether this is essential or whether the array would be better declared as static.

If static and external arrays are not initialized explicitly then all their elements are set to 0. Uninitialized automatic arrays are not given any defined values and contain rubbish.

Multi-dimensional arrays can also be initialized in this way; the style is illustrated by the example:

```
int unit[ ][3] =  {{  1,   0,   0},
                   {  0,   1,   0},
                   {  0,   0,   1}};
```

Notice that, in this case, although the number of rows (the first index) has not been given, the number of columns has been specified. When a multi-dimensional array is being initialized the size of the first dimension may be omitted, and will be deduced by the compiler, but all other dimensions must be specified. The same principle applies when multi-dimensional arrays are passed as function parameters (see section 3.4).

When using an array such as **powers**, defined above, it is sometimes necessary to know how many elements it contains or the value of its upper bound. It is possible to define a separate constant such as

```
#define  UPBpowers 6
```

but this is not very satisfactory; the motive for omitting the size when declaring **powers** was to prevent errors and allow the compiler to provide the correct value, but a **#define** statement such as the one above merely recreates the problem elsewhere.

A solution exists in the form of the operator **sizeof**, which can be used to determine the number of elements in a **static** or external array. One can find the number of elements in **powers** from the expression **sizeof(powers)** / **sizeof(int)**. In general, the size of an array **A** of type **T** will be: **sizeof(A)** / **sizeof(T)** and the upper bound of **A** will be the result of that expression minus 1. The **#define** statement above can now be amended to:

```
#define  UPBpowers  (sizeof(powers) / sizeof(int) - 1)
```

4.8.   Creating 'Triangular' Arrays, Pointers to Pointers

Earlier it was shown how to create the effect of a dynamic array. The same technique may be used to create two-dimensional 'triangular' arrays. The following program fragment shows how this can be done:

```
int *Triangle[n];

for (i = 0;  i < n;  ++i)
    Triangle[i] = (int *) calloc(i+1, sizeof(int));
```

Triangle is declared as an array of **n** pointers to integers (**n** must be a constant) and then **calloc** is called inside a loop to make each element of **Triangle** point to an increasingly large, one-dimensional array. If **n** had the value 5, then the effect of this code would be to create the following situation:

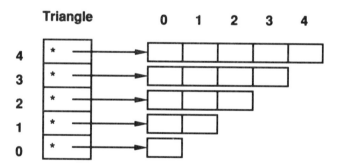

The * in each element of **Triangle** indicates that it is a pointer, in this case to an array of integers. Its elements can be referred to in the usual way, e.g. **Triangle[4][1]**. This works because an array name is really a pointer to the first element of the array. **Triangle[4]** is thus a pointer to the longest array in the diagram above, i.e. its name. Therefore **Triangle[4][1]** is the second element of array **Triangle[4]**.

Exercise 4.3 The same method can be used to create a two-dimensional array with each row being of a different, arbitrary length; such arrays are sometimes called 'ragged' and an important C example, using an array usually called **argv**, is shown in section 5.5. Write and test a program to create such an array, to put values into its elements and to print it. A complication is that you will need to record the length of each row of the array.

It is important to understand the type of **Triangle** in the above example. **Triangle** is an array of pointers, and as an array name is really a pointer, then **Triangle** is a pointer to a pointer to an integer. Consider the following declarations:

```
float    Flotsam = 27, Jetsam = 13, *pBeachComber, *pLookOut,
         **ppLifeGuard, **ppCustomsOfficer;
```

Flotsam and **Jetsam** are float variables, **pBeachComber** and **pLookOut** are pointers to **float** variables and **ppLifeGuard** and **ppCustomsOfficer** are pointers to pointers to **float** variables. After the statements

```
pBeachComber = &Flotsam;
pLookOut = &Jetsam;
```

pBeachComber points to **Flotsam** and **pLookOut** to **Jetsam**. The values of the objects pointed to are found, as usual, by dereferencing:

```
printf("%f %f\n", *pBeachComber, *pLookOut);
```

prints 27 and 13. The next level of indirection is shown by

```
ppLifeGuard = &pBeachComber;
ppCustomsOfficer = &pLookOut;
```

where **ppLifeGuard** and **ppCustomsOfficer** each now contain the address of a variable which itself contains the address of a floating point value. To print the ultimate values of these chains of indirection, it is necessary to doubly dereference:

```
printf("%f %f\n", **ppLifeGuard, **ppCustomsOfficer);
```

It may seem an unnecessary complication to introduce all these seashore characters who spend their time pointing to things that point to other things. However, the value of the technique will emerge in Chapter 7 when lists and other dynamic data structures are discussed, and it will be shown how a customs officer can be made to search a whole regiment of beachcombers to find and remove a single, undesirable individual.

5

Characters, Strings and Files

5.1. Character Order and Lexicographic Order

Single characters are stored in computers as numbers. The particular number that is used to represent some particular character defines what is called the *collating sequence* or the *internal character set* and can vary from one machine to another. However, the most widely used sequence is the ASCII (American Standard Code for Information Interchange, pronounced ass-key) character set which is used as a model in the discussion below.

In the ASCII character set there are 128 characters numbered 0 to 127. The digits (0...9) are contiguous and precede the upper case letters (A...Z) which in turn precede the lower case letters (a...z). Both types of letters are in normal lexicographic order. When characters are compared using ==, >, >=, etc., what are actually compared are their numeric values. Thus 'B' > 'A', '7' < '8', 'n' > 'm' and 'a' > 'A' and 'Z' < 'a'. Ways in which character values, including control characters, may be written are given in section 1.2.

When strings are compared by using the functions below, the comparison starts with the first character of each string and proceeds character by character until a difference is found or the end of either is reached. At this point the order of the strings corresponds to the order of the two differing characters. This is just a complicated way of saying that the method is the same as that used in dictionaries; **"theatre"** comes later than **"theater"**, lexicographically if not historically. However, some results may not be what is expected at first: **"EGG"** comes *before* **"chicken"** because the upper case letters precede the lower case ones. More confusingly, the string **"123"** precedes **"23"** although, of course, the integer **123** > **23**.

There is a set of standard functions available from the header file **ctype.h** to provide common operations such as converting the case of letters or finding whether a character is a letter, digit or punctuation. These functions are listed below and all give integer results indicating a truth value. A result of zero indicates false, and anything else indicates true.

Function name	Condition tested
isalnum(c)	c is alphabetic or a digit
isalpha(c)	c is alphabetic
isascii(c)	c has a value in the range 0...127
iscntrl(c)	c is a control character
isdigit(c)	c is a digit
isgraph(c)	c is a printable character other than space
isprint(c)	c is a printable character including space
ispunct(c)	c is printable but not a letter, digit or space
isspace(c)	c is 'white space' (space, tab, vertical tab, newline, return, formfeed.)
isxdigit(c)	c is a hexadecimal digit (0...9, A...F, a...f)

The remaining functions are used to convert characters:

tolower(c)	converts c to lower case if it is an upper case letter.
toupper(c)	converts c to upper case if it is a lower case letter.

Although we have referred to these as functions they are often implemented as *macros*. Macros are discussed fully in Chapter 13 and usually behave in the same way as functions, but there are circumstances in which they may not always work in the way you may expect. The possible problems are discussed in Chapter 13.

5.2. Basic String Operations

A string is a sequence of characters which in C is always terminated with the null character '\0'. When string values must be written in a program, they are enclosed between double quotes, for example: 'April in Vladivostok'. The null character at the end of strings written in this way is provided automatically by the system. In fact all the standard string manipulation functions provide the null. However, sometimes it is necessary for a programmer to build a string from individual characters and in this case it is essential to attach the terminating null explicitly.

Strings are stored in arrays of characters. Thus,

```
char Name[30], FirstName[30];
```

declares two strings able to hold thirty characters each, one of which will be the terminating null (always remember to allow an extra character for the null). They can be copied using the function **strcpy**:

```
strcpy(Name, "Bloodaxe");
strcpy(FirstName, "Eric");
```

Notice that it is an error to write

```
Name = "Bloodaxe";      /* WRONG */
```

because the operator = does not copy arrays. The effect of the above statement is discussed below.

Strings can be printed by using **printf** and the **%s** conversion character. For example:

```
printf("%s %s", FirstName, Name);
```

The string is printed up to the terminating null character. One way to read a string is to use **scanf** with the **%s** conversion character. For example:

```
scanf("%s", Name);
```

will skip any leading white space characters and then read a string up to the next white space character. In this way it is only possible to read strings which do not contain white space. It is an error if the array into which the string is read is not large enough.

In a declaration such as that of **Name** above, **Name** is actually a pointer and a space of 30 characters is automatically created to which it points. However, **Name** is a *constant* pointer and so cannot be made to point anywhere else. This is why the assignment **Name = "Bloodaxe"** is wrong, as it attempts to make **Name** point to a new location. Such an error should be detected at compile time by a reasonable compiler.

Because pointers and arrays are so intimately related in C, all string operations can be done using character pointers, but care needs to be taken. The declaration

```
char *Hamlet;
```

declares **Hamlet** to be a pointer to a character but does not create any space to which it points. Because **Hamlet** does not point anywhere it is not legal to write

```
strcpy(Hamlet, "Prince of Denmark");
```

as this tries to copy the string into a non-existent space. It is, however, possible to write

> Hamlet = "Prince of Denmark";

because this makes **Hamlet**, a variable pointer, point to a location containing the string **"Prince of Denmark"**.

The function **gets(s)** will read a whole line into a string **s**. The line will be read up to the newline character at the end, but the newline will not be included in the string. Again s must be large enough to hold the whole line. A call to **gets** could be

> gets(Name);

If **gets** encounters an end of file, or an error occurs when reading, it returns the pointer value **NULL**. The following program uses this to count the number of lines in a file, assuming that no line is longer than 132 characters. **Line** is declared as having 133 characters because of the need to store the terminating '\0'.

```
#include <stdio.h>
main() {
    char Line[133];
    int Count = 0;

    while (gets(Line) != NULL)
        ++Count;
    printf("The file contained %d lines\n", Count);
}
```

Strings cannot be assigned or compared by using the standard operators because they are arrays. Consequently operations on strings use a set of functions declared in the header file **strings.h**. Assume two character arrays **s1** and **s2** and an integer variable **n** have been declared. The following functions are available:

strcpy(s1, s2) copies **s2** to **s1**. The assignment operator = would not have the same effect because **s1** and **s2** are really pointers and so **s1 = s2;** would merely make **s1** *point* to the same place as **s2**.

strcat(s1, s2) appends a copy of **s2** to the end of **s1**. It also returns **s1** as its result. For example:

```
char s1[30], s2[30];
strcpy(s2, "Vladivostok");
strcpy(s1 , "April in ");
printf("%s", strcat(s1, s2));
```

would output: **April in Vladivostok**

If **s1** were not long enough to hold the final string, the results are unpredictable and likely to be catastrophic.

strncpy(s1, s2, n) is similar to **strcpy** but only the first **n** characters of **s2** are copied.

strcmp(s1, s2)   compares **s1** and **s2** and returns zero if the strings are equal, a positive integer if **s1 > s2,** and a negative integer if **s1 < s2.** In this context **s1 < s2** implies that string **s1** would come earlier than **s2** in a dictionary, but remember that lower and upper case letters are not equivalent.

strncmp(s1, s2, n) is similar to **strcmp** but only the first **n** characters are compared.

strlen(s)   returns the length of the string **s.** It scans **s** until a null character is found. The null character is not included in the count.

When a string is to be stored in an array of characters, it is important to allow sufficient space for the longest string that can be encountered *plus* the terminating null character. If the array is too small, the error is unlikely to be detected cleanly by your system.

5.3.   Simple Use of Files

File operations are discussed at length in Chapter 14, but it will be useful at this point to describe how characters and strings may be read from, or written to, files. Files are referred to via variables of type **FILE ***, that is pointers to files. A **FILE** is in fact a *structure*, a type of object that will be discussed in Chapter 6. It will contain many internal variables and these will differ between different systems. However, it is not necessary to know such details because **stdio.h** provides a set of functions to perform file operations. The steps needed to use a file are illustrated by the fragment below:

```
FILE *Infile;
Infile = fopen("ExperimentResults", "r");
```

fopen opens a file called **ExperimentResults** for reading and links **Infile** to it. The first parameter of **fopen** is a character array holding the name of the file to be opened; the permitted form of a file name depends upon the operating system in use. The second parameter is also a character array and can be **"r"**, meaning read, **"w"**, meaning write and **"a"** meaning append.

Single characters can be read from a file using **getc**:

```
int ch;
ch = getc(Infile);
```

getc returns the next character from a file or **EOF** if an error occurs or the end of the file is reached. It is defined to deliver an **int** rather than **char** because **EOF** is usually represented by the value -1, which is not a valid character value.

fgets is a similar function to **gets** but is used to read strings from files and has three parameters. An example of a call could be

```
fgets(Line, 133, Infile)
```

which would read one line from **InFile** and store it in the string **Line**. The second parameter is one more than the maximum number of characters to read and should not be greater than the size of **Line**. The difference of one is due to the '\0' character provided on the end of **Line**. A subtle, but important difference between **fgets** and **gets** lies in the handling of the newline character at the end of a line. **gets** reads the newline character but it is not included in the string; **fgets** includes the newline at the end of the string, so that if a string is read using **fgets** and then printed, there will be an automatic newline after it. The result of **fgets** is a character pointer, and normally it will point to the string just read; if an error occurs, however, it will point to **NULL**.

Characters can be written to a file using **putc** which has the definition:

```
int putc(int ch, FILE *Destination)
```

and which prints the character **ch** in the file **Destination**. The value returned will be the character printed unless an error occurs, in which case **EOF** is returned. Whole strings can be printed using **fputs** which is defined as

```
int fputs(char *Line, FILE *Destination)
```

which prints **Line** in the file pointed to by **Destination** and returns zero unless an error occurs, when **EOF** is returned.

ungetc is a standard function which pushes a character back into a file that is being read. Its definition is

```
ungetc(int ch, FILE *FileId);
```

and its effect is to push the character **ch** back into the file **FileId** so that it will be read again at the next call of **getc**, **scanf**, **fgets** or **getchar**. The standard only requires that one character can be pushed back in this way although many implementations are less restrictive.

If it is necessary to 'unget' more than one character, the programmer must provide functions to implement a *buffer* which stores characters that have been 'ungot'. This consists of an array to store the characters and an index to indicate the last 'ungot' character.

The next example program, containing two user defined functions **getch** and **ungetch** (based on similar functions given by Kernighan and Ritchie), shows how this can be done. **ungetch** puts a character at the current position in the buffer and increments the index and **getch** removes the latest character from the buffer, decrementing the index or, if the buffer is empty, it reads a new character using **getc**. This data structure is actually an example of a stack.

The following example illustrates the use of some of the functions and techniques described above. Many programs need to recognize certain words or symbols (here called 'tokens') in their input data. The function **GetToken** shown below takes as a parameter a list of possible tokens, reads the next few characters of input data and compares them with the tokens in the list. If the characters read correspond to one of the tokens then the function delivers the position of the token in the list; if not then it delivers -1. As a example, suppose that a program is to recognize the tokens **left, right, up, down**. A suitable list could be created by declaring:

```
static char *list[ ] = {"left", "right", "up", "down"};
```

A call to **GetToken** could then be:

```
int Direction = GetToken(stdin, list, 4);
```

where the first parameter is the file from which data are to be read, the second is the list of tokens (as an array of pointers to strings) and the third is the number of items in the list.

The **GetToken** function below compares each item in its token list with data read from a file. If one item in the list does not match then the characters which have been read are 'pushed back' using **ungetch** and an attempt made to match the next item. If no match is found then the reading position is unchanged and the calling program can choose to take some other action without loss of data. As tokens are tested in the order in which they appear in the list, it is necessary to ensure that a false recognition is not made through one token being the start of another. For example, if we want to recognize as tokens the words **arcsin** and **arc**, they must be given in that order in the list. Otherwise the **arc** beginning **arcsin** would be wrongly identified. The functions **getch, ungetch** and **GetToken** are:

```
#define BuffSize      100
#define FALSE         0

char Buffer[BuffSize];        /*   Buffer for ungetch */
int BuffPointer = 0;          /*   Next free position in Buffer   */
```

```
int fgetch(FILE *InFile) {
    /*  get a (possibly pushed back) character from InFile  */
    return( (BuffPointer > 0) ? Buffer[--BuffPointer] : fgetc(InFile) );
}

void ungetch(int ch, FILE *InFile) (
    /*  push 'ch' back on 'InFile' */
    if (BuffPointer >= BuffSize)
        printf("ungetch can only unget %d characters\n", BuffSize);
    else
        Buffer[BuffPointer++] = ch;
}

int GetToken(FILE *InFile, char **TokenList, int LenTokenList)  {
    int MismatchFound, TokenNo, CharsRead;
    char **TokenToMatch, *CharToMatch, LastCharRead;

    /*  Scan down each element of TokenList  */
    for (    TokenToMatch = TokenList, TokenNo = 0;
            TokenNo < LenTokenList;
            ++TokenToMatch, ++TokenNo)
    {
        MismatchFound = FALSE;
        CharsRead = 0;
        CharToMatch = *TokenToMatch; /* First char of TokenToMatch  */
        /* Compare each char of 'TokenToMatch' with input from 'InFile' */
        while (*CharToMatch != '\0' && !MismatchFound) {
            ++CharsRead;
            /*  Get one character, store it, compare  with 'CharToMatch', set
                'MismatchFound accordingly , and step 'CharToMatch'
                further down 'TokenToMatch'  */
            MismatchFound = (LastCharRead = fgetch(InFile))
                                != *(CharToMatch++);
        }
        if (MismatchFound) {
            /*  Put back the characters read   */
            for ( ; CharsRead > 1; --CharsRead)
                ungetch(*((*TokenToMatch)++), InFile);
            ungetch(LastCharRead, InFile);
        } else
            /*  Match found, return its list position   */
            return(TokenNo);
    }
    /*  TokenList exhausted   */
    return(-1);
}
```

An example of a use of this function can be found in section 10.5.

5.4. Boyer and Moore's Algorithm: Searching for Strings

A common requirement is to search a file for occurrences of a particular piece of text. A function for doing this can form the basis of a tool for printing or locating all lines of a file which contain some text or for changing all occurrences of one word to another. What is needed for this purpose is a function which could take some string such as **"Isn't it funny how a bear likes honey"**, a substring such as **"funny"** and tell us that the substring occurs in the string at character position 9 (remembering that the first character position is numbered zero). The obvious approach is to scan the string for an 'f' and when one is found check the characters after to see if they match. While this approach is simple, it is not the best way; it involves checking every character of the string, which can be a slow process.

A better approach was devised by Boyer and Moore [BOYE 77]. In their method a table is built from the substring indicating the position of the last occurrence of each character within it; for the word "funny" this would hold the information that 'f' is at 0, 'u' at 1, 'n' at 3 and 'y' at 4. The algorithm then involves searching in the string for the *last* character of the substring in the following way: the substring contains five characters, numbered zero to four, so clearly there is no point checking the string before character number 4, which is a 't'. The table is checked and reveals that there is no 't' in the substring and therefore it is safe to *skip five characters* to the 'f'. This is in the table and is at position zero in the substring, and so four characters can be skipped to the 'y'. This is the character being searched for and so a comparison is made at this point between the whole substring and the appropriate part of the string; this operation finds a match. The diagram below illustrates the process.

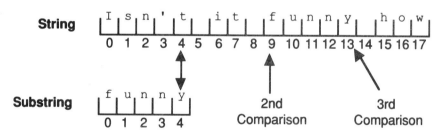

Character	Last Occurrence
f	0
n	3
u	1
y	4

During this entire operation it has been possible to ignore eight characters up to the point where the substring occurs, and in general the number of characters ignored will depend upon the length of the substring; the longer it is, the better.

The program to implement this algorithm will be used to illustrate the program development method known as *stepwise refinement*; this consists of first developing a fairly abstract solution which can easily be seen to be correct and then refining it in steps which are simple enough to be held in the head and which can therefore be checked easily. Each step of this refining process involves making decisions, and the reasons for these decisions should be made as explicit as possible.

Solution 0

```
#define    Absent           -1
#define    CharSetLength    (UCHAR_MAX + 1)

int SubstringPosition( char *String, int StringLength,
                       char *Substr, int SubstrLength,
                       int ContentList[ ]) {

    /*  Searches for Substr (of length SubstrLength) in String (of length
        StringLength) and returns the index of the start of Substr in String
        if it is present and otherwise returns -1.
        ContentList is described below.   */

    int Result = Absent;

    if (StringLength >= SubstrLength) {
        --- 1:   Search for 'substring' in 'string' setting Result
    }
    return(Result);
}
```

This is a 'first-cut' at a solution; decisions have been made about the parameters of the function and some aspects of its internal working. The parameter list has been defined and a decision has been made to pass the lengths of **string** and **substring** as parameters; this may at first seem odd, as the function could use **strlen** to find them for itself, but this particular function is likely to be called many times either to look for different substrings in one string or, more likely, to look for the same substring in many different strings. In this latter case, it is wasteful to calculate the string lengths at each call when in fact they will often be unchanged. Because the representation of a string is a sequence of characters terminated by the character '\0', the **strlen** function is an expensive operation as it needs to scan down its parameter string until the end is found.

ContentList represents the table in the diagram above. It is an array of integers, one for every character in the character set, so that the 65th would correspond to 'A' if the ASCII character set is being used. Since characters are represented as integers, a character can be used directly to index this array. Elements corresponding to characters which occur in **Substr** contain the position of the last occurrence of that character and all the rest contain **Absent**. The array will be given values by a function **MakeContentList**, described later.

Absent, defined at the start of the function, is used both to indicate an absent character in the **ContentList** and the absence of the substring in the string. **CharSetLength** is the number of characters in the machine's character set and so will be one greater than **UCHAR_MAX**, the value of the largest valued character (see section 2.1). The section in bold-face type numbered **1** in the code above is a piece of *pseudocode* which describes the action to be taken by some code which has yet to be written; the next step is to write the piece of code for that subproblem. It involves a special case and a general case.

Subproblem 1:   Search for 'substring' in 'string' setting Result

```
char  FinalChar = Substr[SubstrLength-1];
if (SubstrLength  == 1) {
    --- 2: check for FinalChar in String
}
else {
    --- 3: apply the full algorithm
}
```

The case where it is necessary to find one character in a string is likely to be fairly common and so it is a good idea to treat it as a special case for the sake of efficiency. The variable **FinalChar** is the last character of **Substr.** Next a choice must be made about which of these subproblems to tackle first, and a good rule of thumb is to take the more central or more difficult one, because this is more likely to reveal shortcomings in the development so far; if it should be necessary to back-track on the solution, it is best realized as quickly as possible. With this in mind, the next step is to develop the full algorithm:

Subproblem 3:   Apply the full algorithm

```
int  StringIndex = SubstrLength - 1,
     Result = Absent;
do {
    --- 4: Check for the last character of Substring and move
          StringIndex appropriately if a match is not found.
          If a match is found, check the whole substring and
          set  Result.
} while (StringIndex < StringLength && Result == Absent);
```

Here **StringIndex** is an index to the current position in **String**, and the first character to be checked is at **SubstrLength-1**. It is left to subproblem 4 to decide how to make the necessary adjustments. **Result** will be the eventual result of the function **SubstringPosition**. If it has a value other than **Absent**, then the code of subproblem 4 has found a match.

Subproblem 4 checks the last character of **Substr** against the appropriate place in **String**, identifies a match if there is one and sets **Result** accordingly, and adjusts **StringIndex** if there is no match. In the section of code below, **CurrentChar** is the character of **String** at the position **StringIndex**. Two situations can arise when **CurrentChar** does not match the last character of **Substr**: **CurrentChar** may not be in **Substr** at all, in which case **StringIndex** can be incremented by the whole length of **Substr**, or it is present but is not the last character. In this case **StringIndex** must be incremented by the distance between the end of **Substr** and the last occurrence of **CurrentChar** within it; this is **SubstrLength - PositionInSubstr - 1**. If you find the complicated **if** statement at the start of subproblem 4 a bit daunting you will find it dissected into manageable portions in the next section.

Subproblem 4: Check for the last character of Substring and move StringIndex appropriately if a match is not found. If a match is found, check the whole substring and set Result.

```
if ((PositionInSubstr = ContentList[CurrentChar = String[StringIndex]])
        == Absent)
    /* CurrentChar is not in Substr so StringIndex can be incremented
       by SubstrLength */
    StringIndex += SubstrLength;
else if (CurrentChar == FinalChar) {
    /*  We have a possible match  */
    --- 5: Compare the whole of Substr aligning the last
            character with CurrentChar
}
else  /* CurrentChar is in Substr but not at the end  */
    StringIndex += (SubstrLength - PositionInSubstr - 1);
```

The expression in the first **if** statement is an example of how C allows programs to be compact and efficient but also difficult to read. It is really two assignments and then a comparison. It is equivalent to:

```
CurrentChar = String[StringIndex];
PositionInSubstr = ContentList[CurrentChar ];
if (PositionInSubstr == Absent)
    . . .
```

Subproblem 5 can be easily implemented by using the standard function **strncmp** (see section 5.2), which compares one string with a part of another. At this stage the last character of **Substr** matches the current character in **String**. If the whole of **Substr** is to match the previous **SubstrLength** characters of **String**, the first character of the substring must be at position **StringIndex - SubstrLength + 1** in **String**. If a match is found then **Result** must be set accordingly, and if not **StringIndex** must be moved to the next position of the string move to the next position of the string to continue the process. The program is:

Subproblem 5: Compare the whole of Substr aligning the last character with CurrentChar

```
FirstChar = StringIndex - SubstrLength + 1;
if (strncmp(&String[FirstChar], Substr, SubstrLength) == 0)
    Result = FirstChar;

if (Result == Absent)
    ++StringIndex;
```

It is important to realize why the first parameter to **strncmp** is preceded by **&**; **String[StringIndex - SubstrLength + 1]** is a character somewhere in the middle of **String** and so **& String[. . .]** is the address of that character and can be used as if it were an array in its own right.

Finally we must fill in subproblem 2, for when **Substring** is a single character:

Subproblem 2: check for a single character substring

```
for (StringIndex = 0;
     StringIndex < StringLength && Result == Absent;
     ++StringIndex)
    if (FinalChar == String[StringIndex])
        Result = StringIndex;
```

It is necessary to write a function **MakeContentList** which takes **Substr** and builds **ContentList** from it. This is simple and will not be examined in detail; a solution is found in the program below. Now it only remains to put all these parts together and move a few declarations around to complete the solution. The whole program is:

```
#include <stdio.h>
#include <string.h>
#include <limits.h>

#define Absent      -1
#define CharSetSize (UCHAR_MAX + 1)
```

```
int SubstringPosition(char *String, int StringLength, char *Substr,
                      int SubstrLength, int ContentList[]) {

   /* Searches for Substr (of length SubstrLength) in String (of length
      StringLength) and returns the index of Substr in String if it is
      present and otherwise returns -1.
      ContentList is described in the text paragraph below.  */

   int Result = Absent, StringIndex, PositionInSubstr, FirstChar;
   char FinalChar = Substr[SubstrLength - 1], CurrentChar,
        *StringPointer, *SubstrPointer;

   if (StringLength >= SubstrLength) {
      if (SubstrLength == 1) {
         /* Special treatment for a one character substring  */
         for (StringIndex = 0;
              StringIndex < StringLength && Result == Absent;
              ++StringIndex
              )
              if (FinalChar == String[StringIndex])
                 Result = StringIndex;
      }
      else {
         StringIndex = SubstrLength-1;
         do {
            if ((PositionInSubstr =
                      ContentList[CurrentChar = String[StringIndex]]
                 ) == Absent
              ) /* CurrentChar is not in Substr  */
                 StringIndex += SubstrLength;
            else if (CurrentChar == FinalChar) {
               /*  We have a possible match  */

               FirstChar = StringIndex - SubstrLength + 1;
               if (strncmp(&String[FirstChar],
                       Substr, SubstrLength) == 0
                  )
                  Result = FirstChar;

               if (Result == Absent)
                  ++StringIndex;
            }
            else  /* CurrentChar is in Substr but not at the end  */
               StringIndex += (SubstrLength - PositionInSubstr - 1);
         } while (StringIndex < StringLength && Result == Absent);
      }
   }
   return(Result);
}
```

```
void MakeContentList(char *Substr, int ContentList[]) {

    /*  Sets up ContentList to contain the indices of the characters in
            ContentList  */

    int i;

    /* Initially set all elements of ContentList to Absent   */
    for (i = 0;  i <= CharSetSize - 1;  ++i)
        ContentList[i] = Absent;

    /* Set the indices for the characters in Substr  */
    for (i = 0;  *Substr != '\0';  ++i, ++Substr)
        ContentList[*Substr] = i;

}
```

Below is a simple program intended as an example of how these functions may be used. It searches a specified file for all occurrences of a specified string and prints out the lines which contain that string. The version given is not 'user friendly' in that it is intolerant of user's errors, but it could be easily improved to make a more useful utility, in particular by using *program arguments*, which are described in the next section. Many systems provide such a program as a standard utility. Its principal purpose is to illustrate how to use these functions.

```
main() {
    #define LineLength    132
    #define NameLength    12

    int LineNumber = 1, ContentList[CharSetSize], SearchStringLength;
    FILE *InStream;
    char CurrentLine[LineLength], FileName[NameLength],
            SearchString[LineLength];

    /*  Get the file name and open the file */
    printf("Give the name of the file to be searched\n");
    gets(FileName);
    InStream = fopen(FileName, "r");

    /*  Get the substring   */
    printf("Give the substring to be searched \n");
    gets(SearchString);

    /*  Set up ContentList   */
    MakeContentList(SearchString, ContentList);
    SearchStringLength = strlen(SearchString);
```

```
        while (fgets(CurrentLine, LineLength, InStream) != NULL) {

            if (SubstringPosition(CurrentLine, strlen(CurrentLine),
                                  SearchString, SearchStringLength,
                                  ContentList)
                != Absent
               )
                printf("%6d  %s", LineNumber, CurrentLine);

            ++LineNumber;
        }
    }
```

5.5.   Arguments to Programs

Functions in C programs can be given information in the form of parameters (or arguments). This mechanism can be extended to an entire program and in this sense a C program is like a function which can be called from an operating system, although the precise details of how to achieve this vary between systems. The parameters passed to a program in this way are called *command line arguments*. When a C program is executed, it can be given two pieces of information: the number of command line arguments and a pointer to an array of strings that contain the arguments. By convention these are called **argc** and **argv** respectively.

argc is declared to be of type **int** and **argv** is a pointer to an array of strings. The convention is that **argv[0]** will contain the name by which the program was invoked, **argv[1]** the first parameter, **argv[2]** the second and so on. As an example, consider a program which checks whether a word is a palindrome (has the same spelling forward and backward, for example 'madam'). If the program had been compiled and saved under the name **palindrome** then on some systems a call to the program could take the form:

        palindrome madam

In this case **argc** would be 2 since the name of the program in counted as a parameter, **argv[0]** would be 'palindrome' and **argv[1]** would be 'madam'. It should be noted that not all computer systems allow a program to be invoked in the way shown; some may require a special command or a mouse click to start a program and the parameters may not then be presented in quite the same way. It is necessary to check the documentation for each C system to find the required style.

One possible version of the **palindrome** program is shown below:

```
#include <stdio.h>
main(int argc, char *argv[ ]) {
    if (argc < 2)
        printf("\n No argument has been given\n");
    else if (argc > 2)
        printf("\n Too many arguments have been given \n");
    else {
        int i, j;
        /*  Set i to be the index of the first character of argv[1],
            j to be the index of the last character, and then move i up and
            j down until they meet or the corresponding characters differ  */
        for (    i = 0, j = strlen(argv[1]) - 1;
                 i < j && argv[1][i] == argv[1][j];  /* Compare the ith and jth
                                                         characters of argv[1]   */
                 ++i, --j
            ) /* no loop body   */;

        if (i >= j)
            printf("\"%s\" is a palindrome\n", argv[1]);
        else
            printf("\"%s\" is not a palindrome\n", argv[1]);
    }
}
```

Exercise 5.1   The palindrome program above does not cope with multi-word palindromes or punctuation. For example, it cannot recognize 'Madam, I'm Adam' as a palindrome. Change it so that it can handle such palindromes. Other test data could include 'A man, a plan, a canal Panama' and 'Sex at noon taxes'.

6

Creating Data Types

6.1.   Defining Types

C allows new types to be created, or new names to be given to existing types, through
the **typedef** statement. For example:

```
typedef float real;        /*  ' real' is now another name for the
                               type float   */
typedef char *string;      /*  'string' is a new type which points to a char   */
typedef float vector[3];   /*  'vector' is a new type which is an array of
                               three floats   */
```

Notice the order in which **typedef** statements are written; they look like variable
declarations with the name of the variable replaced by the name of the new type. These
new types can then be used to declare variables in the usual way:

```
real x, Theta;
string Name, Surname;      /*  Note that this does not create any space
                               for the names since 'string' declares a
                               pointer   */
vector  Target, Base;
```

6.2.   Structures

Structures provide a mechanism for grouping items of related information together. For
example:

77

```
struct HeavenlyBody { float Diameter, SolarDistance;
                      int NumberOfMoons;
                      char Name[20];
                    }
Mercury, Venus, Earth, Mars, Jupiter, Saturn, Uranus, Neptune, Pluto;
```

This declares nine variables (**Mercury, Venus** etc.) of type **struct HeavenlyBody**. Each of these variables consists of four components called *members* which are selected by using the dot operator.

```
Mercury.Diameter = 4878.0;
strcpy(Mercury.Name, "MERCURY");
Mercury.NumberOfMoons = 0;
```

Each member is a variable in its own right and can occur anywhere that a variable is allowed. For example:

```
Radius = Mercury.Diameter / 2;
```

The name **HeavenlyBody** associated with the above structure is optional and is called the *structure tag*; it can be used, after the reserved word **struct**, to refer to the structure. This allows the declaration of more heavenly bodies:

```
struct HeavenlyBody   Demos, Phobos;
```

An alternative and rather more neat way of achieving the same effect is to define a new type. Instead of the declaration above it is possible to declare:

```
typedef struct HeavenlyBody {
          float Diameter, SolarDistance;
          int NumberOfMoons;
          char Name[20];
        } Planet;
```

and then the original declaration could be:

```
Planet   Mercury, Venus, Earth, Mars, Jupiter, Saturn, Uranus, Neptune,
         Pluto;
```

Notice again that **Planet** occurs in the **typedef** statement in the same place that a variable would occur in a variable declaration. It is common, in such declarations, to omit the structure tag **HeavenlyBody**.

As **Planet** is a type, it can be used in any of the ways that another type could be used; in particular it is possible to declare an array of **Planet**s:

```
Planet SolarSystem[9];
```

Such an array can be initialized as follows:

```
static Planet SolarSystem[ ] =
            {  {4878,     57.9,     0,   "MERCURY"  },
               {12104,    108.2,    0,   "VENUS"    },
               {12756,    149.6,    1,   "EARTH"    },
               {6778,     228,      2,   "MARS"     },
               {142700,   778.4,    16,  "JUPITER"  },
               {121000,   1427,     21,  "SATURN"   },
               {52400,    2869.6,   5,   "URANUS"   },
               {44600,    4496.6,   2,   "NEPTUNE"  },
               {3000,     5965.2,   1,   "PLUTO"    }
            };
```

Members of elements of this array can be referred to using the style illustrated by:

```
printf("The mean distance to the Sun from %s is %f million kilometers\n",
    SolarSystem[2].Name, SolarSystem[2].SolarDistance );
```

6.3.   Unions

A union is declared with the same syntax as a structure except for the use of the reserved word **union**.

```
union Versatile {  int iVal;
                   float fVal;
                   char *sVal;
                } MultiFacet;
```

declares a variable **MultiFacet** of type **union Versatile** which has three members: **iVal**, **fVal** and **sVal**. The difference between this union and a structure, however, is that while **MultiFacet** has three members, just as if it were a structure, only one of them exists at any given time; in other words, **iVal**, **fVal** and **sVal** occupy overlapping storage locations, the amount of storage used being that of the largest member.

An assignment to a member of **MultiFacet** could be:

```
MultiFacet.iVal = 27;
```

Now **MultiFacet** holds an integer but it does not know it; it is up to the programmer to keep track of which member is currently in use. Following the statement above a compiler would allow:

```
x = MultiFacet.fVal;
```

but the effect would be unpredictable and is not likely to be useful. In order to simplify the task of keeping track of the currently active member of a union, one can use an extra variable which is most conveniently declared as a member of a structure containing the union; to do this the above declaration should be changed to:

```
struct  Versatile {  enum {INT, FLOAT, STRING} uType;
                union {  int iVal;
                         float fVal;
                         char *sVal;
                      } uValue;
              } MultiFacet;
```

Now the assignment becomes:

```
MultiFacet.uType = INT;
MultiFacet.uValue.iVal = 27;
```

and extracting a value from **MultiFacet** could take the form:

```
switch (MultiFacet.uType) {
    case INT     :    printf("%d", MultiFacet.uValue.iVal);   break;
    case FLOAT   :    printf("%f", MultiFacet.uValue.fVal);   break;
    case STRING  :    printf("%s", MultiFacet.uValue.sVal);   break;
}
```

Note that the names **FLOAT, INT** and **STRING** have no intrinsic significance; they have been chosen arbitrarily as enumeration values. We could have used **TOM, DICK** and **HARRY** with the same effect but the program would be less transparent. The enumeration constants above are written in capital letters in order to prevent them clashing with the reserved words **int** and **float**.

The use of unions is appropriate when certain items in a data structure are not relevant in all circumstances. Suppose we wish to represent information about students and staff in a university. All people have a name, address and date of birth but students also have academic data such as the number of credits, an intended degree and a home address while staff have a rank, salary and department. We could create a structure with members for all possible data but this would clearly be wasteful and a more economical representation for a person would be:

```
struct Person { char * Surname, *FirstNames, *Address;
               int BirthDay, BirthMonth, BirthYear;
               enum {Staff, Student} Classification;
               union {struct { float GradePointAverage;
                               int Credits;
                               char *HomeAddress, IntendedDegree;
                             } StudentData;
                      struct { float Salary;
                               char *Rank, *Department;
                             } StaffData;
                     } Details;
             }
```

A small, but select university could then be declared as:

```
struct Person UniMember[2];
```

Then a few members could be introduced:

```
UniMember[0].Surname = "Socrates";
UniMember[1].Surname = "Plato";
```

One of these will be a staff member and the other a student:

```
UniMember[0].Classification = Staff;
UniMember[1].Classification = Student;
```

The staff member needs a salary:

```
UniMember[0].Details.StaffData.Salary = 1000000;  /*  Drachmas
presumably */
```

And the student needs a subject:

```
UniMember[1].Details.StudentData.IntendedDegree = "Politics";
```

The member **Classification** indicates which part of the union is active for each person, but it is the programmer's responsibility to ensure that he does not cause offense by writing, for instance:

```
UniMember[1].Details.StudentData.GradePointAverage = 1.0;
```

Section 10.5 shows how unions can be used in the representation and evaluation of algebraic expressions.

7

List Manipulation

Chapter 4 explained how to create 'dynamic' arrays which give a degree of flexibility in the way information is stored by allowing the size of an array to be decided as a program runs. Many applications, however, require even more flexibility: they need a data structure that can grow and shrink without restriction (apart from purely physical memory constraints, of course). The most basic of these is the linked list.

To illustrate a typical application for a linked list, suppose that a program needs to store a set of integers in numerical order, but new numbers need to be added and old ones removed. It would be possible to use an array for this purpose, values being inserted by moving array elements up to make space, and values being deleted by shuffling elements down again. The disadvantages of this approach are that insertion and deletion would be expensive operations, and the size of the set of numbers would be limited by the array bounds. The linked list solves both these problems.

7.1. A Simple List

The next diagram illustrates a linked list holding an ordered set of integers; the list consists of *nodes* (the outer boxes) with each node holding a value and a link to the next node in the list. The links are pointers, which is why each one on the diagram is marked with an asterisk. The earth (ground) symbol at the end of the list denotes the value **NULL**, which is conventionally used to terminate a list, and **Root** is a pointer to the start of the list. NULL is defined in **stdio.h**, and has the value zero, but it has the special property that it is automatically coerced to any pointer type when necessary. Shadows on some elements indicate that they are held on the heap. The space for such elements needs to be explicitly allocated and freed by the programmer.

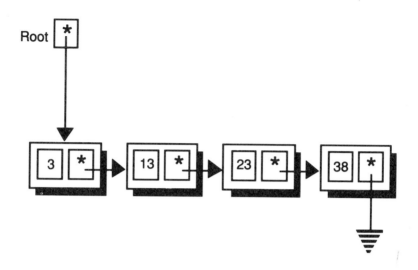

Insertion involves cutting the link between two nodes and 'splicing in' a new node. The diagram below shows the situation after inserting the value 18 into the list above:

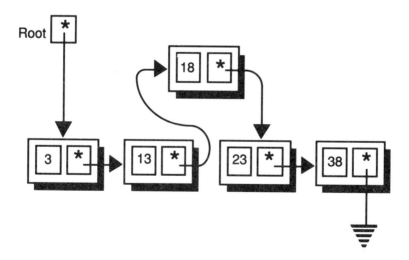

Deletion requires only the movement of a link pointer to by-pass the node that is no longer required; the diagram shows how the value 23 would be removed from the list.

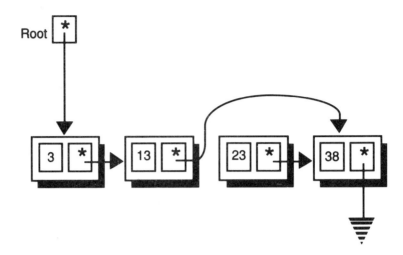

Discussion of the ultimate fate of the deleted node (23 in the above case) will be left until section 7.7.

A type definition for a node of a list is typically of the form:

```
typedef struct ListNode {  int Value;
                          struct ListNode *Next;
                      }   ListNode;
```

Notice that the definition seems to be recursive; the structure **ListNode** contains a member (**Next**) which is a pointer to a **struct ListNode**. This does not create any problems for a C compiler because **Next** is a pointer. It is not permissible to declare a structure which contains a member of the same type as the structure, but a member which *points* to a member that is the same type of structure is permissible.

Confusion can arise over why the name **ListNode** appears both before and after the structure declaration. The first use, **struct ListNode**, is the structure tag and is needed so that the declaration of the member **Next** can refer to a type that has been already declared; the use of **ListNode** after the } gives a name to the new structure type. These two names can be different and many programmers would prefer to declare this as, say:

```
typedef struct LISTNODE { int Value;
                         struct LISTNODE *Next;
                     } ListNode;
```

A list is normally started by declaring its first node and making it point to NULL:

```
ListNode *Root = NULL;
```

This defines **Root** to be a pointer to a **ListNode** and initially to contain the value **NULL** (point to nothing).

If **p** is a pointer to a **ListNode** then the **Value** member of the node to which it points can be referred to as (***p).Value**. Thus a program may contain a statement such as:

```
(*p).Value = 27;
```

Because dereferencing a pointer to a structure and then selecting one of its members is very common, a special operator -> is provided. With this the statement above is usually rewritten:

```
p -> Value = 27;
```

7.2. Constructing an Unordered List

A list is a dynamic data structure since it changes size as a program runs and so space is normally allocated on the heap for each of its nodes (see section 4.4). When making lists, or indeed any other dynamic data structure, it can simplify matters to have a special purpose function to allocate space for the nodes; for example the function **AllocListNode** below creates a new list element, sets the values of its two members and returns a pointer to the new element:

```
ListNode *AllocListNode(int Value, ListNode *Next)  {

    /*  Declare a pointer to a list node and allocate space for it  */

    ListNode *NewOne = (ListNode *) malloc (sizeof(ListNode));

    /*  Set the values of its members   */
    NewOne -> Value = Value;
    NewOne -> Next = Next;
    return(NewOne);
}
```

The easiest way to build a list is simply to insert every element at the start of the list and often, if the values do not have to be in a special order, this all that need be done. The process is illustrated by the function **InsertAtHead** below:

```
void InsertAtHead(int Value, ListNode **List) {
    *List = AllocListNode(Value, *List);
}
```

A call to this function, given **Root** declared as above, could be:

    InsertAtHead(i, &Root);

Notice that the *address* of **Root** must be passed to the function **InsertAtHead** because a new element is added at the beginning which changes the value of **Root**. **List** is declared with two asterisks since it is the address of (a pointer to) a pointer; it points to **Root**, which in turn points to the first node of the list.

7.3.   Printing a List

The function below will print the values stored in a list.

```
void PrintList (ListNode *List) {
    ListNode *p;

    for (p = List;  p != NULL;  p = p -> Next)
        printf("%d\n", p -> Value);
}
```

Notice that **List** is declared here as only a single pointer (*) and not as a pointer to a pointer, since nothing will be changed when a list is printed.

Some C programmers would write the loop above as:

    for (p = List;   p;   p = p -> Next)

This works because the loop continues for as long as **p** has a non-zero value and stops when it becomes zero (**NULL**); the motivation programmers give for using this type of construction is that they believe that a compiler may generate better code (one less comparison). However, such constructions are much harder to read and can easily lead to mistakes; moreover, any but the most simple compiler would not generate code for the comparison because **NULL** is known to be zero. Therefore the only advantage is a miniscule reduction in typing time at the cost of a less readable program, with consequent penalties later during debugging or program modification. A similar idiom is to type

    if (p == NULL) ...

as

```
if (!p) ...
```

but we will not use this cryptic style.

The variable **p** in the above function is not strictly necessary; an alternative form could be:

```
void PrintList (ListNode *List) {
    for ( ;  List != NULL;  List = List -> Next)
        printf("%d\n", List -> Value);
}
```

This version makes use of the fact that **List** is a copy of the actual parameter given to **PrintList** and so the function can safely use it as a local variable. This style is commonly found in C programs.

7.4. Ordered Lists: Using Pointers to Pointers

Often it is necessary to add elements to a list in some order (e.g. alphabetical), a process which involves breaking the links to insert a new element at its proper place. A simple case involves creating an ordered list of integers with no repetitions. The process of inserting a value **V** at its proper place in a list involves the following steps:

```
Set a pointer (called Tracer here) to point to the start of the list;
Move Tracer along  the list until it finds an element preceding one which
holds  a value >= V or the end of the list;
if V was found then
    the value is already in the list and need not be added
else
    Make a new node;
    Put V in its Value member;
    Make its Next member point to the next element in the list;
    Set the Next member of the previous element in the list to point to the
        new element;
end if
```

The problem is how to stop at the element preceding the one wanted. A too simple-minded approach leads to all sorts of problems dealing with special cases, i.e. a list with no elements, inserting at the end of the list or at the beginning. One method, beloved of Pascal programmers, is to use two tracers, one lagging behind the other, although this does not remove all the problems; in C this is unnecessary and a shorter, more efficient function is possible by using a single tracer which is a pointer to a pointer. This technique is illustrated by the function below and is explained in detail in the next few pages.

```
void Insert(int Val, ListNode **List) {
/*   A list insertion function which inserts a value "Val" into an ordered
     list provided it is not already present. */

/*   Declare Tracer and make it point to the root of the list   */
ListNode **Tracer = List;

/*   Move along List until the following item is the end or a node is
     found containing a value greater than or equal to Val   */
while (*Tracer != NULL && (*Tracer) -> Value < Val)
    Tracer = &(*Tracer) -> Next;

/*   Insert Val in List if it not already present   */
if (*Tracer == NULL || (*Tracer) -> Value != Val)
    *Tracer = AllocListNode(Val, *Tracer);
}
```

A call to this function could be:

```
Insert(27, &Root);
```

Tracer in the above function, is a pointer to a pointer. After the statement

```
ListNode **Tracer = List;
```

it contains not the address of the first element of the list but the address of the address of the first element of the list (**Root**, in this case).

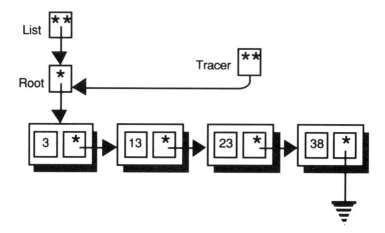

The value of doing this is illustrated above. Suppose we want to insert the value 27

2200 Eastridge Loof
San Jose   95122
Bone Marrow   11:00
3:0

CMS Quad

2355 oakland Rd

1 7 9 7 1

1 3 3 1

1 2 1

1 1

1

1 = 1

0 = 1

1156 Hi.by St

into the list {3, 13, 23, 38}. After the initialization of **Tracer** we have the situation shown. In the diagram some elements are shadowed; these are on the heap and have been created by calls to **malloc**. **List** and **Root** are usually **static** and are normally declared globally (that is, outside any function) and **Tracer** is **auto**. The elements marked ** are pointers to pointers to nodes and the elements marked * are pointers to nodes. The convention requires that a pointer points to an element with one less * than itself; bearing this in mind makes it possible to draw similar diagrams involving pointers of any complexity.

The loop moves **Tracer** down the list after first checking that the end of the list has not been reached and then that the current node is smaller than **Val**. The order of the two tests in the loop condition is important; if the element to which **Tracer** points is the last in the list then it is essential not to refer to the non-existent **Value** member of the next node. The expression takes advantage of the fact that if the left-hand side of **&&** is false then the right-hand side will not be evaluated. Notice that **Tracer** does not point to a node, but to a pointer member within a node, i.e. the member **Next**. Thus **(*Tracer) -> Value** refers to the value stored in the following node (38 in the diagram) and **&(*Tracer) -> Next** is the address of the **Next** member of the following node.

After obeying the loop we have:

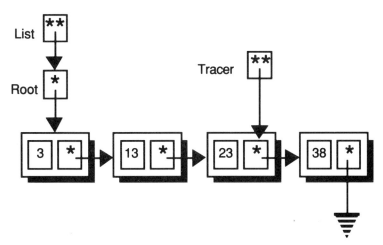

Notice that **Tracer**, a two star location, is not pointing to the element containing 23 but is actually pointing inside it to the **Next** field, a one star location. This satisfies the convention above and is crucial to the next step of inserting a new element, illustrated by the next diagram.

This situation is created by the statement:

```
*Tracer = AllocListNode(Val, *Tracer)
```

Here, **AllocListNode** creates a new node, puts **Val** in its **Value** member, sets its **Next** member to point to the next node in the list and delivers the address of this new node. This address is assigned to ***Tracer**, which is the **Next** member of the preceding node.

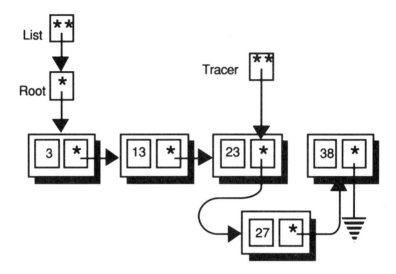

7.5.   Appending to a List

Another common operation is to append an element to the end of a list. The **Insert** function above is easily modified and, in fact, becomes simpler:

```
void Append(int Val, ListNode **List) {
    /* Append "Val" to "List". */

    ListNode **Tracer = List;

    while ((*Tracer) != NULL)
        Tracer = &(*Tracer) -> Next;
    *Tracer = AllocListNode(Val, *Tracer);
}
```

Exercise 7.1 Modify the function **Append** so that it only appends a value to a list if it is not already present.

Exercise 7.2 If our need is to append a value to a list without regard to whether it is already present, then it is more efficient to keep a global pointer to the end of the list in order that adding an element can be done without scanning the list. Write an **Append** function (and whatever global declarations are necessary) to implement this approach.

7.6. Using Recursion to Simplify List Operations

Many operations on lists can be greatly simplified by using recursion. This may not always be the most efficient method in terms of computer time or space, but it can be a lot simpler than iteration. As an example, suppose that we have a list starting at **Root**, as in the examples above, and want to make a copy of it pointed to by a variable **CopyOfRoot**. One may be tempted to write:

```
CopyOfRoot = Root;
```

but this would be wrong; it would merely copy the contents of **Root** (the address of the first list element) into **CopyOfRoot**. Thus **CopyOfRoot** would not hold a copy of the list but would be another pointer to the start of the same list. To make a copy of a linked list it is necessary to allocate new space for all the elements. This is done in the example below:

```
ListNode *CopyOfList(ListNode *Source) {
    if (Source == NULL)
        return(NULL);
    else
        return(AllocListNode(Source-> Value, CopyOfList(Source-> Next)));
}
```

A call to this function could be:

```
CopyOfRoot = CopyOfList(Root);
```

To understand this function, it is helps to think of a list as a head node and a tail which is the remainder of the list. This tail is itself a list with a head and a tail, and so on to the end of the list. Therefore to copy a list it is necessary to create a copy of the head node, and a copy of the tail.

The call of **AllocListNode** generates a new node with a copy of the **Value** member from the head node of **Source** and a pointer to a copy of the tail of **Source**, generated by the recursive call to **CopyOfList**. Working through an example will show you that **CopyOfList** will deliver a copy of any list, including an empty one.

The same function can be written using iteration but the code is far less transparent. There is, however, a cost: the recursive function will call itself once for each element in the list and each of these recursive calls will stay active until the last element has been copied; this may require a lot of memory if the list is long. Choosing between an iterative or a recursive solution to a problem such as the above is a design decision that must be made on the basis of the length of the list, the amount of available memory, the importance of program size, etc. For other dynamic data structures such as trees (described in Chapter 8), the cost of recursion can be slight and the clarity of a recursive solution is well worth the overhead.

7.7. Deleting an Element

Deleting an element from a list involves finding the doomed element, adjusting the **Next** member of the previous element in order to bypass it, and then freeing the space occupied by the defunct element. The use of pointers to pointers makes this particularly easy:

```
void DeleteNode(int Val, ListNode **List) {

    /* A function to delete "Val" from "List".  */

    ListNode **Tracer = List, *DefunctNode;

    /*   Scan the list until Val is found or the end reached   */
    while (*Tracer != NULL && (*Tracer) -> Value != Val)
        Tracer = &(*Tracer) -> Next;

    /*   At this point Tracer is pointing to the Next field of the node
         before the one to be removed, provided it is present  */

    if (*Tracer != NULL){
        /*  Set DefunctNode to point to the element to remove   */
        DefunctNode = *Tracer;

        /*   Adjust the Next field of the node preceding DefunctNode
             to point to the one succeeding it   */
        *Tracer = (*Tracer) -> Next;
        free(DefunctNode);
    }
}
```

7.8. Disposal and Comparison

Disposing of an entire list is not difficult but requires a little care. Simply writing

```
Root = NULL;
```

will detach **Root** from its list, making the list inaccessible but not making its space available for re-use. The function below shows how a list can be properly removed from memory:

```
void DeleteList(ListNode **List)   {
    /* A function to delete the list "List".   */

    ListNode *NextToGo;

    /*   Repeat until List is empty   */
    while ((*List) != NULL) {
        /*   Set NextToGo to point to the current element then
             move List to the next element; notice the two
             assignments   */

        *List = (NextToGo = *List) -> Next;

        /*   Free the previous element   */
        free(NextToGo);
    }
}
```

A call could be:

```
DeleteList(&Root);
```

The function moves **Root** along the list until it reaches **NULL** with **NextToGo** following one step behind and pointing to the element to be freed.

Exercise 7.3 Testing a function such as **DeleteList** is not as easy as it may seem since ***List == NULL** at the end does not guarantee that any space has been freed. Suppose that, because the implementer of your C compiler is lazy, the **free** function does nothing; devise a way of testing **DeleteList** that would show this fact. Test your method by suppressing **free** in **DeleteList**. (Hint: you cannot do this from within the program; you must think about how a running program would behave if space were not freed.)

The next function will compare two lists for equality. Here again, recursion is used to simplify the problem; this solution may use more memory than an iterative version but it easy to see that it is correct. It is left as an exercise to the (energetic) reader to produce an iterative version; this task may be simplified by looking at the solution to the next exercise.

```
typedef enum {FALSE, TRUE} boolean;
boolean ListsAreEqual(ListNode *List1, ListNode *List2) {
    /* Compare two lists */

    if (List1 == List2)  /*   which will happen if both point to NULL and hence
                                 the ends of both have been reached   */
        return(TRUE);
    else if ((List1 == NULL) || (List2 == NULL))
        /*   The end of only one list is reached   */
        return(FALSE);
    else if ((List1 -> Value) == (List2 -> Value))
        /*   The heads of the lists are equal   */
        return(ListsAreEqual(List1 -> Next, List2 -> Next));
    else              /*   The heads are unequal   */
        return(FALSE);
}
```

Exercise 7.4   The function **ListsAreEqual** above uses several return statements and an 'if' statement. In fact, it can be simplified to just one return statement with no 'if'. Produce a version of **ListsAreEqual** which contains just one statement (a **return** statement).

8

Trees

The most commonly used dynamic data structures are lists (discussed in the previous chapter) and *trees*. Lists have disadvantages when storing large amounts of information because searching for an item in a list of N nodes will require the inspection, on average, of about N/2 nodes, provided there is an equal chance of the item being anywhere in the list. A tree allows faster searching at the expense of a little more storage space.

A tree comprises nodes, each of which holds some data and pointers to two or more *descendant* nodes; the tree grows from a root node, which is normally (if unbiologically) depicted at the top in diagrams, and grows downwards; nodes without descendants are called *leaves* and represent the ends of a branch. The number of nodes between the root and the leaf at the end of the longest branch is called the *height* of the tree.

The most commonly used tree is the *binary* tree consisting of nodes with no more than two descendants (called the left and right children) and is particularly easy to implement.

8.1. Binary Trees

Binary trees are normally ordered according to the value of one of the data items stored in a node. The small tree shown below is ordered alphabetically: everything to the left of a node is alphabetically earlier than everything to its right. A suitable type definition for a node of such a structure could be:

```
typedef struct TreeNode {char *Value;
                    struct TreeNode *Left, *Right;
                    } TreeNode;
```

and a declaration for **Root** would then be:

TreeNode *Root = NULL;

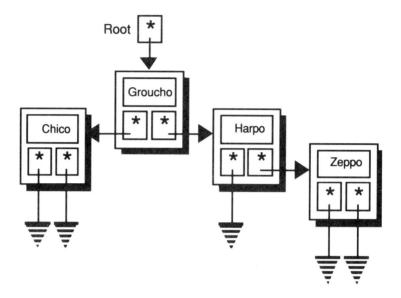

In order to grow a tree it is convenient, as with lists, to have a function to generate a tree node and to give it values. A suitable function is **AllocTreeNode**, below:

```
TreeNode *AllocTreeNode(char *Entry) {
    /*  Deliver a pointer to a new, initialized tree node   */
    TreeNode *NewOne = (TreeNode *) malloc (sizeof(TreeNode));

    NewOne -> Value = Entry;
    NewOne -> Left = NewOne -> Right = NULL;
    return(NewOne);
}
```

Notice that this function does not create any space for the member **Value**. Instead it sets the **Value** member of the new node to point to the same string as **Entry**. This is efficient, but may not be what is required in a particular application. If it is necessary to create space for a new copy of each string then the relevant line can be changed to:

strcpy((NewOne -> Value = (char *)malloc(strlen(Entry) + 1)), Entry);

which allocates space for the **Value** member (+1 is to allow for '\0' at the end) and then copies **Entry** into it.

Tree structures are fundamentally recursive; any node that is not a leaf is itself the root of a subtree. This leads to a particularly simple function for inserting a node in an alphabetically ordered binary tree (often called a *binary search tree*):

```
void AddToTree(char *Entry, TreeNode **ThisTree) {
    /* Insert "Entry" in "ThisTree" if not already present.    */

    if (*ThisTree == NULL) /* Have found a leaf    */
        *ThisTree = AllocTreeNode(Entry);
    else {
        int Comp = strcmp(Entry, (*ThisTree) -> Value);

        if (Comp != 0)   /*   Strings not equal, continue searching   */
            AddToTree(Entry, Comp < 0    ?  &(*ThisTree) -> Left
                                         :  &(*ThisTree) -> Right);
    }
}
```

A call to **AddToTree** could be:

```
AddToTree(Surname, &Root)
```

where **Surname** is a string variable. **AddToTree** inspects each node starting at **Root** and compares the value of **Surname** with the value of the **Value** member of the current node. If **Surname** is alphabetically earlier than the value in the current node it searches the left subtree, if later it searches the right subtree, if equal it does nothing because **Surname** is already in the tree, and if it finds a leaf (which it recognizes as a pointer to null) then it inserts a node containing **Surname** at that point. Notice the use of the **? :** to choose the subtree to be searched.

The tree shown in the diagram above would be created if the data were entered in the order: **Groucho, Harpo, Chico, Zeppo**. Notice that the first value entered would become the root node. This behavior may be a problem; if the data had been entered in the order **Chico, Groucho, Harpo, Zeppo** the tree would degenerate into a list. The function above will work well if the data are well mixed, but if there are large amounts of data which are already in order (or reverse order) then it can perform poorly. In general, in the worst case (the degenerate case mentioned above), a tree of N nodes would have a depth of N; in the best case its depth would be $\log_2 N$. Thus, for a tree of 16,000 nodes, in the worst case inserting an element at the end will require 16,000 nodes to be inspected and in the best case about 14. This represents an improvement of over a thousand-fold. Algorithms exist for ensuring that a tree remains optimally balanced, but they greatly complicate the insertion process and so are not often used unless a tree will be large and there is a strong likelihood that data will arrive in such a way that a highly unbalanced tree will result.

The contents of a binary tree can be printed in alphabetical order by the function:

```
void PrintTree(TreeNode *t) {
    if (t != NULL ){
        PrintTree(t -> Left);
        printf("%s\n", t -> Value);
        PrintTree(t -> Right);
    }
}
```

The function **PrintTree** above is an example of an 'in-order' tree traversal; this means that a left subtree of a node is printed, then the node and finally the right subtree. In general, tree traversal algorithms are classed as pre-order (node, left subtree, right subtree), in-order (left subtree, node, right subtree) and post-order (left subtree, right subtree, node).

Exercise 8.1. It is sometimes necessary to be able to print a tree in a way which reveals its structure. This can be done by printing a node and, indented under it, its left and then right subtrees. As an example, an alphabetically ordered, binary tree formed from the input: James James Morrison Morrison Weatherby George Dupree can be printed as:

```
James
    George
        Dupree
            - - -
            - - -
        - - -
    Morrison
        - - -
        Weatherby
            - - -
            - - -
```

Here '- - -' indicates a null node. Write a version of **PrintTree** that will print a tree in this manner.

8.2.   Searching Binary Trees

Having created a tree it is usually necessary to search it. The next function will search an ordered, binary tree for a node containing a specified string and will deliver a pointer to the node, if it exists, or **NULL** otherwise:

```
TreeNode *Search(char *Query, TreeNode *ThisTree) {
    /*  Searches for "Query" in "ThisTree" and returns a pointer
        to the node containing it, if it there.  Otherwise it
        returns NULL.  */

    if (ThisTree == NULL)
        return(NULL);
    else {
        int Comp = strcmp(Query, ThisTree -> Value);

        if (Comp == 0)  /* Node found */
            return(ThisTree);
        else
            return(Search(Query, Comp < 0  ?  ThisTree -> Left
                                           :  ThisTree -> Right));
    }
}
```

Notice that the second parameter is declared as **TreeNode *ThisTree**, a pointer to a **TreeNode**, whereas the equivalent parameter in **AddToTree** was declared as a pointer to a pointer to a **TreeNode**, i.e. **TreeNode **ThisTree**. This is because inserting into a tree involves changing the value of a root pointer, and so the address of the root of the tree must be known to the function. Simply searching a tree does not involve any changes and so the extra level of indirection is not necessary.

8.3. Deleting a Node

Deleting a node from a binary tree involves a certain amount of restructuring of the tree. To illustrate what needs to be done, consider the first tree shown below. Deleting a node with fewer than two children is simple. As an example we will delete the node containing R. **NodeToRemove** is made to point to the node of the tree which must be deleted, and **ParentPointerOfNodeToRemove** to the pointer in the parent node which points to the node to remove (called the 'parent pointer'). The latter is shown, in the second diagram, with two asterisks because it is a pointer to a pointer. Removal of the node then involves moving the pointer coming from 'M' and freeing the defunct node. In the case of a defunct node with one child the parent pointer needs to be moved to that child. If the defunct node has no children the value of either child pointer can be copied into the parent pointer as they will both be **NULL**. In either case the space of the defunct node can be freed.

Removing a node with two children is harder. Such a node is the root of a complete tree, and so its removal will leave two subtrees without a common root. It is necessary to choose a node from within either subtree which can be promoted to be the new root.

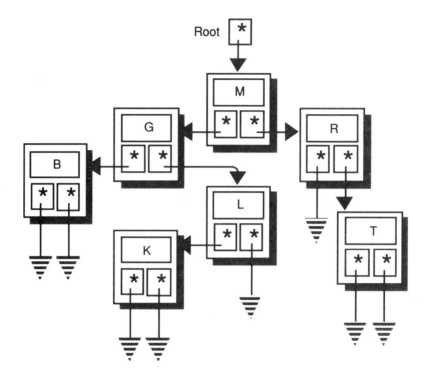

The other nodes belonging to the same subtree as the new root must be rearranged so that they all become the subtree at one side of the new root. The second unattached subtree must then be joined to the other side of the new root. The new root can now be joined to the main tree in the place of the deleted node.

In principle any node could be chosen as the new root, but some choices would make readjusting the new tree quite difficult. For example, if the node containing 'M' in the first figure were to be removed and it was decided to make 'B' the new root, then major movement of nodes would be necessary to move 'G', 'K' and 'L' to their correct positions in the new right subtree.

Several strategies are possible to simplify the operation, but one that also helps keep a well balanced tree is to choose as the new root either of the two nodes which are closest to the deleted node in value, in other words the next lower or next higher valued nodes. In the case of deleting M these are L or R. L is the right-most node of the left subtree and R is the left-most node of the right. What makes these nodes good candidates for being the new root is that everything in the left subtree has a lower value than L and everything in the right is larger than R, so choosing either of these nodes for promotion does not strongly influence the balance of the tree. Since both nodes provide the same advantage the choice is arbitrary; in this example the node containing L (the right-most node of the left subtree) will become the new root.

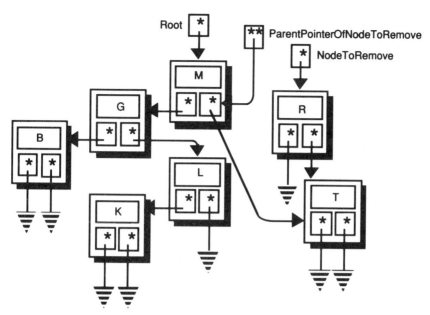

The diagram below shows the situation before rearrangement of the tree if the node to be deleted is the root node (containing M).

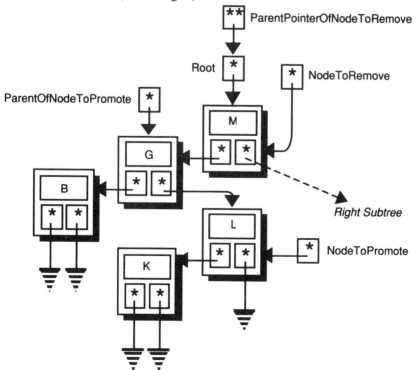

In this case the parent pointer is **Root** and the rearranged tree will have **Root** pointing to a new root node. As the right subtree of 'M' is not involved in the rearrangement, except in so far as it about to acquire a new parent, it is not shown in the diagram. The necessary pointer movements are described by the following pseudocode version of the algorithm:

```
Find the node to remove (M) and its parent pointer (Root);
If the node to remove does not have two children then
    Adjust the parent pointer as in Figure 8.3;
else
    Find the node to promote ('L') and its parent node ('G');
    Adjust the parent pointer of the node to remove (Root) to point to
        the node to promote (L);  (The new root is now in its place)
    If the node to promote is not a child of the node to remove then
        Attach the parent pointer of the node to promote to that
            node's left subtree (attach 'K' to the right of 'G');
        Attach the left subtree of the node to remove to the left of the
            node to promote (the left pointer from 'L' now points to 'G');
    end if
    Attach the right subtree of the node being removed (everything to the
        right of 'M') to the right of the node to be promoted ('L');
end if
free the node to remove;
```

Notice the special case: if the node being promoted is a child of the node being removed then the two adjustments are not necessary. The final tree is shown below. The original right subtree of M, consisting of R and T, is now the right subtree of L.

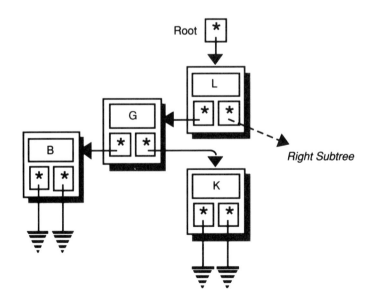

The first step in the pseudo-code requires us to find the node to be removed. This can be done with a slightly modified version of the **Search** function given in section 8.2. **FindNodeToRemove** below delivers the parent pointer of the node about to be removed, which is more useful for our current purposes than a pointer to the node itself.

```
TreeNode **FindNodeToRemove(char *Value, TreeNode **ThisTree) {
    /*   Searches for 'Value' in 'ThisTree' and returns a pointer
         to the parent pointer of the node containing it, if it is there.
         Otherwise it returns NULL.  */

    if (*ThisTree == NULL)
        return(NULL);
    else {
        int Comp = strcmp(Value, (*ThisTree) -> Value);
        if (Comp == 0)  /* Node found */
            return(ThisTree);
        else
            return(FindNodeToRemove(Value,
                           Comp < 0   ?    &((*ThisTree) -> Left)
                                      :    &((*ThisTree) -> Right)));
    }
}
```

The rest of the operations in the pseudocode can be translated into C fairly directly, with the exception of finding the node to promote. This is done by starting from the left child of the node to be removed and following all the right links up to the last one; this is the purpose of the **while** loop in the function **DeleteFromTree** shown below:

```
void DeleteFromTree(char *Entry, TreeNode **ThisTree) {
    /* Delete 'Entry' from 'ThisTree'. */

    TreeNode  *NodeToRemove, **ParentPointerOfNodeToRemove,
              *NodeToPromote, *ParentOfNodeToPromote;

    if ((ParentPointerOfNodeToRemove =
            FindNodeToRemove(Entry, ThisTree)) != NULL)
    {
        NodeToRemove = *ParentPointerOfNodeToRemove;
        /*  First check if NodeToRemove has one or no children  */
        if (NodeToRemove ->Left == NULL)
            *ParentPointerOfNodeToRemove = NodeToRemove -> Right;
        else if (NodeToRemove ->Right == NULL)
            *ParentPointerOfNodeToRemove = NodeToRemove -> Left;
        else {
            /*   It has two children.  Find the node to promote i.e. the
                 rightmost node of the left subtree of the node to remove */
```

```
                    NodeToPromote =
                        (ParentOfNodeToPromote = NodeToRemove) -> Left;
                    while ((NodeToPromote -> Right) != NULL) {
                        ParentOfNodeToPromote = NodeToPromote;
                        NodeToPromote = NodeToPromote -> Right;
                    }
                    *ParentPointerOfNodeToRemove = NodeToPromote;
                    if (NodeToRemove -> Left != NodeToPromote) {
                        /*  NodeToPromote is not a child of NodeToRemove so
                            rearrange the nodes of the left subtree   */
                        ParentOfNodeToPromote -> Right = NodeToPromote -> Left;
                        NodeToPromote -> Left = NodeToRemove -> Left;
                    }
                    /*  Attach the right subtree of NodeToRemove to new root   */
                    NodeToPromote -> Right = NodeToRemove -> Right;
                }
            free(NodeToRemove);
            }
    }
```

A call to delete 'M' from the tree shown in the diagrams would be:

```
        DeleteFromTree("M", &Root);
```

9

Bit Manipulation

One of the reasons that C is widely used is that it allows programs to manipulate data at a very low level, and the lowest level of all is the binary digit or *bit* which corresponds to a binary one or binary zero. (If you are not familiar with binary number systems, logical and shift operations, the way in which numbers are stored in computers and the operations which are applied to them, then you should read Appendix 1.) In order to speed operations bits are organized into groups such as a *byte*, which is normally eight bits or a *word* which is normally several bytes. Word sizes vary from machine to machine; on commercially available computers they range from 16 bits at the lower end to 64 bits on some large, scientifically oriented machines. In C an **unsigned int** would normally correspond to a machine word and is the most natural type to use if bits are being manipulated, although signed **int** is sometimes used.

In the examples below, values are written in C's octal notation; thus the binary number 01101011 is written 0153. To make the operations clearer it may help, in the beginning, to convert the octal values to binary and back again, but after a little practice this will become unnecessary.

9.1.　Basic　Operations

The operations available on words considered as bit values are the logical operations and various types of shift. The logical operations are:

    &   Bitwise AND. Each bit of the left-hand operand is logically ANDed with each bit of the right-hand operand. ANDing two bits together gives the result zero unless both bits are one.
                012 & 014 gives **010**.

    | Bitwise inclusive OR. Each bit of the left-hand operand is logically

ORed with each bit of the right-hand operand. Inclusively ORing two bits together gives the result one if either of the two bits is one and otherwise gives zero.

012 | 014 gives **016**.

^ Bitwise exclusive OR. Each bit of the left-hand operand is exclusively ORed with each bit of the right-hand operand. Exclusively ORing two bits together gives the result one if either, but not both, of the two bits is one.

012 ^ 014 gives **06**.

~ Bitwise complement (also called NOT). This is a monadic operator (i.e. has no left-hand operand) and it reverses each bit of its operand.

~012 gives **0177765** on a 16-bit machine.

C provides shift operations on either signed or unsigned integers. The operation on an unsigned quantity is a logical shift and on a signed quantity may be an arithmetic or a logical shift depending upon the implementation. In the examples unsigned values are assumed.

The shift operations in C are:

L << R **L** is a bit pattern and gives a result equal to **L** shifted left by **R** places. **L** and **R** can be expressions. **R** must be a positive value.

012 << 2 gives **050**

L >> R Behaves in the same way except that the shift is to the right.

012 >> 2 gives **02**

The operators **&=**, **|=**, **^=**, **<<=** and **>>=** are also available with the obvious meanings.

A common use for the logical operations is to set or test individual bits within a word: suppose that we have a sixteen bit word and need to set the left-most eight bits to zero while leaving the right-most eight unchanged. As an example, given the binary number 1101 1100 0101 1100 (shown split into fours for readability), and the need to extract the last eight bits (i.e. produce 0000 0000 0101 1100), one can perform an AND operation between this value and the binary pattern 0000 0000 1111 1111. Patterns used in this way are called *masks* and in C are usually written as octal or hexadecimal constants. If the value above were in a variable **v** then we could write the operation as **v &= 0x00FF**. A similar technique can be used to test individual bits or groups of bits. For example, **if (v & 1) ...** will test the right-most bit of **v**. In fact this last operation can be used to write a function to test if a number is odd or even. All odd numbers have a binary representation that has one as the right-most bit and so the following function will return zero (false) if its parameter is even and unity (true) if it is odd.

```
int odd(int n) {      /* Test if n is odd */
    return(n & 1);
}
```

OR operations can be used to set bits in a word. For instance, to set the first four bits of a sixteen bit integer **v** to 1, leaving the others unchanged, it is possible to use the expression **v |= 0xF000**.

9.2.   Bit Counting

Logical and shift operations can be used for many tasks but the best ways of using them are not always obvious. A simple practical example involves trying to count the number of bits in a word which are set to one, a problem which can arise in data communications. The obvious approach is to write a loop which tests every bit position and performs an operation similar to the **if** statement in the previous section in order to find whether or not it is a one; for a sixteen bit word this would involve sixteen iterations, sixteen tests and sixteen shifts. While this approach will work, a better method can be based on the less obvious observation that if a value is ANDed with itself minus one the result will have one fewer one-bit. For example if **v** holds the bit pattern 0110, then **v-1** is 0101 and **v & (v-1)** is 0100; the least significant one-bit has disappeared. If this operation is repeated until **v** is zero then the number of repetitions will be equal to the number of one-bits. The function **BitsIn** below accomplishes this:

```
int BitsIn(register unsigned n) { /* Count the 1-bits in n  */
    register int Count = 0;

    while (n > 0) {
        ++Count;
        n &= (n - 1);
    }
    return(Count);
}
```

Because the contents of the **while** loop are only executed once for each one-bit in **n** this function is much faster than the 'obvious' solution. Incidentally, this is an example of when a register declaration can be worthwhile. Since there are only two variables which are simple integers and are both referred to within a loop, they are excellent candidates for register variables.

9.3.   Parity and Data Transmission

When characters are being transmitted from one computer to another by means of a serial connection (a link between two machines through which only one bit is transmitted at a time) they are normally sent in the form of eight-bit bytes. An ASCII character requires only seven bits (all ASCII characters have values in the range 0...127) and so it would appear that a bit is being wasted. But computer engineers are economical people and in fact the extra bit is provided to permit error checking. To do this, the sender and receiver agree on a *parity* for all the characters. That is, they agree that each character will have an odd number of one bits if they choose odd parity or an even number if the parity is to be even; the extra bit is used to force the parity to be correct.

Suppose that the agreement is to use even parity; in other words there will be an even number of bits in each transmitted character. In the ASCII character set the letter 'A' is represented by 01000001 which has an even number of bits, 'B' is 01000010 which also has even parity, but 'C' is 01000011 which contains three bits and therefore has odd parity. Before transmitting a 'C' the sender would force the parity to be even by putting a one-bit in the parity position (the left-most bit) producing 11000011 (inclusive OR the character with 0200, which is 10000000 in binary). The receiver checks the incoming characters and if a character arrives with odd parity, then there must have been an error in transmission and some suitable action must be taken; if the parity is correct then the receiver will change the parity bit to zero to restore the original ASCII character.

The function below, which uses both **odd** and **BitsIn** defined above, will change a character to be even parity:

```
char SetEvenParity(char  n) {
    if (odd(BitsIn(n)))
        return(n | 0200); /*  Set the left-most bit to 1   */
    else
        return(n);
}
```

Exercise 9.1 Write a function to check the parity of a received character, to restore it to seven-bit ASCII (i.e. left-most bit equal to zero) if the parity is even, and to produce some error action if it odd.

Parity checking in the form described here can only detect an error if it occurs in a single bit; a double error would escape detection. More sophisticated schemes such as error-correcting codes, cyclic redundancy checks and checksums are used to provide more effective error checking when data integrity is particularly important. Andrew Tannenbaum gives a detailed account of these and related subjects in [TAN 81].

9.4.   Huffman Codes: Data Compression

When a large amount of information is to be transmitted over a communications link or stored in a file, it becomes worthwhile to try to find a way of compressing it in order to reduce transmission time or storage space. Normally each character is represented as an eight-bit byte. Frequency dependent codes are based on the realization that this figure could be reduced if one were to use short codes for characters which occur often and longer codes for rarer characters. The problem then is to find an unambiguous set of such codes to represent characters; the Huffman algorithm is a way of doing this.

As an example, suppose that a character set consists of only the first ten letters of the alphabet and that in a sample text the number of occurrences of each letter is as shown in the table below:

Character	Number of Occurrences
A	5
B	3
C	0
D	7
E	8
F	2
G	9
H	11
I	13
J	4

The Huffman algorithm involves constructing a binary tree from the leaves down to the root. First nodes are made, one for each character of the character set, each node containing the frequency of occurrence of the corresponding character. Then the two nodes with the lowest frequencies are located and joined to a parent node which contains their combined frequencies. In this example the first two characters that would combine would be **C** and **F** and the combined frequency would be 2. **C** and **F** now no longer play a part as individual characters but are both represented by their common parent node. Repeating this process, the next two lowest frequencies are **B** and the **CF** parent and so these are combined into another node. The repetition continues until there is one final node which is the root of the tree. The value held in this node will be the sum of the frequencies of all the characters. If two nodes contain the same frequencies then it is not important which is chosen. The final tree for this example is shown in the next diagram.

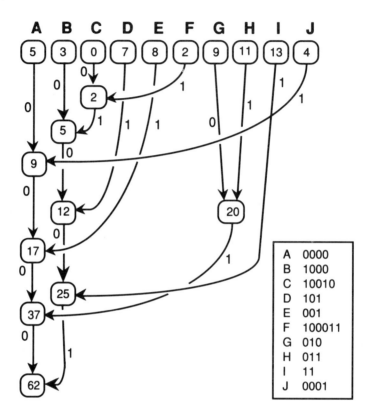

When the complete tree has been constructed each left branching link is marked with a zero and each right link with a one. The code for any character can be found by tracing the path from the root to the leaf node containing that character and reading off the bits. The diagram below gives the codes produced for each character in the table above. Notice how the letter **I**, which is the most frequently used has a two bit code while **C** takes five bits, but also that no code occurs as the start of any other (**I** is 11 for instance and no other code starts with 11). This last property, known as the prefix property, is clearly essential as otherwise it would not be possible to decode the information.

A system using Huffman codes needs three parts: a program to construct codes from a reasonably representative example of the type of data to be handled, a program to use those codes to encode the data and a program which uses the same codes to decode them; examples of each of these three programs will be developed.

The obvious way to write the first program is to construct a binary tree, in the usual way, with pointers, and then to scan it in order to produce the codes, but in practice the solution produced by this approach is complicated and a different way is possible. This alternative approach uses a table in the form of a one-dimensional array, with one element for each character in the character set. Each element of the array is a structure of the form:

```
struct {int Occurrences;
        BinCode Code;
        int Link}
```

where **Occurrences** is the number of occurrences of the corresponding character in the sample text, **Code** is the Huffman code for it (which is to be constructed as the program runs; the type **BinCode** will be described later) and **Link** is the index of a node's right brother when that has been found. For example, **H** is the right brother of **G** in the diagram above, and **E** is the right brother of the intermediate node formed by combining **A** and **J**.The **Occurrences** value of a parent node is equal to the sum of its two children. Because the frequencies of the children are no longer needed once the parent has been created, one can store **Occurrences** of the parent in the place of one of its children. In this program the left child is used, but the choice is arbitrary. With the **Occurrences** of a left child replaced by that of its parent, it is necessary to keep a link to the right child from the parent This is the purpose of the **Link** member in the above structure; it holds the index of the right child (or, equivalently, the brother of the suppressed node).

When a parent node is created, the children are no longer candidates for selection as one of the two smallest nodes. With the left child there is no problem, because it has been replaced by its parent, which is a valid candidate. It is important, however, to ensure that the right child is never again chosen; this can be done by setting **Occurrences** of the right child to the largest number the computer allows.

The creation of a parent node also requires the addition of a bit to the codes for each of its children and their descendants; a zero bit must be added to the code of the left child and all its descendants, and a one bit to the right child and all of its descendants.

Representing this diagrammatically, the initial state of the table is:

	A	B	C	D	E	F	G	H	I	J
Occurrences	5	3	0	7	8	2	9	11	13	4
Code										
Link										

After the first step it has changed to:

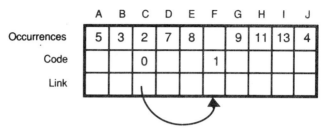

where **C** and **F** have been joined and have been allotted the last bits of their codes (notice that the codes are generated from right to left). After the next step the situation is:

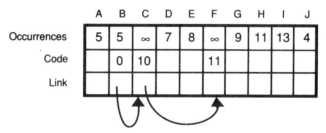

A one bit has been added to the codes for **C** and **F**, a zero bit to the code for **B**, and **B** is now linked to **C**, which in turn is linked to **F**. The right children (**C** and **F**) have had their **Occurrences** changed to infinity to ensure that they never again are considered to be children in need of parents. This process continues until all nodes are linked; all the steps are shown in the table below.

In the pseudocode version below, **Table** is the array and **Left** and **Right** are integer variables:

```
Initialize the table;
Calculate the frequencies of each character in the sample text;
repeat CharSetLength - 1 times
    Put the indices of the two nodes with the smallest frequencies in
        variables Left and Right;
    Add the Occurrences of Table[ Right] to Table[Left];
    Set Occurrences of Table[Right] to infinity to ensure it is never
        re-used;
    Attach a zero bit to the code of the Left node and all nodes linked to it;
    Link the end of the chain from the Left node to the Right node;
    Attach a one bit to the code of the Right node and all nodes linked to it;
end of the loop;
Output the codes to a file;
```

Notice that the pseudocode says 'Link the end of the chain from the **Left** node to the **Right** node'. The process of linking a right node to a left node is complicated by the

the fact that left nodes are already often linked, in which case it is necessary to find the end of the chain from a left node and link it to the new right brother.

To illustrate this algorithm, the table below shows the state of the program at each step for the example given on page 98. The process of linking already linked left nodes by finding the end of the chain is shown at step 5. The infinity symbol (∞) represents a very large number, larger than any possible number of occurrences of a character.

Index		0	1	2	3	4	5	6	7	8	9
Character		A	B	C	D	E	F	G	H	I	J
Step											
0	Occurrences	5	3	**0**	7	8	**2**	9	11	13	4
	Code										
	LinkTo										
1	Occurrences	5	**3**	**2**	7	8	∞	9	11	13	4
	Code			0			1				
	LinkTo			5							
2	Occurrences	**5**	5	∞	7	8	∞	9	11	13	**4**
	Code		0	10			11				
	LinkTo		2	5							
3	Occurrences	9	**5**	∞	**7**	8	∞	9	11	13	∞
	Code	0	0	10			11				1
	LinkTo	9	2	5							
4	Occurrences	**9**	12	∞	∞	**8**	∞	9	11	13	∞
	Code	0	00	010	1		011				1
	LinkTo	9	2	5			3				
5	Occurrences	17	12	∞	∞	∞	∞	**9**	**11**	13	∞
	Code	00	00	010	1	1	011				01
	LinkTo	9	2	5			3				4
6	Occurrences	17	**12**	∞	∞	∞	∞	20	∞	**13**	∞
	Code	00	00	010	1	1	011	0	1		01
	LinkTo	9	2	5			3	7			4
7	Occurrences	**17**	25	∞	∞	∞	∞	**20**	∞	∞	∞
	Code	00	000	0010	01	1	0011	0	1	1	01
	LinkTo	9	2	5	8		3	7			4
8	Occurrences	**37**	**25**	∞	∞	∞	∞	∞	∞	∞	∞
	Code	000	000	0010	01	01	0011	10	11	1	001
	LinkTo	9	2	5	8	6	3	7			4
9	Occurrences	62	∞	∞	∞	∞	∞	∞	∞	∞	∞
	Code	0000	1000	10010	101	001	10011	010	011	11	0001
	LinkTo	9	2	5	8	6	3	7	1		4

In this table a blank entry represents an undefined value; in implementing the algorithm we need an explicit way of representing such values. The program which follows uses the constant **Unlinked** with the value -1 to represent a link that has not yet been made.

Underlined values represent two nodes which are to be combined.

A binary representation of a code is a **BinCode** which is a structure declared as:

```
struct{ int NumberOfBits;
        Bits Representation;
      } BinCode;
```

The type **Bits** is here made a synonym for **unsigned**. Although **unsigned** is an adequate representation for most purposes, it may be necessary to change it to a more general type, such as **long unsigned**, for some applications. The bit pattern is held at the least significant end of **Representation** and occupies **NumberOfBits** bits. The bit pattern is built up one bit at a time and it may be helpful to see how. Suppose **r** is a **BinCode**, then **r.Representation** is a pattern of **r.NumberOfBits** bits. Suppose also that **Bit** is an integer holding either zero or one, which is to be added to the most significant end of **r.Representation**. **Bit** can be made into a suitable mask by shifting it left by **r.NumberOfBits** positions, which will make the important bit line up with the required position in **r.Representation**. A logical OR operation (addition would work as well) will then copy it into **r.Representation**. This whole operation can be done by the expression:

```
r.Representation |= (Bit << r.NumberOfBits++);
```

A problem with applying the Huffman algorithm precisely as described earlier is that there are valid characters, such as ASCII control characters which occur very rarely in normal text, and may never occur in the sample text used to create the codes. Such characters will be given an **Occurrences** value of zero which can lead to them being assigned an unreasonably long representation. In the program below every character in the set is treated as if it occurs at least once, in order to avoid this problem. If the sample text is sufficiently large, the inefficiency caused by this subterfuge will be trivial.

As was mentioned, three programs are needed to implement a full system, one to generate suitable code tables, one to encode data and one to decode data. Each of these programs will have certain declarations in common and so these parts can be combined by using **#include**. The first step is to write a header file containing the common parts. This file is called **Huffman.h** and is shown below.

Initially it defines some machine dependent constants. It may be thought, at first, that these constants should be those in **<limits.h>** but this is not the case. The computer used to generate the codes may not be the same as that which is used to run the encoding and decoding programs. For example, **CharSetLength** is defined as 129 but this value should be set to the appropriate value on the machine that will use the codes, not the machine generating the codes. The file **Huffman.h** is:

```
/* Implementation limitations and details which could be changed
      on different machines although these values are probably adequate
      for most purposes */

#define    CharSetLength    129
#define    EndText             (CharSetLength - 1)
#define    BitMax          16      /*  Smallest possible number of bits
                                          in an integer */
#define    Infinity        32767   /*  Smallest possible maximum int */
#define    MaxFileName 32          /*  Max characters in a file name */
#define    CodeFormat    "%d %o\n" /*  Should match 'Bits': see
                                          function 'OutputCode  */
typedef    unsigned  Bits;

/*  End of the 'implementation dependent' part */

#include <stdio.h>
typedef struct{int NumberOfBits;
                Bits Representation;
                } BinCode;

void RequestAndOpenFile(FILE **FileId, char *Mode)
```

The function **RequestAndOpenFile** is used by all parts of this system. It gets a file name from the user and attempts to open it. If it fails, it halts the program with a message. It should be compiled separately and is:

```
void RequestAndOpenFile(FILE **FileId, char *Mode) {

    char FileName[MaxFileName];

    gets(FileName);
    if ((*FileId = fopen(FileName, Mode)) == NULL) {
        printf("Unable to open the file %s\n", FileName);
    exit(0);
    }
}
```

It may seem, at first, that the type of **FileId** in the function parameter list should only be a pointer rather than a pointer to a pointer. However, when a file is opened, **fopen** creates an object of type **FILE** and delivers a pointer to it. The argument corresponding to **FileId**, which will have type **FILE ***, has to be changed to point to this object. As the argument to be changed is a pointer its address must be passed to the function. The address of a pointer variable is a pointer to a pointer.

The above version of **Huffman.h** assumes the ASCII character set and further assumes that no letter's code will be longer than sixteen bits. The reason that 129 characters are permitted, is to allow for all 128 ASCII characters plus a special character to indicate the end of data.

Given **Huffman.h** it is possible to create the first program, which reads a sample text and generates Huffman codes using the algorithm given earlier:

```
/* Program 1: reads a sample text and constructs a Huffman code from it   */
#include <stdio.h>
#include <stdlib.h>
#include "Huffman.h"

#define     Unlinked        -1

struct {unsigned   Occurrences;
        BinCode    Code;
        int        Link;
        } HuffTable[CharSetLength];

FILE *SampleText, *CodeFile;

void ClearTable(void) {
    int i;
    for (i = 0; i < CharSetLength; ++i) {
        HuffTable[i].Occurrences = 1;
        HuffTable[i].Link = Unlinked;
        HuffTable[i].Code.NumberOfBits = 0;
        HuffTable[i].Code.Representation = 0;
    }
}

void FindLeftAndRight(int *Left, int *Right) {
    /*   Find the smallest and next smallest values in HuffTable and
         set Left and Right to their indices   */
    int i, MinIndex = 0, MinValue = Infinity, NextMinIndex,
        NextMinValue, Occurrences;

    for (i = 0; i < CharSetLength; ++i) {
        Occurrences = HuffTable[i].Occurrences;
        if (Occurrences < MinValue) {
            NextMinIndex = MinIndex;
            NextMinValue = MinValue;
            MinIndex = i;
            MinValue = Occurrences;
        }
        else if (Occurrences < NextMinValue) {
            NextMinIndex = i;
            NextMinValue = Occurrences;
        }
    }
```

```
        if (MinIndex < NextMinIndex) {
            *Left = MinIndex;
            *Right = NextMinIndex;
        }
        else {
            *Right = MinIndex;
            *Left = NextMinIndex;
        }
}

void AddBitToCodesLinkedTo(int Index, int Bit, int *ChainEnd) {
    /*  Add  'Bit' (0 or 1) to the code of the character in
           'HuffTable[Index]' and all elements linked to it.  On
           exit 'ChainEnd' holds the index of the last linked element  */

    do {
        if (HuffTable[Index].Code.NumberOfBits == BitMax) {
            printf("A code is too long to be represented in %d bits\n",
                    BitMax);
            exit(0);
        }
        HuffTable[Index].Code.Representation |=
            (Bit << HuffTable[Index].Code.NumberOfBits++);
        *ChainEnd = Index;
        Index = HuffTable[Index].Link;
    } while (Index != Unlinked);
}

void OutputCodes(void) {
    int i;

    for (i = 0; i < CharSetLength; ++i)
        fprintf(CodeFile, CodeFormat, HuffTable[i].Code.NumberOfBits,
                                HuffTable[i].Code.Representation);
}

main() {
    char ch;
    int NodesRemaining, Left, Right, ChainEnd;

    ClearTable();

    /*  Open the input and output files   */

    printf("Sample text file name?\n");
    RequestAndOpenFile(&SampleText, "r");
    printf("Code file name?\n");
    RequestAndOpenFile(&CodeFile, "w");
```

```
/*  Calculate the number of occurrences of each character in the sample
    text.  Ignore characters outside the defined character set size.  */

while ((ch = getc(SampleText)) != EOF)
    if (ch < CharSetLength)
        if (HuffTable[ch].Occurrences++ == Infinity) {
            printf( "The number of occurrences of character %c"
                " exceeds %d\n", ch, Infinity);
            exit(0);
        }

/*  Work out the code  */

for (   NodesRemaining = CharSetLength;
        NodesRemaining > 1;
        --NodesRemaining)
{
    FindLeftAndRight(&Left, &Right);
    HuffTable[Left].Occurrences += HuffTable[Right].Occurrences;
    HuffTable[Right].Occurrences = Infinity;
    AddBitToCodesLinkedTo(Left, 0, &ChainEnd);
    HuffTable[ChainEnd].Link = Right;
    AddBitToCodesLinkedTo(Right, 1, &ChainEnd);
}
OutputCodes();
}
```

The program above can be used to produce a table of Huffman codes from a specimen file which should consist of text which is statistically similar to the type to be compressed, for instance English text, French text, C programs, numeric data, etc. As an example, suppose a word-processor is being written intended for the English language and to save disc space it will use Huffman coding when storing text. In that case a suitable sample of English would be used to create tables which would be incorporated into the word processor.

The next program uses the codes constructed by the previous program in order to provide a simple data transmission link with data compression. In such use it is possible to store tables for some of the more likely types of file to be transmitted (English, C code etc.) and to request the user to select, perhaps from a menu, the type of file to be sent.

In writing such a program, the lowest level requirement is a function to transmit a byte (assuming that a byte is the unit of communication). Such a function can be very complicated as it can depend upon hardware details and transmission protocols. For our purposes it is not necessary to understand the detail of how transmission works; the function **Transmit** merely prints each byte, in a humanly readable style, in a file. It will be noticed that **Transmit** takes an integer parameter and prints one character. It does this by masking all but the last seven bits in order to ensure a seven-bit character value.

The Huffman codes are read from a file and stored in **HuffTable**, which contains, for each character, the number of bits required and the code in the form of an integer. These values are passed to **OutputHuffCode**, which packs the variable length codes into 8-bit bytes and then passes them to **Transmit**.

In order to perform the packing, **OutputHuffCode** breaks the code into individual bits which are then appended to a bit pattern in the global variable **Accumulator**. When **Accumulator** is full (contains eight bits) its contents are transmitted bits are once more accumulated. Notice that a single Huffman code can split across more than one byte.

The last character provides a problem because, when it is to be transmitted, it is unlikely that **Accumulator** is full; in this case the function **Flush** fills the remaining bit positions with zeros and transmits the last byte.

The final program is:

```
/* Program 2:  encode and transmit data using Huffman codes constructed
               by program 1. */

#include <stdio.h>
#include "Huffman.h"

BinCode HuffTable[CharSetLength];

FILE *Text, *CodedFile, *HuffCodes;

void ReadCodes(void) {
    /*  Read the Huffman codes from a file created by program 1 */
    int i;

    for (i = 0;  i < CharSetLength;  ++i)
        fscanf(HuffCodes, "%d %o", &HuffTable[i].NumberOfBits,
                                   &HuffTable[i].Representation);
}

int BytesSent = 0, CharsSent = 0;

void Transmit(int Byte) {
    /*  This is an illustrative version of this function; a practical
        version would need modification.   */

    fprintf(CodedFile, "%o \n", Byte & 0377);
    BytesSent++;
}

int BitsAccumulated = 0, Accumulator = 0;
```

```
void OutputHuffCode(BinCode h) {
    Bits Mask = 1;

    /*  Initially set Mask to match the first significant bit of h and then
        move it right to scan successive bits .. see the text */

    for (Mask <<= (h.NumberOfBits - 1);  Mask != 0; Mask >>= 1) {
        Accumulator <<= 1;
        if ((Mask & h.Representation) != 0)
            Accumulator |= 1;
        if (++BitsAccumulated == 8) {
            Transmit(Accumulator);
            BitsAccumulated = Accumulator = 0;
        }
    }
    CharsSent++;
}

main() {
    char ch;

    /*  Open the input and output files and read the codes  */

    printf("Text file name?\n");
    RequestAndOpenFile(&Text, "r");
    printf("Output file name?\n");
    RequestAndOpenFile(&CodedFile, "w");
    printf("File containing the codes?\n");
    RequestAndOpenFile(&HuffCodes, "r");
    ReadCodes();

    while ((ch = getc(Text)) != EOF)
        OutputHuffCode(HuffTable[ch]);

    Flush();
    printf("Characters = %d, Bytes  = %d, Ratio = %f\n",
            CharsSent, BytesSent, (float)BytesSent / (float)CharsSent);
}
```

The for-loop in **OutputHuffCode** is a good example of the flexibility of this control statement in C. In order to understand it, suppose that the binary **Representation** of some character is say 01101. On a sixteen-bit computer this would be held as 0000000000001101 and the **NumberOfBits** would be five. The first eleven bits are not part of the code and need to be ignored. To read off the relevant bits from **Representation** we can use a mask that initially has the value 0000000000010000 to select the first bit, then 0000000000001000 and so on. The initialization statement of the loop creates this mask. **Mask** has the value 0000000000000001 from its declaration and then the initialization statement shifts this left by four places (for this example) to produce the required pattern. Once the body of the loop has been obeyed the update statement of the for-loop shifts **Mask** right by one position before the next iteration. After five iterations the update statement shifts the bit in **Mask** off the right end, the whole value becomes zero and the loop stops.

To demonstrate the effectiveness of Huffman coding the first program was used to construct a suitable table for English text using the first few pages of this book as a sample; when the encoding functions above were used to encode another piece of English the compression was 40% (in fact 660 characters were stored in only 393 bytes).

The decoding of a Huffman encoded text involves taking the input (from a file or communications link) bit by bit to build up a code. As each bit is received it is appended to an accumulated code which is then compared with a table of valid codes to see if it can be recognized; if it is valid then the appropriate character can be produced and the accumulation starts again from the beginning, but if not then another bit is added and the process repeated. In this way a character encoded as seven bits will have its first bit checked against the one bit codes, then the first two against the two bit codes and so on until a match is found in the seven bit codes. If the codes were held in the same data structure as the previous program, that is as an array in order of ascending character value, then finding a seven bit code in this way would involve about 800 comparisons.

A better way is to hold the codes in a list, in increasing order of length. First will come the group of one-bit codes, then the two-bit codes and so on. The diagram is illustrated in the next diagram.

A pointer **CodeList** points to the first element of the list and when the first bit of a message is received it can be compared with the one-bit codes by moving the pointer down the list until it finds a match or finds the start of the two-bit codes (for an alphabet of more than two characters there can only be a single one-bit code, but the principle still applies). When one group has been checked the pointer will point to the first code of the next group so that when the next bit is known the program is ready to read the appropriate group of codes. In this way the maximum number of comparisons will be equal to the number of codes and as the most likely codes come first, the average number of comparisons to find any particular code will be significantly less that half the total number of codes.

When writing programs of this type it is often difficult to separate all the different, unrelated subproblems. The program has to receive the incoming data in some format, read the Huffman tables in another format, represent these as a list, compare bit patterns with the stored list to test for matches and so on. In these circumstances it is helpful to create levels of abstraction; each level presents to the level above it a simplified view of the level below. This approach has been adopted in the next program. Thus in the main program there are calls to a function **GetDecodedChar** which delivers the next character from the input stream or some indication that the stream has ended. At this level it is not necessary for the program to 'know' details of the file formats, coding scheme used or internal representation of the codes; it 'sees' an abstraction - the input is a stream of already decoded characters.

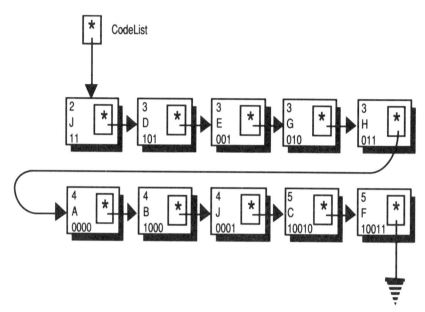

The function **GetDecodedChar** is easiest to design if we think of the input as a stream of bits; it needs to be able to read a bit, attach it to a code and to compare it with the patterns already known. It does this by calling **GetBit**, which presents the input stream as if it were a sequence of bits.

   GetBit in turn assumes that input is actually in the form of bytes and calls **Receive** to present it with the next byte of input. **Receive** deals with the details of input and in a fully fledged version might handle transmission errors, line time-outs or any of the myriad other things that afflict communication between machines. The important thing to realize is that each level is as self-contained as possible. A good point of view to take when trying to work out the tasks for each level is to regard each set of functions that provide a particular level of abstraction as potentially replaceable and potentially re-usable. Thus **Receive** could be replaced by an enormous piece of program to handle some sophisticated communications protocol but this change would only affect **Receive** and the rest of the program would not need modification. Furthermore, if such a sophisticated version of **Receive** were written, it could easily be taken and used in a different program to deal with an utterly different type of application. To make this separation of roles as effective as possible the interface between the different levels should be simple but general.

The whole program is shown below, and an explanation of each of the more complicated functions is given immediately afterwards.

```
/*  Program 3: decodes data encoded by program 2  */

#include <stdio.h>
#include <stdlib.h>
#include "huffman.h"

typedef struct ListNode{int Length;
                        int CharValue;
                        Bits Code;
                        struct ListNode *Next;
                        }ListNode;

FILE *Output, *CodedFile, *HuffCodes;
ListNode *CodeList = NULL;
int MaxCodeLength = 0;   /* The length of the longest code used.  */

/* The next variables are used in AllocListNode and ReadCodes  */

int Length, CharValue;
Bits Code;

ListNode *AllocListNode(ListNode *Next) {
    ListNode *NewOne = (ListNode *) malloc (sizeof(ListNode));
    NewOne -> Length = Length;
    NewOne -> CharValue = CharValue;
    NewOne -> Code = Code;
    NewOne -> Next = Next;
    return(NewOne);
}

void Insert(ListNode **List) {
    ListNode **Tracer = List;
    while (*Tracer != NULL && (*Tracer) -> Length < Length)
        Tracer = &(*Tracer) -> Next;
    *Tracer = AllocListNode(*Tracer);
}

void ReadCodes(FILE *TableFile) {
    for (CharValue = 0; CharValue < CharSetLength; CharValue++) {
        fscanf(TableFile, CodeFormat, &Length, &Code);
        Insert(&CodeList);
        if (Length > MaxCodeLength)
            MaxCodeLength = Length;
    }
}
```

```
int Receive(void) {

    /*   Gets one byte from the input stream which may be a transmission
         link or a file; The version shown here is just suitable for
         testing purposes.   */

    int byte;
    if (fscanf(CodedFile, "%o", &byte) == EOF)
        return(EOF);
    else
        return(byte);
}

void Error(char *Message) {
    printf("An error has occurred - %s -\n", Message);
    exit(0);
}

int GetBit(FILE *HuffFile) {
    /*   return the next bit from the file HuffFile   */

    static int mask = 0;
    static int byte;

    if ((mask >>= 1) == 0) {
        mask = 0200;
        if ((byte = Receive())  == EOF)
            return(EOF);
    }
    return( (mask & byte) == 0 ? 0 : 1 );
}

int GetDecodedChar(FILE *HuffFile) {
    /*   Reads one Huffman coded character, one bit at a time
         and decodes it   */
    Bits Accumulator = 0;
    int Length = 0, Bit;
    ListNode *NextCode = CodeList;

    while ((Bit = GetBit(HuffFile)) != EOF) {
        Accumulator = (Accumulator << 1) | Bit;
        if (++Length > MaxCodeLength)
            Error("Code is too long");
        for (;;) {  /*  Ends with "break" or "return"  */
            if (NextCode == NULL)
                Error("List exhausted");
            if (NextCode -> Length > Length)
                break;
            if (((NextCode -> Length) == Length)
```

```
                    && ((NextCode -> Code) == Accumulator))
                        return(NextCode -> CharValue);
                    NextCode = NextCode -> Next;
            }
        }
        return(EOF);
    }

    main() {
        int ch;
        /*  Open the input and output files and read the codes  */

        printf("Input file name?\n");
        RequestAndOpenFile(&CodedFile, "r");
        printf("Output file name?\n");
        RequestAndOpenFile(&Output, "w");
        printf("File containing the codes?\n");
        RequestAndOpenFile(&HuffCodes, "r");

        ReadCodes(HuffCodes);

        while ((ch = GetDecodedChar(CodedFile)) != EOF && ch != EndText)
            fputc(ch, Output);
            exit(0);
    }
```

The table of codes is read from a file by **ReadCodes**, which calls **Insert** to create the list mentioned above. **Insert** is a modified version of the ordered list insertion function given in Chapter 7.

GetBit has to deliver the input as single bits and when necessary it calls **Receive** to get the next group of eight. If the input came in some other form (60-bit words, smoke signals) then only these two functions would need to be changed. The static variables **byte** and **mask** respectively store the last byte read and the position of the next bit to be used. **mask** starts with the binary value 10000000 (0200 in octal), and is shifted right by one position at each call. When it becomes zero it is re-initialized with its original value.

GetHuffc is responsible for reading one encoded character and decoding it. It calls **GetBit** to find the next bit, attaches it to **Accumulator** and checks against the codes of the appropriate length. If it does not find a match between **Accumulator** and any of the codes, it takes in an extra bit and tries again until a match is found or it realizes that a code is in error. (The program does not do exhaustive error checking; making it robust against all the mistakes that could occur will be left as an exercise to the indefatigable reader.) The while-loop in the function is responsible for adding successive bits to **Accumulator** and the inner for-loop compares **Accumulator** to the appropriate group from the list of codes.

9.5.   Bit Fields

One of the principal uses of bit manipulation is to store several items of information within one machine word in order to reduce storage space. This can be done by using a combination of bitwise logical operations using masks and shifts, but *bit fields* provide a more convenient mechanism. However, just as with using masks, using bit fields can make a program machine dependent.

As an example consider a sports club with a computer system to record details of members; among the information to be held for each member is the birth date (day, month, year), sex (male = 0, female = 1), whether the member is active in a club team (no = 0, yes = 1) and whether club dues are paid (no = 0, yes = 1). This can be done with the following declaration (which would normally form part of a larger record):

```
struct {
    unsigned int BirthDay      : 5;
    unsigned int BirthMonth    : 4;
    unsigned int BirthYear     : 7;
    unsigned int Female        : 1;
    unsigned int Active        : 1;
    unsigned int PaidUp        : 1;
} PersonalDetails;
```

The structure members in this case are bit fields. The numbers after the colon following each field represent the number of bits to be allowed for the field. Thus five bits for the BirthDay allow values in the range 0...31, which is enough for the longest months.

The fields can now be used completely as if they were structure members e.g.

```
PersonalDetails.BirthDay = 27;
```

assigns a value to the **Birthday** member, and

```
if (PersonalDetails.Active && !PersonalDetails.Female)
    . . .
```

would select active, male members of the club.

The same effect could be achieved by using logical and shift operations to unpack the fields; using a bit field causes the compiler to generate the required shifts and saves programmer effort. It does not save computer effort though, and access to a bit field will take more machine operations than to a member of a normal structure.

Bit fields are often used to map onto some hardware feature (for instance, a serial communications controller). When doing this there may be certain bit positions which are not used, or not required. Unnamed fields can be used to provide padding in these cases. For example,

```
struct {
    unsigned int Ready      : 1;
                            : 4;
    unsigned int Received   : 3;
} Status;
```

defines a structure which could map onto a single, eight-bit byte. If the implementation stores the fields from left to right within the byte, then **Ready** would be the first (left-most) bit of **Status** and **Received** the last three bits on the right. The second to fifth would not be used.

This example shows a problems with bit fields: the order of the fields within a storage location are not defined by the ANSI standard. On one machine the fields may be stored left-right and on another right-left. Similarly it is not defined whether a field can cross a word boundary and, of course, the size of a word varies between machines. To reduce the chance of portability problems, avoid fields of more than sixteen bits and never make assumptions about the order of storage.

An unnamed field of width zero forces the next field to begin on a word boundary. For example,

```
struct {
    int Part1   : 5;
                : 0;
    int Part2   : 5;
} Henry4;
```

would be stored with **Part1** occupying five bits of one word and **Part2** five bits of the next.

Fields can be only of type **int** (signed or unsigned), but as they are only part of a word they do not have addresses, and so cannot be used with the address (**&**) operator.

Section 13.4 gives further examples of bit manipulation to reduce storage space and Chapter 10 shows how bit operators can be used to implement common operations on sets.

10

Pointers to Functions

10.1. Pointers to Functions

All pointers seen so far point to values (numbers, structures, the first element of an array etc.). The C language allows more than this; a pointer can point to a function enabling us to create some interesting objects: arrays of functions, function variables, records containing functions, and so on. As such objects are not available in many languages, the ways of using them need some explanation.

Consider two functions declared as:

```
int Add(int i; int j) {
    return(i + j);
}

int Multiply(int i; int j) {
    return(i * j);
}
```

Both these functions have the same type, because they deliver the same result and take identical parameters. A pointer to functions of this type can be declared as

```
int (* Arith) (int, int);
```

This says that **Arith** is a pointer to a function with two integer parameters and delivering an integer. **Arith** can be made to point to **Add** by the statement:

```
Arith = Add;
```

Now the statement

```
printf("%d\n", (*Arith)(2, 3));
```

will print the result 5. Notice the syntax of the call. **Arith** points to a function so that ***Arith** is the function to which it points. To call this it must be enclosed in parentheses producing **(*Arith)** and then followed by the arguments, as in the example. Notice how the call to **Arith** matches the declaration. It may not be obvious why the parentheses are necessary, but the declaration

```
int * Arith (int, int);
```

says **Arith** is a function with two integer parameters, delivering a pointer to an integer, not the same thing at all. If now we give the statements

```
Arith = Multiply;
printf("%d\n", (*Arith)(2, 3));
```

the program will print 6. **Arith** now points to a different function and so a seemingly identical call produces a different result. The rest of this chapter shows more powerful uses for this technique.

10.2.   Functions as Parameters to Functions

The most common use of pointers to functions is to pass one function as a parameter to another. As an example of this, consider a program which performs operations on lists; one of its operations involves changing all the elements in some way (squaring them in the example below) whilst another is to print the list. We could write each of these operations (and any others that may be involved) as separate functions but would find that the list processing part (checking for the end of the list, moving the tracing pointer, etc.) was identical in each function. If we adhere to the maxim that any programming done twice is done once too often we may want to try to write a general list scanning function that is able to apply any specified action to each element of the list. The function **ForEachNodeOf** in the program below shows how this can be done. The interesting feature of this function is the parameter **Action** which is defined, not completely transparently, as **void (*Action)(ListNode *)** in the argument list. Working from the inside out we see that **Action** is a pointer to a function which delivers no result (i.e. **void**) and which has one argument which is a pointer to a **ListNode**.

The two actions used in this example are **PrintNode**, which prints the value of a single list node, and **SquareNode** which replaces the **Value** member of a node by its square. **ForEachNodeOf** scans the list and applies its parameter **Action** to each node. The **Insert** function is that found in section 7.4 and is used to create an ordered list. The **main** function is intended merely as an example of how to use the functions.

```
#include <stdio.h>
#include <stdlib.h>

typedef struct ListNode {  int Value;
                             struct ListNode *Next;
                           } ListNode;

void ForEachNodeOf(ListNode **List, void (*Action)(ListNode *))
    ListNode *ThisEntry = *List;
    while (ThisEntry != NULL) {
        (*Action)(ThisEntry);
        ThisEntry = ThisEntry -> Next;
    }
}

void PrintNode(ListNode *n) {
    printf("%d\n", n -> Value);
}

void SquareNode(ListNode *n) {
    n -> Value = n -> Value * n -> Value;
}

main() {
    int i;
    ListNode *Root = NULL;
    printf("Type several integers and terminate with 0\n");
    while (scanf("%d", &i), i != 0)
        Insert(i, &Root);
    printf("\nThe list is:\n");
    ForEachNodeOf(&Root, PrintNode);
    ForEachNodeOf(&Root, SquareNode);
    printf("\n\nand after squaring is:\n\n");
    ForEachNodeOf(&Root, PrintNode);
}
```

The actual function parameters in the calls of **ForEachNodeOf** are not preceded by the address operator **&**; the operator is unnecessary, although some compilers will accept it, because the compiler 'knows' that the parameters are functions and therefore graciously provides an address.

The statement:

```
(*Action)(ThisEntry);
```

in **ForEachNodeOf** is the call of the function **Action**. The indirection operator ***** means 'find the function to which **Action** refers' with **ThisEntry** as the parameter.

The parentheses around ***Action** are necessary because ***Action(ThisEntry)** would mean 'dereference the result of a call to **Action** with **ThisEntry** as the parameter', as () has a higher priority than *****; this will cause a compilation error because **Action** is not a function but a pointer.

The **main** function above makes use of the sequence operator in a way we have not seen before. The statement

```
while (scanf("%d", &i), i != 0)
        Insert(i, &Root);
```

uses the fact that the sequence operator (,) not only causes its operand statements to be obeyed in the order written but also delivers the value of the last statement as its result. Hence **(scanf("%d", &i), i != 0)** reads an integer **i** and then delivers the result of the expression **i != 0**.

It is important to be clear about the difference between passing a function as a parameter to another function and using a function in an expression which appears in a parameter list. In the statement:

```
y = sin(exp(Theta));
```

exp is not being passed to **sin** as a function but is being called, with the parameter **Theta**, to yield a result which is then passed to **sin**.

10.3.   Sorting and Searching

The standard library **<stdlib.h>** contains, among other things, the definition of a function **qsort** for sorting arrays of any type of data and a function **bsearch** to search a sorted array for an element having a particular value. As the two functions will accept arrays of any type they can be said to be *generic* sorting and searching functions.

Any sorting or searching algorithm needs to be able to compare values, but the method of comparing values depends upon the type of the values: strings can be compared by using **strcmp**, integers by ==, != etc. and structures by comparing one or more members. This would seem to create an insurmountable obstacle to writing a generic sorting function. A way of circumventing the problem is illustrated by the definition of **qsort**, which is:

```
void qsort( void *Array, size_t NumElements, size_t ElemSize,
            int (*Compare) (const void *, const void *));
```

The array to be sorted is **Array** and it being defined as having type **void *** means that the corresponding actual parameter can be a pointer to any type, and hence can point to the start of any type of array. This array has **NumElements** elements each of size **ElemSize**, and **Compare** is a pointer to a function provided by the user which compares its two arguments that are each pointers to objects of the same type as the array elements. **Compare** must return a negative value, zero or a positive value according to whether its first argument is less than, equal to, or greater than its second argument. The type **size_t** is also defined in **<stdlib.h>** and is an integer of the same type (short, long etc.) as the return value of **sizeof**. This means that the corresponding actual parameter can be something like **sizeof(AnyType)**.

To illustrate the use of **qsort** we will develop a simple program which reads a file containing student names and the corresponding percentage grades. It first prints the data in alphabetical order and then in order of ascending grade. A sample of the start of the input file (for a collection of music students) could be:

```
Schubert 73
Arnold 35
Bach 94
Mozart 83
. . .
```

It is necessary to read these entries and store them in a suitable array. It is convenient to define a type student:

```
typedef struct {char Name[20];
                float Grade;
               } Student;
```

The following two functions compare students by name and by grade respectively and return an appropriate value:

```
int NameCompare(Student *Stud1, Student *Stud2) {
    return(strcmp(Stud1 -> Name, Stud2 -> Name));
}

int GradeCompare(Student *Stud1, Student *Stud2) {
    return(Stud1 -> Grade - Stud2 -> Grade);
}
```

The first of these makes use of the fact that **strcmp** returns a result which directly satisfies our requirements, and the second uses subtraction of grades to give a suitable value. Given these definitions the rest of the program might be:

```
#include <stdlib.h>
#include <stdio.h>

main() {
#define ClassSize 30

    Student ClassList[ClassSize];
    int i;

    /*  Open the input and output files    */
    FILE   *StudentFile = fopen("GRADES", "r"),
            *Output = fopen("RESULTS", "w");

    /*  Read the list of students   */
    for (i = 0; i < ClassSize; ++i)
        fscanf(StudentFile,
                "%s %f\n", ClassList[i].Name, &ClassList[i].Grade);

    /*  Print alphabetically    */
    qsort(ClassList, ClassSize, sizeof(Student), NameCompare);
    fprintf(Output, "Alphabetical list\n\n");
    for (i = 0; i < ClassSize; ++i)
        fprintf(Output,
                "%-20s    %5.1f\n", ClassList[i].Name, ClassList[i].Grade);
    fprintf(Output, "\n\n\n");

    /*  Print by grade */
    qsort(ClassList, ClassSize, sizeof(Student), GradeCompare);
    fprintf(Output, "List by grade\n\n");
    for (i = 0; i < ClassSize; ++i)
        fprintf(Output,
                "%-20s    %5.1f\n", ClassList[i].Name, ClassList[i].Grade);
}
```

A similar function to **qsort** is **bsearch**, which searches for a value in a sorted array. Its definition is:

```
void *bsearch(const void *Key, void *Array,
            size_t NumElements, size_t ElemSize,
            int (*Compare) (const void *, const void *));
```

Key is a pointer to a value to be sought in **Array**. **Key** must have the same type as the element type of **Array**. The other arguments are identical to those of **qsort**.

bsearch searches **Array** to find an element which (according to **Compare**) is equal to **Key**. If it finds one it returns a pointer to it, otherwise it returns **NULL**. It is important to notice that the definition of **qsort** begins **void qsort(...)** and that the definition of **bsearch** starts **void *bsearch(...)**. **qsort** therefore returns no result, but **bsearch** returns a pointer to **void**, i.e. a generic pointer. It is important that the array being searched is first sorted.

To illustrate the use of **bsearch**, consider a modification to the previous program in order to make it read the file of students records and then answer queries about the grades of named students. The program fragment below reads queries, one at a time, in the form of student names and gives the corresponding grades. The program terminates if a ***** is typed. The main part of the program, after reading and sorting the data, can be replaced by:

```
Student *StudentFound;
char Query[20];

qsort(ClassList, ClassSize, sizeof(Student), NameCompare);

/*  Handle queries and terminate on " * " */

while (scanf("%s", Query), strcmp(Query, "*") != 0) {
    StudentFound = bsearch(Query, ClassList,
                        ClassSize, sizeof(Student), NameCompare);
    if (StudentFound == NULL)
        printf("%s is not in the list\n", Query);
    else
        printf("The grade of %s is %5.1f\n",
                Query, StudentFound -> Grade);
}
```

10.4.   Finite State Automata

Pointers to functions can be used to construct table driven programs, that is, programs whose actions are not written directly as program statements, but instead are encoded as data tables. The logic of such a program is contained only in these tables and so it is easy to adapt the program to other tasks by modifying the tables.

An example of such a program is a table driven, finite state automaton (FSA). An FSA is usually represented by a diagram such as the one below, with circles, representing states, and curved lines (called *edges*) representing changes of state (called *transitions*). Each edge is labelled with characters which, if encountered in the input stream, cause that edge to be followed. The automaton moves from its initial state by receiving one symbol, choosing the edge labelled by that symbol, and following that edge to another state, from where the process is repeated until the terminal state is reached. If the terminal state is reached successfully then the automaton is said to have recognized a sentence in the language for which it was designed.

To take a concrete example, consider a function to read an integer which can take the three styles used in C, i.e. 123 is a decimal number, 0123 is an octal number, 0x123A is a hexadecimal number. The rules for recognizing valid numbers of these styles can be represented by the diagram below.

This diagram shows six states: the initial state (the circle labelled 0), the terminal state (the double circle), one for each of the possible types of number (states 1, 3 and 4) and an intermediate state (state 2). The edges are labelled with the characters which cause them to be followed and some with an action that is to be taken when following a transition; these actions are labelled with a capital letter (**A**, **B**, **C** etc.).

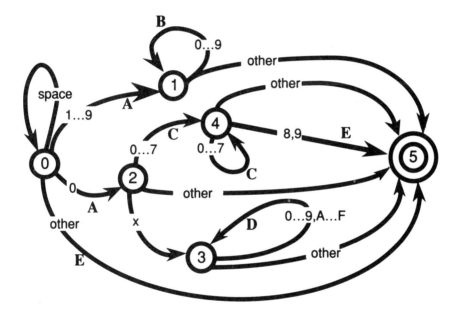

The actions, in this case, calculate the value of the number being recognized. Assume that **Value** is a global variable and that **Digit** is the current character read by the automaton; then the actions are:

> *A:* **Value** = Numerical value of **Digit**
> *B:* **Value** = 10***Value** + decimal value of **Digit**
> *C:* **Value** = 8***Value** + octal value of **Digit**
> *D:* **Value** = 16***Value** + hexadecimal value of **Digit**
> *E:* Print an error message.

The characters fall into seven groups: **space**, **zero**, **1** to **7**, **8** or **9**, **x** or **X**, **A** to **F** and

other. Using these groups the *transition table*, which determines the state change and action for each combination of state and input, is shown below:

Input \ State	0	1	2	3	4
other	5 - E	5 -	5 -	5 -	5 -
0	2 - A	1 - B	4 - C	3 - D	4 - C
1...7	1 - A	1 - B	4 - C	3 - D	4 - C
8,9	1 - A	1 - B	5 - E	3 - D	5 -
x	5 - E	5 -	3 -	5 -	5 -
A...F	5 - E	5 -	5 -	3 - D	5 -
space	0 -	5 -	5 -	5 -	5 -

The columns are labelled with the states and the rows with the character groups. Each cell of the table contains the number of the next state and an action to take during the transition. The absence of an action implies that there is none, although the implementation below will use an 'empty' function to simplify programming.

The function for recognizing a number has to read a character, classify it, and index the table with the character class and the current state. This gives it an action, which it performs, and a new state, to which it makes a transition. This process is repeated until the terminal state is reached. The function **GetValue** in the program below carries out these operations.

In this program the transition table is stored in a two dimensional array called **TransitionTable**, each element of which has the type **TransitionEntry** and contains the number of the next state and a pointer to a function which will perform the required action. Notice how the table is initialized.

The classification of characters is simply done by indexing the array **ClassOf** which has an element for each character in the character set. **ClassOf** is declared globally and so all its elements are initially zero. As a consequence all the elements initially contain the enumeration value **Other** because they have the enumeration type **CharClass**. This is convenient, as most possible characters belong to this class. A call to the function **InitCharClassOf** sets the other elements to their appropriate values.

```c
#include <stdio.h>
#include <ctype.h>
#include <limits.h>

#define    CharSetSize   SCHAR_MAX+1
int Value, ch;

void ActionA(void)    { Value = ch - '0'; }
void ActionB(void)    { Value = 10*Value + ch -' 0'; }
void ActionC(void)    { Value = 8*Value + ch -' 0'; }
void ActionD(void)    { Value = 16*Value +
                                    (isdigit(ch) ? ch - '0' : ch - 'A' + 10); }
void ActionE(void)    { printf("Error: inappropriate character\n"); }
void ActionF(void){ /*  The null action   */ }

enum CharClass {Other, Zero, OneToSeven, EightOrNine, x, HexDigit,
                Space};

enum CharClass ClassOf[CharSetSize];  /* All elements are zero by
                                    default i.e. Other      */

void InitCharClassTable(void) {
    ClassOf['0']   = Zero;           ClassOf['1']   = OneToSeven;
    ClassOf['2']   = OneToSeven;     ClassOf['3']   = OneToSeven;
    ClassOf['4']   = OneToSeven;     ClassOf['5']   = OneToSeven;
    ClassOf['6']   = OneToSeven;     ClassOf['7']   = OneToSeven;
    ClassOf['8']   = EightOrNine;    ClassOf['9']   = EightOrNine;
    ClassOf['x']   = x;              ClassOf['X']   = x;
    ClassOf['A']   = HexDigit;       ClassOf['B']   = HexDigit;
    ClassOf['C']   = HexDigit;       ClassOf['D']   = HexDigit;
    ClassOf['E']   = HexDigit;       ClassOf['F']   = HexDigit;
    ClassOf[' ']   = Space;
}

typedef  struct{int NextState;
                void (*Action)();
                }TransitionEntry;

TransitionEntry TransitionTable[7][5] =
    {{{5, ActionE},    {5, ActionF},    {5, ActionF},    {5, ActionF},    {5, ActionF}},
     {{2, ActionA},    {1, ActionB},    {4, ActionC},    {3, ActionD},    {4, ActionC}},
     {{1, ActionA},    {1, ActionB},    {4, ActionC},    {3, ActionD},    {4, ActionC}},
     {{1, ActionA},    {1, ActionB},    {5, ActionE},    {3, ActionD},    {5, ActionF}},
     {{5, ActionE},    {5, ActionF},    {3, ActionF},    {5, ActionF},    {5, ActionF}},
     {{5, ActionE},    {5, ActionF},    {5, ActionF},    {3, ActionD},    {5, ActionF}},
     {{0, ActionF},    {5, ActionF},    {5, ActionF},    {5, ActionF},    {5, ActionF}}};

#define    ClosingState  5
```

```
int GetValue(FILE *Input) {
    int State, Class;
    for (State = 0;
        State != ClosingState;
        State = TransitionTable[Class][State].NextState
        )
        (*TransitionTable[Class = ClassOf[ch = getc(Input)]][State].Action)  ();

        return(Value);
}
```

GetValue uses a for-statement to drive the automaton through its various states, the update statement of the loop making the transitions. The statement within the loop is a call to the appropriate function to perform an action. As this is complicated it might help to break it down into its components. The expression

> ch = getc(Input)

reads and stores the next character from the input file, so

> ClassOf[ch = getc(Input)]

is the class of the character read and is one index to the transition table, so that

> TransitionTable[Class = ClassOf[ch = getc(Input)]][State].Action

gives a pointer to the required function and

> *TransitionTable[Class = ClassOf[ch = getc(Input)]][State].Action

is the function itself. To call it we enclose it in parentheses and give it an empty parameter list:

> (TransitionTable[Class = ClassOf[ch = getc(Input)]][State].Action)();

InitCharClassTablemust be called before the first call of **GetValue**. A possible call could be:

> i = GetValue(stdin);

For the case of merely recognizing numbers, it could reasonably be argued that a simpler solution could be obtained by using the diagram for the automaton to write an *ad hoc* function, without the need for the tables. However, in practice such diagrams are usually much larger than this. Programs exist which will read some representation of a diagram for an automaton and generate the tables automatically. These tables can then be used to drive a function such as **GetValue**. Such programs are typically used to generate lexical analyzers for compilers.

10.5.   Evaluating Algebraic Expressions

The next example involves writing a program to read algebraic expressions from data and evaluate them. The technique could be used in writing an interpreter for some language, a spreadsheet program or a program to draw graphs of formulae. The expressions allowed have the style:

```
2*x^2+3*(x/sin(x))^2;
```

They can contain one independent variable (called **x**), numbers, parentheses, the arithmetic operators +, -, *****, / and ^ (^ meaning raise to power), the functions **sin**, **cos, tan, arcsin, arccos, arctan, log** and **exp** and they terminate with a semicolon.

   It is first necessary to choose a method of representing each of the components of an expression. If we accept a wide definition of an operator as including the usual arithmetic operators, parentheses, the independent variable **x** and the terminating semicolon, then an element of an expression is a number, operator or function call. Given a suitable way to represent each of these three types of element, we can use a union to represent a general element. Thus given **ElemClass** declared as:

```
typedef enum {RealElem, OpElem, FuncElem} ElemClass;
```

and **func** declared as a pointer to a function delivering a **double** (because all the mathematical functions in C return a **double** value), viz

```
typedef double (*func)();
```

each element of an expression can be represented by a structure containing a union:

```
typedef struct {ElemClass uType;
                union {float Value;
                       int Operator;
                       func Function;
                       } uValue;
                } Element;
```

uType is an element's class (number, operator or function pointer), and **uValue** its value .

An expression is an array of **Element**s and is made from symbols denoting the operators and function names. These can be one-character tokens (*, +, /, etc.) or longer ones, such as **sin, cos, arctan** and so on. To read these we can use the function **GetToken** defined in section 5.3. We can define the tokens to be recognized in an array of strings and use an enumeration to name them:

```
typedef enum { Semicolon, RightParen, Plus, Minus, Times, Div,
               Power, LeftParen, IndepVarSy, SinSy, CosSy, TanSy,
               ArcsinSy, ArccosSy, ArctanSy, LnSy, ExpSy, RealValue
             } SymbolClass;

static char *Symbols[] = { ";" , ")" , "+" , "-" , "*" , "/" , "^" , "(" , "x" , "sin" ,
                           "cos" , "tan", "arcsin", "arccos", "arctan", "ln",
                           "exp", "" };

#define    NoOfSymbols (sizeof(Symbols) / sizeof(char *))
```

Given these definitions the formula **3*sin(x)** will be stored in an array as:

Index	uType	uValue
0	RealElem	3.0
1	Operator	Times
2	FuncElem	pointer to **sin**
3	Operator	LeftParen
4	Operator	IndepVarSy
5	Operator	RightParen

Now we must write a function **ReadFormula** which reads a formula from some data stream and converts it to a suitable array of **Element**s. The parameters are a pointer to a **FILE** structure and a pointer to an array of **Element**s that will contain the expression after reading. **ReadFormula** needs to check matching parentheses, make sure that a formula is not too long, and to classify each token as it is read. It is shown below, along with a function **SkipSpaces** which is used to ignore 'white space' characters. In **ReadFormula** the do-loop reads characters and converts them to formula elements until either a semicolon is read or an error occurs. Errors detected are mismatched parentheses, invalid number formats or an overlong formula. **ReadForm** returns 0 if an error occurs and otherwise it returns a non-zero value.

```
void SkipSpaces(FILE *f) {
    char ch;
    do {ch = fgetc(f); } while (ch == ' ' || ch == '\t' || ch == '\n');
    ungetc(ch, f);
}
```

```c
#define    MaxFormula    100
#include   <math.h>

int ReadFormula(FILE *InFile, Element *Form) {
    /* Reads a formula terminated by ';' from 'InFile' into 'Form'.
       Delivers 0 if an error occurs and 1 otherwise. */

    int i = 0, Token, Brackets = 0;
    do {
        SkipSpaces(InFile);
        Token = GetToken(InFile, Symbols, NoOfSymbols);
        if (Token <= IndepVarSy) { /* Operator found */
            Form[i].uType = OpElem;
            Form[i].uValue.Operator = Token;
            if (Token == LeftParen)
                Brackets++;
            else if (Token == RightParen)
                if (--Brackets < 0)
                    return(0);   /* Bracket mismatch  */
        }
        else if (Token >= SinSy && Token <= ExpSy) { /* Function found */
            Form[i].uType = FuncElem;
            Form[i].uValue.Function = (Token == SinSy)      ? sin   :
                                      (Token == CosSy)      ? cos   :
                                      (Token == TanSy)      ? tan   :
                                      (Token == ArcsinSy)   ? asin  :
                                      (Token == ArccosSy)   ? acos  :
                                      (Token == ArctanSy)   ? atan  :
                                      (Token == LnSy)       ? log   :
                            /* (Token == ExpSy) */            exp   ;
        }
        else { /* assume it is a floating point constant */
            Form[i].uType = RealElem;
            /* fscanf returns the number of values read.  If this is
               not one then an error must have occurred  */
            if (fscanf(InFile, "%f", &Form[i].uValue.Value) != 1)
                return(0);   /* error on failure to read one value */
        }
        if (++i == MaxFormula)
            return(0);   /* Formula too long  */
    } while (Token != Semicolon);
    return(Brackets == 0);   /* Error if brackets don't match  */
}
```

Notice how a cascade of conditional expressions give a value to **Form[i].uValue.Function**.

Having read an expression and put it into a suitable representation we next need to evaluate it. Before writing the function for this, first let us imagine how we are going to use it. The type of main function we might have in mind could be:

```
main() {
    FILE *Inf = fopen("text", "r");
    int i;
    float x;
    Element Form[MaxFormula];

    if (ReadFormula(Inf, Form) != 0) {
        for (x = 0; x < 5.0; x += 0.5)
            printf("Value for x = %f is %f\n", x, Evaluate(Form, x));
    } else
        printf("Formula error\n");
}
```

which reads an expression and prints its value for all **x** from 0.0 to 5.0 in steps of 0.5. It remains to write the function **Evaluate**. To see how this can be done consider the expression:

$$x*(2+sin(3*x)/x)$$

This expression is seen to contain within itself the expression **2+sin(3*x)/x**, which in turn contains the expression **sin(3*x)/x** which also contains **3*x**. Since expressions can contain other expressions, one anticipates that the evaluation algorithm will be recursive. The algorithm also needs the order of priority of operators. To this end the order of the symbol classes in the type **SymbolClass** defined above is not accidental; it corresponds to increasing priority.

The function **Evaluate**, which is defined below, is rather trivial. It calls **fEval** to do the serious work and **fEval** takes four parameters: a pointer to an array containing the formula, the value of the independent variable **x**, the position within the array of the start of an expression and a priority. Consider the steps involved in evaluating the above expression; at the first call of the function **Position** and **Priority** will both be zero. The first symbol is **x**, the value of which is known and which can be stored. Moving along the formula the next symbol is ***** which has a priority higher than zero. This means that the right-hand operand must now be evaluated and **fEval** calls itself with **Position** pointing to the subexpression on the right of ***** and with **Priority** set to the priority of *****. Whenever **fEval** encounters an operation with a priority lower than **Priority** it must have fully evaluated a left-hand operand and so can return a value. The process will stop when the operator with the lowest priority of all (semicolon) is reached.

```
float fEval(Element *Formula, float x, int *Position, int Priority) {
    float Value, RightHandSide;
    int OpSymbol, CurrentOperator;
    Element *CurrentElement = &Formula[(*Position)++];

    if ((*CurrentElement).uType == RealElem)
        Value = (*CurrentElement).uValue.Value;
    else if ((*CurrentElement).uType == OpElem) {
        CurrentOperator = (*CurrentElement).uValue.Operator;
        if (CurrentOperator == IndepVarSy)
            Value = x;
        else if (CurrentOperator != LeftParen) {
            printf("Formula error\n");
            return(0.0);
        }
        else {
            Value = fEval(Formula, x, Position, 0);
            ++(*Position);
        }
    }
    else /* (*CurrentElement).uType == FuncElem */ {
        ++(*Position); /*  skip parenthesis before parameter  */
        Value = (*(*CurrentElement).uValue.Function)
                    (fEval(Formula, x, Position, 0));
        ++(*Position); /*  skip parenthesis after parameter  */
    }

    for ( ; ; ) /* Loop until exit via return */
        if (((OpSymbol =
                Formula[(*Position)++].uValue.Operator)-2) < Priority) {
            --(*Position);
            return(Value);  /* This is the only way out of the loop  */
        }
        else {
            RightHandSide = fEval(Formula, x, Position, OpSymbol-1);
            Value =
                (OpSymbol == Plus)      ?   Value + RightHandSide :
                (OpSymbol == Minus)     ?   Value - RightHandSide :
                (OpSymbol == Times)     ?   Value * RightHandSide :
                (OpSymbol == Div)       ?   Value / RightHandSide :
                /*  (OpSymbol == Power) */      pow(Value, RightHandSide) ;
        }
}

float Evaluate(Element *Formula, float x) {
    int Start = 0;
    return(fEval(Formula, x, &Start, 0));
}
```

11

Using the Pre-processor

The C pre-processor reads and manipulates the text of a program before it is compiled. Sometimes it is part of the compiler but on some systems it is a completely separate program which reads a program and outputs it in modified form to a file. It can be thought of as an editor to which commands are given by means of directives embedded in the program text. These directives all begin with the character #, which must be the first non-space character on a line (some non-standard compilers require that it be the very first character on a line). Pre-processor directives can stretch over several lines in which case all but the last line must end with backslash (\ ). For example

```
#define    ArraySize    (NoOfElements\
                         *ElementSize)
```

11.1.   File Inclusion: #include

Examples of **#include** have appeared in almost all the programs so far because most use the standard header file **<stdio.h>**. An example of a header file created by a programmer can be seen in section 9.4, where prototypes, constants and types which are common to the three, independent programs that form the Huffman coding system are defined in the file **Huffman.h**. Apart from saving typing this has the advantage that a change to any of the definitions in the included file is made available to all sections of the system.

When the pre-processor encounters a **#include** directive at some point in a program it substitutes the contents of the named file at that point. An included file can itself contain **#include** directives.

Section 12.6 gives more information about using **#include** to help split programs between files, but some useful principles will be mentioned here because there are traps for the unwary. A header file used by different modules of a program should contain definitions of types, constants and function prototypes which are common to some of the modules. It should not contain declarations of variables or complete functions.

To illustrate the problem caused by variable declarations, consider a program which comprises two modules in files called **module1.c** and **module2.c**, and a header file which is included in both of them called **common.h**. The content of **common.h** is:

```
typedef   float   real;
real SharedValue;
```

Now suppose that **module1.c** contains

```
#include   "common.h"
real x;
main() {
    funcA();
    x = SharedValue;
}
```

and **module2.c** contains

```
#include   "common.h"
void funcA(void) {
    SharedValue = 27;
}
```

It might at first be thought that **module1.c** will see the same **SharedValue** as **module2.c** and therefore that **x** might take the value 27. This is not the case and to see why consider the text of the two modules as seen by the compiler. After completing the **#include** directive the first module looks like

```
typedef   float   real;
real SharedValue;
real x;
main() {
    funcA();
    x = SharedValue;
}
```

and the second like

```
typedef   float   real;
real SharedValue;
void funcA(void) {
    SharedValue = 27;
}
```

What has happened is that each module contains a declaration of **SharedValue** and so two, completely independent variables exist, one in each module. The type definition however creates no problem, because this merely gives information to the compiler.

A similar argument applies to including a complete function declaration in header files. Each file which includes the header file will contain a copy of the function. For the correct way of handling such situations see section 12.6.

As computer operating systems differ in the ways that files are organized. Some have hierarchical directories organized as trees, with long pathnames to needed to identify files in remote directories, others have an essentially flat file structure. The places where a C compiler searches for a file depend upon the implementation. However, some indication of where to look can be given by the programmer. The command

```
#include <filename>
```

will, on most systems, search initially in some system directory while

```
#include "filename"
```

searches first in the same directory as the program being compiled. But as there are systems which do not have directories it is necessary to check the documentation with each implementation to be sure what will happen.

The ANSI standard also requires that the file name in the first example cannot contain a > or a newline and there may be odd, but undefined effects if it contains ", ', \ or /*. The style of the second example permits > in the name. However, as a general rule, because some systems may object to file names containing punctuation characters, it is a good idea to keep names simple and not too long (there are systems which limit file names to as few as eight characters).

11.2.   Macros: #define

#define has already been seen in statements such as:

```
#define   pi      3.1415927
```

where it defines a constant. In fact **#define** is much more powerful than this, but first it is necessary to understand some terminology. In the above example **pi** is called a *macro* and 3.1415927 is its *replacement string*. A macro name has the same form as any other identifier. Whenever **pi** is used in a program the pre-processor replaces it by the text of its replacement string.

Even though this type of use of **#define** is very simple, it is very important. By defining **pi** in this way it is guaranteed that should an inadvertent effort be made to change it, the compiler will detect a syntax error. For instance, the statement

    pi = 4;

appears to the compiler as

    3.1415927 = 4;

which is certain to be detected as an error, whereas the statement

    float pi = 3.1415927;

does not offer the same security. In this second case **pi** is a variable and, moreover, needs to be accessed at runtime as well as occupying space in runtime memory.

Expansion by means of textual replacement is the basis of the power of macros, but can lead to unexpected effects, for example

    #define   Four   2+2

seems harmless enough, but the subsequent expression

    j = Four*Four;

will produce the value 8, not 16. The reason is that macro expansion produces

    j = 2+2*2+2;

and * has higher priority than +. The solution is simple, the definition should be

    #define   Four   (2+2)

A related hazard is the detection of syntax errors. If the expansion of a macro produces a syntax error a compiler will show the error at the position of the macro call, not its definition. As compilers do not normally show the expansion of a macro such errors can be difficult to recognize. The general rule is that if your compiler indicates an error in a statement which, after serious thought, seems correct, check to see if the statement involves macros. If it does, work out what the statement looks like after the macro call has been expanded.

Macros can take parameters written in parentheses immediately after the macro name. For example, the macro defined as

```
#define    max(x,y)  ((x) > (y) ? (x) : (y))
```

when called with the statement

```
j = max(c + d, 3*x);
```

will expand into

```
j = ((c + d) > (3*x) ? (c + d) : (3*x));
```

Although this looks like a function call it is important to realize that it is not; each reference to **max** generates 'in-line' code. This may be faster than a function call but will usually take more space. In fact, for the case above, one of the expressions **c + d** or **3 * x** will be evaluated twice, which is not very efficient.

Because **max** is not a function, the type of its arguments are not specified and so can be anything that is textually appropriate in its expanded form; the same version of **max** could be used with integer, floating point or character arguments.

When a macro is being declared there can be no intervening spaces between the macro name and the parenthesis starting the formal parameter list, but there can be spaces between parameters. Thus

```
#define    max(x,  y)     ((x) > (y) ? (x) : (y))
```

is valid, but

```
#define    max  (x,y)     ((x) > (y) ? (x) : (y))
```

is not.

Notice that in **max** the arguments, when used internally, are enclosed in parentheses; this is good practice in order to avoid problems with operator priority similar to those described above. Consider

```
#define    TIMES(x,y)    x*y
```

with the call

```
a = TIMES(r+1, s+1);
```

The expansion is:

```
a = r+1*s+1
```

which does not produce the correct result at all. A good principle when writing a macro that produces an expression is to enclose the whole macro body in parentheses and also each of the argument references. Even with this precaution macros can still produce surprises; consider the call:

    s = max(a[i++], m);

The expansion is

    s = ((a[i++]) > (m) ? (a[i++]) : (m));

which increments **i** twice if the condition is true. The problem is that an expression such as **(a[i++]) > (m)** has two effects, its main one of comparing two values, and a side-effect of incrementing **i**. The principle is to avoid side effects when passing arguments to macros. Particular care should be taken when using the standard functions; many of them (e.g. **getc, putc**) are often implemented as macros and so may cause problems if arguments with side-effects are used.

The ANSI standard includes two new operators which can only be used in macros. These are **##**, which concatenates text and **#**, which allows quoted text to contain substituted parameters. To demonstrate **##**, the macro

    #define decl(p1,p2)   int p1##p2

if called by

    decl(North, West);

generates

    int NorthWest;

The **#** operator, when preceding a macro parameter name, causes the name to be expanded and then enclosed in quotes. For example,

    #define   monitor(var)   printf(#var" = %d\n", var);

can be called by

    monitor(size);
    monitor(index);

which generates:

```
printf("size"" = %d\n", size);
printf("index"" = %d\n", index);
```

The two adjacent strings are automatically concatenated by the compiler. The **#** operator is needed because macro parameter substitution does not occur inside strings. For example, the macro

```
#define    monitor(var)   printf("var = %d\n", var);
```

if called by the statement

```
monitor(size);
```

would merely produce output such as

```
var =  3
```

The pre-processor does not look inside strings and so does not substitute **var**.

Once a name has been defined it stays defined until the end of the file being compiled, although a subsequent **#define** can give a new meaning to the name. Sometimes it is necessary to remove a defined name, for instance if a standard header file defines a name that you wish to use for your own purposes. **#undef** is used to do this, as in

```
#undef    max
```

This frees the name **max** for other use.

Sections 11.4 and 14.4 give examples of relatively more advanced uses of macros.

11.3.   Conditional Compilation: #if and #ifdef

When writing a large program to be run on different computer systems it is common to find that certain parts of the program have to be adapted to suit some aspect of each of the systems in question. A particular compiler might have a bug in some construction, or might offer some machine dependent way of achieving a great saving of space or time. One way to cope with this is to have a different version of the program for each system, but this makes maintenance much more difficult and increases the likelihood that different versions may become inadvertently incompatible. A much better way is to include all the different versions of a piece of program in the correct place in the appropriate files and to use the pre-processor to select the appropriate version during compilation. This can be achieved by using the pre-processor directives **#if**, **#else**, **#elif** and **#endif**.

As an example, suppose a program has to exist in two versions which work on two different types of screen, one small and one large. The fragment below could be used to create both versions of the program:

```
#define    Model    Small
#if Model == Small
    #define MaxX  512
    #define MaxY  490
    #define Colors 2
#elif   Model == Large
    #define MaxX  1024
    #define MaxY  1024
    #define Colors 8
#endif
```

In this case the first set of definitions will be used, but by changing only **Small** to **Large** in the first line the second set could be substituted. It is well to be aware that some old compilers require # to be the first character on a line, rather than the first non-space character.

It should be noted, by users of non ANSI compilers, that many old compilers would not accept the indented use of **#define** above. Some such compilers require the # to be the first character on a line, not the first non-space character.

As well as the directives mentioned there is **#ifdef**, which tests if a name has already been defined and **#ifndef**, which tests if a name is not defined. The following segment defines the macro **Model** only if it has not been defined earlier:

```
#if ndef Model
    #define Model  Small
#endif
```

The effect of **#ifdef** can also be obtained by using the expression **defined()**, which is new to the ANSI standard. The above example can be written as:

```
#if !defined(Model)
    #define Model  Default
#endif
```

#if statements can also make debugging code optional. When writing programs one often includes testing code for printing variables, checking values against limits, and so on, but this code needs to be removed for the production version of the program. If one removes this code completely one finds, only too often, that a new bug emerges and the debugging code has to be retyped. One way to avoid this situation is illustrated below:

```
#define   Debug
   . . .
#if defined(Debug)
    printf("Index = %d\n", i);
#endif
```

For the production version the first line can be removed. Notice that **Debug** is not given a value here; a name can be defined even without a value. Such names often serve as flags to denote the version of a program to use.

A similar approach can be used to avoid known compiler bugs or limitations; if it is known, for instance, that a certain expression is implemented incorrectly by some system, then **#if ... #endif** can be used to provide alternative coding without penalizing correct compilers.

11.4.   Pre-defined Names

The following names are provided by standard systems and can be used to aid debugging or record keeping.

_ _LINE_ _   Contains the number of the current line in the source file.

_ _FILE_ _   Contains the name of the current source file in the form of a character string.

_ _DATE_ _   Contains, as a string, the date when the program was compiled in the form illustrated by '12 27 1945' (month, day, year).

_ _TIME_ _   Contains the compilation time as a string in the form illustrated by '11:45:23' (hours, minutes, seconds).

_ _STDC_ _   Should contain the constant 1 only if the system conforms to the ANSI standard. It can be used by a programmer to check if a system conforms.

The fragment below illustrates one way these definitions might be used:

```
if (Index > ArrayMax) {
    printf("Array index error at line %s, file %s\n", __LINE__, __FILE__);
    exit(0);
}
```

11.5. Other Pre-processor Directives

Some of the directives below may not be implemented by compilers which do not conform to the standard although most have been available for some time in many implementations.

> #error *Message*

makes the compiler print *message* in a diagnostic message during compilation. For example

> #if !defined(SYSTEM)
>   #error   You forgot to define SYSTEM
> #endif

would cause a compilation error, with the message, if SYSTEM were not defined.

The directive

> #pragma *text*

is used to pass a command to a compiler to produce some system defined action. For instance a compiler might have an optimizing mode which can be turned on by

> #pragma OPT

The valid texts that can follow **#pragma** are implementation dependent, but if a compiler finds a pragma that it does not recognize then it will ignore it.

The directive

> #line *constant*

tells the compiler to regard the current line as having the line number given by *constant* when producing error messages. It is even possible to tell the compiler to pretend that the name of the current source file is different by:

> #line *constant* "*file name*"

The principal application of this is in pre-processors for C programs. For instance, one may be writing a program to generate a C program from a file containing commands to a data-base management system. Line 27 of the command file could be something like

> REQUEST Age AS INTEGER IN RANGE 0..120.

and the program which processes this may have to generate several lines of C program to print a message, take a response and check its validity. The user of this program writes only in the command language and is not concerned that a C program is produced as an intermediate stage. However, should an error be made in the command language he will expect to see line numbers in the error message which refer to his original text, and not the C translation. If the generated C program includes **#line** directives then this can be achieved. For instance, the program generated by the above command could begin:

```
#line   27
printf("Please give Age\n");
     . . .
```

so that if the C system produces any error messages, they will refer to line 27, which is in the original command file, and not to the generated C text.

11.6.   Portability and the Pre-Processor

When a program has to run on many different systems there are usually problems created by differences between precision of floating point numbers or the maximum size of different types of integer. For example, using 32 bits for a floating point value gives a precision of about 7 decimal digits, 48 bits about 11 digits and a 96 bit representation typically gives about 20.

If one is writing a program which needs at least ten decimal digits for floating point numbers it is possible to declare all floating point variables with type **double**. However, a large machine might have a default size for **float** larger than ten digits, and a **double** could have more than twenty, which is probably more than necessary but slower than need be. A solution is to write a header file which contains synonyms for the types which are adequate. It could contain, for instance:

```
#define   real      double
#define   integerlong int
```

with any other definitions necessary for unsigned values etc. One must now take care always to use the synonyms, as in

```
integer i, j, k;
real x, y;
```

To move the program to some generously endowed number cruncher it is only necessary to change the header file to

```
#define    real       float
#define    integer    int
```

Typically the header file would also contain relevant numeric constants and string constants with print formats. Using a defined name as an alias for a type is safe in this case, but the following is not a good practice:

```
#define    intp    int *
```

This will work for a declaration such as

```
intp    pm;
```

but not for

```
intp    pm, pn;
```

which, when expanded, is

```
int *pm, pn;
```

Therefore **pm** is a pointer to an integer, but **pn** is an integer. The solution is to use **typedef** instead of **#define** to create an alias for complicated types.

11.7.   Splitting Programs between Files

When the source file (the file containing C text) of a program module is compiled the compiler produces a *link-ready* (sometimes called *object*) version of the module which contains the compiled code of each of the functions in the module in a form close to the final binary code needed for a program. It also contains information about the location of variables which can be used by other modules. When all the modules of a program have been compiled the link-ready modules are passed to a *link-editor* which joins them together, checks for name conflicts or missing functions, scans any libraries that may be required and produces the final, binary version of the program.

The ways in which a linker is invoked, the commands used to control it, the location of the link-ready modules and the way in which libraries of pre-compiled modules are specified are not part of the C language and vary between computer systems, or even between different C compilers on the same computer system. However, it is important to realize that link-ready files do not normally contain information about types of variables, arguments of functions or details of structures; in other words, the information that is so valuable in helping a compiler ensure consistent and correct use of objects is lost once a module has been compiled. The C programmer therefore uses header files to provide this necessary information to the compiler.

In order to illustrate the use of this technique, consider a simple graphics package which provides a function **GraphOpen** to open some drawing medium (a window or a plotter, perhaps), **GraphClose** to close it and **Move(x, y)** and **Line(x, y)** to relocate the 'pen' and to draw a line to the point (x, y). The origin of the coordinate system is the bottom left-hand corner of the drawing medium. The size of the drawing area is defined by **xMax** and **yMax**, the x coordinate of the right-hand edge and the y coordinate of the top of the drawing area respectively. The necessary definitions can be provided in a header file **graphs.h** as follows:

```
#define    xMax   1000.0
#define    yMax   1000.0
void GraphOpen(void);
void GraphClose(void);
void Move(float, float);
void Line(float, float);
```

This file describes the public interface, or specification of the package. It contains all objects (functions, global variables, constants, types) that a user of the package is allowed to use. The body of the program can be stored in a file **graphs.c** and could have the structure illustrated below. The row of dots '. . .' is not part of the program; it is intended to imply that a programmer will write some appropriate C code to be inserted at this point.

```
#include <graphs.h>
static float CurrX, CurrY;

void GraphOpen(void) { . . . }

void GraphClose(void) { . . . }

void Move(float x, float y) { . . . }

void Line(float x, float y) { . . . }

static void DevOpen(void) { . . . }

static void DevClose(void) { . . . }
```

The functions **DevOpen** and **DevClose** are lower level functions to open and close physical devices and must not be called directly by a package user; packages of this type often contain many such functions. By declaring them to be static they are only accessible within this file. Similarly the variables **CurrX** and **CurrY**, which should not be changed except by calls to **Move** and **Line**, are private to the graphics package. To make this package available the file **graphs.c** needs to be compiled and stored in a library or file according to whatever system dependent method is used, and **graphs.h** needs to be placed in whatever system directory is required. Any user can now call the package. The following program, in the file **square.c**, shows how to draw a square.

```
/* File square.c */
#include <graphs.h>
main() { /* Draw a square */
    GraphOpen();
    Move(100.0, 100.0);
    Line(100.0, 900.0);
    Line(900.0, 900.0);
    Line(900.0, 100.0);
    Line(100.0, 100.0);
    GraphClose();
}
```

If a file forming part of a package is modified it is important to be aware of which files need to be recompiled and when relinking is necessary. For the package above the requirements are:

1. If the **square.c** is modified then it alone must be recompiled. Relinking is then needed.
2. If **graphs.c** is modified (but not **graphs.h**) then **graphs.c** must be recompiled and relinking is necessary but **square.c** does not need recompiling.
3. If **graphs.h** is modified then both **graphs.c** and **square.c** need to be recompiled and relinked. They may also need modifications themselves; for instance, if the function **GraphOpen** is given arguments in a new version then **square.c** and **graphs.c** need modification to allow for the new definition.

Clearly, modifying a header file involves more subsequent work than any other operation and for this reason such files should be designed carefully. Some systems are able to keep track of all the dependencies and cause automatic recompilation and relinking of only the necessary files. This can be important in large systems containing possibly thousands of files.

In the example above, consistency between the graphics package and the user program is ensured by using **graphs.h** to specify the public parts of the package; however, C does not force this mechanism upon programmers and it is possible for a programmer to include incorrect specifications for these functions. In this case the error will not be detected by the system and the result will be a failure of the program in a way that can be very difficult to diagnose. Some languages (Modula-2 and Ada, among others) have mechanisms for ensuring that such errors cannot happen. They also have a clearer, more precise and safer way of specifying which objects are imported from other modules and which should remain private to the current module. It is possible to achieve some of this clarity by defining macros such as:

```
#define   PRIVATE static
#define   EXPORT
#define   IMPORT  extern
```

Using these, **graphs.c** could be rewritten:

```
#include   <graphs.h>
PRIVATE   float CurrX, CurrY;
PRIVATE   void DevOpen(void) { . . . }
PRIVATE   void DevClose(void) { . . . }
EXPORT    void Move(float, float) { . . . }
EXPORT    void Line(float, float) { . . . }
EXPORT    void GraphOpen(void) { . . . }
EXPORT    void GraphClose(void) {. . . }
```

These macros do not provide any extra level of protection, but they do emphasize the programmer's intention and make errors less likely.

Suppose that it would be useful for the package user to be able to refer to the variables **CurrX** and **CurrY**. Then in **square.c** the definition of **CurrX** and **CurrY** would be changed to:

```
EXPORT   float CurrX, CurrY;
```

and **graphs.h** should now include the line

```
IMPORT   float CurrX, CurrY;
```

A programmer can now use these variables, but there is no way of preventing statements which modify them, such as

```
CurrX = 3.7;
```

which would upset the 'house-keeping' of the graphics package. A project leader could tell programmers not to write statements such as the above, but in a large system written by many programmers, the rule is hard to enforce. One solution is to use *encapsulation*. Encapsulation involves providing functions which are the only way of referring to public variables or data structures. As an example, the first part of

graphs.c can be changed to

```
PRIVATE  float CurrX, CurrY;
EXPORT   float CurrentX(void) { return(CurrX) }
EXPORT   float CurrentY(void) { return(CurrY) }
```

and the following two lines added to **graphs.h** changed to

```
float CurrentX(void);
float CurrentY(void);
```

These functions allow a programmer to inspect the values of **CurrX** and **CurrY** but have no way of changing them except by the intended mechanism of calling **Move** and **Line**. The references will take slightly longer, as they now involve a function call, but program security is enforced.

When constructing a program with many header files, it becomes possible that a file may inadvertently be included more than once. For example, suppose that the file **common.h** is included in two header files **first.h** and **second.h**. Then a program with the statements

```
#include  "first.h"
#include  "second.h"
```

has included **common.h** twice. Kernighan and Ritchie suggest a technique for avoiding this by writing **common.h** in the following style

```
#if !defined(CommonPresent)
   #define CommonPresent
   /* give the contents of common.h here */
   . . .
#endif
```

The first time **common.h** is included in a program, the name **CommonPresent** will not be defined and so the subsequent statements are obeyed, including the definition of **CommonPresent**. Later inclusion of **common.h** will find **CommonPresent** already defined and therefore the pre-processor will skip the body of the file.

11.8. Program Testing with 'assert'

The standard header file **<assert.h>** contains a macro **assert** for helping with program testing. The argument of **assert** is an expression which, if it has the value zero when the macro is executed, will cause the program to stop and to write out an error message to **stderr**. The message should include the filename and line number of the assertion.

To illustrate its use, consider a program which contains the declarations

        int Data[100], Lower, Upper;

Lower and **Upper** are to be used as indices to **Data** in statements such as

        if (Data[Lower] > Data[Upper]) . . .

Because of programming errors it is not uncommon for one of the indices in statements such as this to stray outside the permitted range of 0 to 99. This can be tested by including **<assert.h>** at the beginning of the program file and changing the statement to:

        assert(Lower >=0 && Lower < 100);
        assert(Upper >=0 && Upper < 100);
        if (Data[Lower] > Data[Upper]) . . .

Now if either assertion is false the program will stop and produce a message such as

        FALSE ASSERTION "Lower >=0 && Lower < 100" AT LINE 99 OF FILE test.c

This type of testing can be invaluable, but once a program has been thoroughly tested it might slow down performance unacceptably. In this case it is not necessary to go through all the program files removing the **assert** statements. If the macro name **NDEBUG** is defined when **<assert.h>** is included the calls of the macro will be ignored. Therefore all the assertions in a file can be suppressed by putting

        #define   NDEBUG

at the start of the file.

12

Further Data Structures

Earlier chapters have shown how to implement fundamental data structures such as lists and trees. Similar techniques can be used to implement an abstraction such as a set, queue or stack. If an implementation provides such abstract data structures in a way in which the implementation details are hidden then it is said to be *encapsulated*. If it makes no assumptions about the types of the component elements of the structure then it is said to be *generic*.

12.1. Abstract Data Structures

An abstract data structure is defined by a set of operations and a description of the effect these operations have on the subsequent state of the data structure. As an example, a *stack* is a structure to which elements may only be added at the top and removed from the top, and is often likened to a stack of plates in a cafeteria. All operations on any data structure can be classed under the broad headings, CREATE, DELETE, MODIFY and INSPECT. For a stack the MODIFY operations are called PUSH (add a plate) and POP (remove a plate). Whichever operation is used only affects the top element. In a pure implementation of a stack the only INSPECT operations would be EMPTY (is the stack empty?) and FULL (is the stack full?), but in practice it is useful to allow the inspection of any element given a position relative to the top of the stack.

A *queue*, on the other hand, defines a structure where elements can only be added at the tail and removed from the head (this concept is more readily understood in some countries than others). In this case the modify operations are ENQUEUE (add an element at the tail of the queue) and DEQUEUE (remove an element from its head). The inspection operations FULL and EMPTY may be defined as they are for a stack.

When implementing such a data structure, care should be taken to isolate the implementation details from the operations which can be applied to the structure. This has several advantages: the implementation can be changed without affecting the program

161

which uses the data structure; the person implementing the abstract data structure can be sure that if only the standard set of operations has been used, and those operations are correctly implemented, the internal integrity of the data structure is guaranteed and finally a module which defines a full set of operations on a fundamental data structure is more likely to be re-usable in another program. In fact, writing well defined, comprehensive packages of tools for manipulating standard data structures is an important way of reducing programming effort.

The re-usability of an abstract data structure can be enhanced if a generic implementation is provided. The term generic implies an implementation that will work for any type of data (stacks of **int**, **float**, or **struct**, for example) or from which it is possible to derive instances of the data structure for particular types. For example, from a set of functions and a data structure implementing a generic stack one can derive an implementation of a stack of **int**s; this process is usually called *instantiation*. An example of how useful this approach can be was seen earlier in section 10.3 which described two standard library functions, **qsort** and **bsearch** which can sort or search any type of array. These functions can be used directly, or can be used to write functions or macros to sort or search arrays of any specific type. In this sense then, **qsort** and **bsearch** are generic sorting and searching functions and any function derived from them for a particular type is an instantiation. A way in which such functions can be written will be explained in section 12.5.

12.2.   Stacks

A stack is often described as a last in-first out structure; elements can only be added and removed at the top. They are used, among other things, to recognize languages which involve nesting of matching symbols (for example, **begin** ... **end** or { ... }), to represent algebraic expressions and to implement recursion. A stack can be implemented as an array or as a linked list.

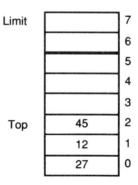

The diagram above illustrates a typical array implementation of a stack of integers which, at the point shown in the diagram, contains three values. In this diagram **Top** is the index of the top element of the stack and **Limit** is the limit to which the stack can grow.

To implement such a stack one must write a header file **Astack.h** (for 'array stack') to define the public interface of the stack module. First it is necessary to define the data structure for the stack. It must hold the stack itself (or in this case a pointer to it), the stack top and the limit to which the stack can grow. A suitable structure is shown in the header file **Astack.h**, which is:

```
/*  Header file for an integer stack implemented as an array  */

typedef struct{    int Top;
                   int *Body;
                   int Limit;
               }Stack;

typedef enum {False, True} Bool;

/* The modifying functions      */

void    InitStack(Stack *s, int Size); /*    Initialize stack 's'  */
void    DeleteStack(Stack *s);         /*    Delete stack 's'  */
void    Push(int i, Stack *s);         /*    Push 'i' on to stack 's'  */
int     Pop(Stack *s);                 /*    Delete top of 's' and return its
                                             value  */

/* The inspection functions      */

Bool    StackEmpty(Stack s);           /*    Test for an empty stack  */
Bool    StackFull(Stack s);            /*    Test for a full stack  */
```

The function **InitStack**, as well as setting **Top** and **Limit**, must also generate the space for a suitable array and set **Body** to point to it. A suitable implementation for all these functions can be defined in the file **Astack.c** as shown below:

```
/*  Implementation file for an integer stack implemented as an array  */

#include  <stdio.h>
#include  <stdlib.h>
#include  "Astack.h"

void Error(char *Message) {
    fprintf(stderr, "%s\n", Message);
    exit(0);
}
```

```
void    InitStack(Stack *s, int Size)   /*   Initialize stack 's'   */ {
    s -> Top    = -1;
    s -> Limit = Size - 1;
    s -> Body = (int *) malloc(Size * sizeof(int));
}

void    DeleteStack(Stack *s)           /*   Delete stack 's'   */ {
    s -> Top = s -> Limit = -1;
    free(s);
}

void    Push(int i, Stack *s)           /*   Push 'i' onto stack 's'   */ {
    if (StackFull(*s))
        Error("Stack is full");
    else
        s -> Body[++(s -> Top)] = i;
}

int     Pop(Stack *s)                   /*   Return top of 's'; pop 's'   */ {
    if (StackEmpty(*s))
        Error("Stack is empty");
    else
        return(s -> Body[(s -> Top)--]);
}

Bool   StackEmpty(Stack  s)             /*   Test for an empty stack   */ {
    return(s.Top < 0);
}

Bool   StackFull(Stack  s)              /*   Test for a full stack   */ {
    return(s.Top == s.Limit);
}
```

The rather trivial program below shows how these functions may be used. It reads from a file a set of up to 100 integers and prints them in reverse order.

```
#include    <stdio.h>
#include    "Astack.h"
main() {
    Stack Pile;
    int Value;
    InitStack(&Pile, 100);
    while (scanf("%d", &Value) == 1)
        Push(Value, &Pile);
    while (!StackEmpty(Pile))
        printf("%d\n", Pop(&Pile));

}
```

This implementation is effective but has disadvantages: the size of the stack is limited to the value specified at the initialization of a stack, the type of stack is limited to integers and the mechanism for handling errors is primitive. From the point of view of reliability it has a major problem: the file **Astack.h** contains a definition of the structure **Stack** and so the internal organization of the stack is visible to a program using the package. The correct working of the functions depends therefore upon a programmer agreeing not to tinker with the members of **Stack**. It would be more secure if the internal workings of a **Stack** were completely hidden from a user. Section 12.5 shows a way of avoiding all these problems.

Exercise 12.1 As an exercise in using the above implementation of a stack, write a program which uses it to recognize correct 'sentences' in the following 'language': a correctly formed sentence is a sequence of any length of the symbols (,), [,], {, }, < and > arranged in such a way that matching symbols nest correctly. Correct sentences could be '([ ] < ( ) { } >)' or '< < < ( ) [< < > [ ] >] > > ( ) >'. Incorrect sentences are illustrated by '< [>]', '< < < [ ] { } > >' and '[< > ({) }]]'. Your program should read a sentence (up to one line long) and print a message stating whether or not it is correctly formed.

Exercise 12.2. Modify the function **Push** so that if a stack becomes full it automatically creates a new one twice the size. **realloc** can be used for this.

12.3. Queues

A queue is a first-in/first-out data structure. Elements are added at the tail and removed from the head. Examples of queues may be found in simulation systems, operating system schedulers and type-ahead buffers on computer keyboard drivers. As with stacks, they can be implemented by using arrays or by using pointers. An array implementation is presented here, and a linked list representation is left as an exercise in section 12.5.

The operations on a queue, are CREATE, DELETE, ENQUEUE, which adds a new element at the tail of the queue, DEQUEUE, which removes one from the head and FULL and EMPTY, with obvious meanings. The next diagram shows an array implementation of a queue.

An implementation of a queue must allow space freed by dequeueing to be available for subsequent enqueueing. This is achieved by providing 'wrap-around'; when the tail reaches the end of the array it is moved to the front, if space is available. In fact a queue implemented in this way is a circular array.

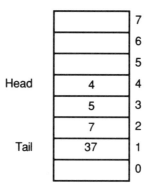

The header file **Aqueue.h** for an array implementation of a queue of characters is:

```
/*  Header file for an integer queue implemented as an array */

typedef struct{int Head;          /* index of queue head  */
               int Tail;          /* index of queue tail */
               int Limit;         /* maximum queue size */
               int Elements;      /* current number of elements  */
               int *Body;} Queue;
typedef enum{False, True}Bool;

/* The modifying functions     */

void   InitQueue(Queue *q, int Size);   /* Initialize queue 'q' */
void   DeleteQueue(Queue *q);           /* Delete queue 'q'  */
void   Enqueue(int i, Queue *q);        /* Enqueue 'i' onto queue 'q'  */
int    Dequeue(Queue *q);               /* Dequeue the head of 'q'  */

/* The inspection functions     */

Bool   QueueEmpty(Queue s);     /* Test for an empty queue  */
Bool   QueueFull(Queue s);      /* Test for a full queue */
```

The corresponding implementation is:

```
/*  Implementation of an integer queue using an array   */

#include "Aqueue.h"
#include <stdio.h>
#include <stdlib.h>

void Error(char *Message) {
    fprintf(stderr, "%s\n", Message);
    exit(0);
}
```

```
/* The modifying functions    */

void    InitQueue(Queue *q, int Size) /*   Initialize queue 'q'  */ {
    q -> Body   = (int *) malloc(Size * sizeof(int));
    q -> Head = q -> Tail = q -> Elements = 0;
    q -> Limit = Size - 1;
}

void    DeleteQueue(Queue *q)    /* Delete queue 'q'  */ {
    free(q -> Body);
    q -> Head = q -> Tail = q -> Limit = q -> Elements = 0;
}

void    Enqueue(int i, Queue *q) /*    Enqueue 'i' onto tail of 'q'  */ {
    if (QueueFull(*q))
        Error("Queue is full");
    else {
        q -> Body[q -> Tail] = i;
        if (q -> Tail == q -> Limit)
            q -> Tail = 0;
        else
            (q -> Tail)++;
        (q -> Elements)++;
    }
}

int    Dequeue(Queue *q) /*  Dequeue the head of 'q'  */ {
    if (QueueEmpty(*q))
        Error("Queue is empty");
    else {
        int Result = q -> Body[q -> Head];
        if (q -> Head == q -> Limit)
            q -> Head = 0;
        else
            q -> Head++;
        q -> Elements--;
        return(Result);
    }
}

Bool    QueueFull(Queue q)  /* Test for a full queue */ {
    return(q.Elements == q.Limit+1);
}

Bool    QueueEmpty(Queue q) /* Test for an empty queue */ {
    return(q.Elements == 0);
}
```

12.4.   Sets

A set is a mathematical object which is provided, in a restricted form, by a number of programming languages, for example, Pascal. To simplify matters, the discussion here initially involves only sets of small integers, but the mathematical principles apply to more general sets. Given the two sets

$A = \{1, 2, 3, 5, 7, 9\}$
$B = \{3, 4, 5, 6\}$

then the following operations are defined on them:

The *union* of A and B is $\{1, 2, 3, 4, 5, 6, 7, 9\}$
The *intersection* of A and B is $\{3, 5\}$
The *difference* of A and B is $\{1, 2, 7, 9\}$

C does not provide built-in types or functions for sets, but they are easy to implement. For sets of small integers a 'bit string' is a particularly convenient method of representation. For example, if we need sets of integers limited to the range 0 to 9 then the set A above can be represented by the binary number

0111010101

where the left-most bit represents the number 0, the right-most the number 9, a 0 in a bit position shows that the corresponding set member is absent, a 1 shows it is present. In this notation B is therefore represented by

0001111000

Set operations can now easily be expressed in terms of bitwise operations **and, or** and **not** (written as **&,** | and **~** in C). The union of A and B is **A | B**, the intersection is **A & B** and the difference is **A & (~ B)**. To test whether a value is a member of a set involves testing the corresponding bit position.

This approach to set operations will be used to implement a package called **BitSet**. Before beginning it is necessary to decide what is meant by 'small integer'. The value of ten mentioned above is too restrictive to be useful. The package below uses 128 values (0 to 127), as this covers the range of ASCII characters, but this can easily be changed.

Clearly some type of integer is needed to hold the bits representing a set. Efficiency implies that **long int** would be most suitable, as one **long int** can hold at least 32 bits. However, the problem arises of precisely knowing how many bits can be stored in a particular length of integer. The standard header file **limits.h** contains a constant **CHAR_BIT**, which is the number of bits in a character. It does not, unfortunately contain any equivalent constant for other lengths of integer. Therefore in the implementation below a set is represented as a sufficient number of characters; if a character is eight bits then sixteen characters will be used to represent a set of up to 128 elements.

```
/*  Header file for package 'BitSet'    */

#include    <limits.h>

#define    MaxBitSet          127
#define    BitSetArraySize   (MaxBitSet/CHAR_BIT+1)

typedef char BitSet[BitSetArraySize];
typedef enum{False, True}Bool;

/*  All the following functions except 'IsIn' put their result in
    the first parameter  and return a pointer to it  */

BitSet *AddToSet(BitSet s, int i);
    /*  Add 'i' to the set 's';    e.g. AddToSet(Primes, 7);  */

BitSet *ClearSet(BitSet s);
    /*  Empty the set 's'  */

BitSet *AddRangeToSet(BitSet s, int i, int j);
    /*  Add all the integers between 'i' and 'j' inclusive to the set 's'.
            e.g. AddRangeToSet(Letters, 'A', 'Z');      */

BitSet *Unite(BitSet s1, BitSet s2);
    /*  Replace 's1' by the union of 's1' and 's2'  */

BitSet *SubtractSet(BitSet s1, BitSet s2);
    /*  Replace 's1' by the difference of 's1' and 's2'  */

BitSet *SubtractElement(BitSet s, int i);
    /*  Remove 'i' from set 's'  */

BitSet *SubtractRange(BitSet s, int i, int j);
    /*  Remove the range 'i' to 'j' from 's'  */

BitSet *Intersect(BitSet s1, BitSet s2);
    /*  Replace 's1' by the intersection  of 's1' and 's2'  */

Bool IsIn(BitSet s, int i);
    /*  Test for the presence of 'i' in 's'  */
```

As a simple example of how such a package may be used, a program which included the statements:

```
BitSet Vowels;
char ch;

ClearSet(Vowels);
AddToSet(Vowels, 'A');
AddToSet(Vowels, 'E');
AddToSet(Vowels, 'I');
AddToSet(Vowels, 'O');
AddToSet(Vowels, 'U');
```

could then test whether a character **ch** is a vowel with, for example, a statement such as:

```
if (IsIn(Vowels, ch) ) {. . .}
```

As an illustration of why the functions all return a pointer to the modified set, the sequence above can be replaced by:

```
AddToSet(*AddToSet(*AddToSet(*AddToSet(*AddToSet(*ClearSet(Vowels)
    , 'A'), 'E'), 'I'), 'O'), 'U');
```

This may be readable to Lisp programmers. For a version which may be better for the rest of us see exercise 12.3.

The implementation of this package is shown below. The macro **Throughout** is particularly important. It is a convenient way of applying any operator to each matching array element of two sets. It illustrates one way of using a macro to achieve an effect that is not possible with a function. A function cannot take an operator as an argument, but a macro argument can be any group of characters, including the characters which constitute an operator.

Expressions such as the following, found in the function **AddToSet**, are used to select the proper bit from the appropriate array element:

```
s[i/CHAR_BIT] |= (1 << (i % CHAR_BIT));
```

Set element **i** is located in array element **i/CHAR_BIT** and is at bit position **i%CHAR_BIT**. The last part of the statement makes a one-bit mask aligned with the required bit of the array element by shifting left a single one-bit (the number 1 is a sequence of zeros followed by a one-bit) by **i%CHAR_BIT** places. The OR operation **|=** then places that bit at the appropriate place.

```
#include "BitSet.h"

#define    Throughout(s1,s2,op) {int i;\
                           for (i = 0; i <= BitSetArraySize-1; i++)\
                               (s1[i]) op (s2[i]);\
                           }

BitSet *ClearSet(BitSet s) {
    int i;
    for (i = 0; i < BitSetArraySize; i++)
        s[i] = 0;
    return((BitSet *)s);
}

BitSet *AddToSet(BitSet s, int i) {
    s[i/CHAR_BIT] |= (1 << (i%CHAR_BIT));
    return((BitSet *)s);
}

BitSet *AddRangeToSet(BitSet s, int i, int j) {
    int n;
    for (n = i; n <= j; n++)
        AddToSet(s, n);
    return((BitSet *)s);
}

BitSet *Unite(BitSet s1, BitSet s2) {
    Throughout(s1, s2, |=);
    return((BitSet *)s1);
}

BitSet *SubtractSet(BitSet s1, BitSet s2) {
    Throughout(s1, ~s2, &=);
    return((BitSet *)s1);
}

BitSet *SubtractElement(BitSet s, int i) {
    s[i/CHAR_BIT] &= ~(1 << (i%CHAR_BIT));
    return((BitSet *)s);
}

BitSet *SubtractRange(BitSet s, int i, int j) {
    int n;
    for (n = i; n <= j; n++)
        SubtractElement(s, n);
    return((BitSet *)s);
}
```

```
BitSet *Intersect(BitSet s1, BitSet s2) {
    Throughout(s1, s2, &=);
    return((BitSet *)s1);
}

Bool IsIn(BitSet s, int i) {
    return(s[i/CHAR_BIT] & (1 << (i%CHAR_BIT)));
}
```

Exercise 12.3. Earlier a set of vowels was created by repeated calls to **AddToSet**, which is clumsy and unattractive. Another way of achieving the same end is to nest calls in a single statement, but the result is hard to read. A better way than either of these is to use the variable argument list technique explained in section 3.8 to create a function **VarAddToSet** which can take an arbitrary sequence of values and add them to a set. The first argument of the function can indicate the number of other arguments, simplifying the program fragment above to:

```
VarAddToSet(5, 'A', 'E', 'I', 'O', 'U');
```

Write and test such a function.

It is not uncommon to need sets of values other than integers; for example sets of coordinate pairs may be useful in a graphics program. In these cases bit sets are inappropriate, but a set can be implemented using other data structures such as ordered lists or trees. The abstract operations on sets can still be implemented using such structures, although the individual functions are more complicated. The next section shows a technique which could be applied to write a general set package.

12.5.   Generic Data Structures

The implementations of stacks and queues shown so far were specifically for integers. If a program needs many stacks of various different types of object (integers, structures and arrays, for instance) then it will need a version of the stack package for each type of stack element. Apart from the rewriting required, with the consequent waste of time and possibility for error, such an approach wastes space. A truly abstract implementation of a stack would not contain any restriction about the type of its elements; it would provide the stack operations and allow a programmer to use them to produce particular *instances* of stacks of any data type. Some languages, for example Ada, have the concept of *generic* data types from which such instances may be derived. Generic packages are not explicitly part of the C language, but the same effect can be produced.

A general package for manipulating a stack needs to provide a flexible mechanism for handling errors. In the implementation below a user of the package can provide his or her own function to be called on stack underflow or overflow, or can allow a default action to be taken. This is the purpose of the parameter **OnError** of the function **InitStack**. The user can provide, as parameter, a pointer to any function of the appropriate type and this will be called if an error occurs, but if no function is provided (indicated by a **NULL** parameter) then a simple, default error function will be used.

In the implementation shown all the stack elements are generated on the heap. This creates the problem of when to free them; should it be the responsibility of the package or of the user of the package? The problem on this case attaches to the pop operation. This could copy the top element of the stack into a user supplied variable and free the space it occupied. Alternatively it could deliver a pointer to the object on the stack top and leave it to the user to free it. The first option is more convenient from the user's point of view, but if the objects on the stack are large the cost of copying into a user's variable could be significant. The implementation below takes the second option, but could easily be modified if this were not deemed desirable.

The stack and its associated function are defined in the header file **Lstack.h** as:

```
/*  Header file for a generic, linked stack implementation */

typedef void *Stack;
typedef enum{False, True}Bool;
typedef enum{Underflow, Overflow}StackErrorType;

/* The modifying functions     */

void    InitStack(Stack *s, int ElemSize, void OnError(StackErrorType));
        /*  Initialise stack 's', each element of which has a size of
            'ElemSize' bytes. If 'OnError' is NULL then a default error
            function will be provided; otherwise a user can provide a routine
            to be called on stack underflow or overflow.   */

void    DeleteStack(Stack *s);
        /*  Delete the stack 's'   */

void    Push(void *NewElem, Stack *s);
        /*  Push 'NewElem' onto stack 's'. 'NewElem' is a pointer to the
            element to be inserted.   */

void    *Pop(Stack *s);
        /*  Remove the top element from the stack 's' and return a pointer
            to it. The result will need to be cast to the appropriate type.
            As the result is a pointer to an object on the heap, it is the
            responsibility of the calling function to free the object
            when it is no longer needed. If the stack is empty then call
            the error function with 'Underflow' as an argument.   */
```

```
/* The inspection functions   */

Bool    StackEmpty(Stack s);  /* Is 's' empty? */
Bool    StackFull(Stack s);  /* Is 's' full? */
void    *StackElement(unsigned n, Stack s);
    /*   Return a pointer to the 'n'th element of stack 's', where the
         top element is number zero, the next one, and so on. If 'n' is
         greater than the size of the stack than the 'OnError' function
         of 's' will be called with parameter 'Underflow'.   */
```

Notice how this header file provides an interface to a set of stack operations but does not specify the type of the elements of the stack. Instead a stack is defined as a pointer to **void**, a generic pointer and the implementation must provide a suitable structure to which this can point. In this way the implementation details are hidden and so the implementation can be changed without affecting the programs which use it.

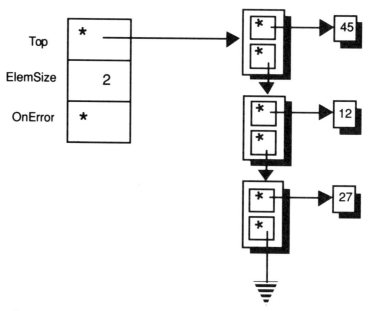

The type **StackDescriptor** below contains all the information about a particular instance of a stack except the type of the stack element. **Top** points to the top element of the stack, **ElemSize** is the size of a single element and **OnError** points to a function that is to be called if an error occurs. The structure is:

```
typedef struct ListNode {void *Element; struct ListNode *Next;} ListNode;
typedef struct{ListNode *Top;
        int ElemSize;
        void (*OnError)(StackErrorType);
        } StackDescriptor;
```

The type **ListNode** needs some explanation. The lists described in Chapter 7 were based on a structure which contains both the value stored in a node and a pointer to the next element in the list. Such an approach cannot be used in this case because the type of the stack element cannot be specified in advance. A solution is to use a list of pointers, each node of which contains a pointer to an element and a pointer to the next node. The diagram above shows a stack of integers made using this technique.

It is important to realize that the elements of the stack are held on the heap (the elements with shading) because these elements must be freed when no longer needed. This is illustrated in the implementation of **DeleteStack** below.The complete implementation is:

```c
#include    <stdio.h>
#include    <stdlib.h>
#include    <string.h>
#include    "Lstack.h"

void DefaultError(StackErrorType e) {

    switch (e) {
        case Underflow:   fprintf(stderr, "Stack underflow\n");   break;
        case Overflow:    fprintf(stderr, "Stack overflow\n");   break;
    }
    exit(0);
}

typedef struct ListNode { void *Element;
                          struct ListNode *Next;
                          }
                          ListNode;

typedef struct{ListNode *Top;
               int ElemSize;
               void (*OnError)(StackErrorType);
               }
               StackDescriptor;

void    InitStack(Stack *s, int ElemSize, void OnError(StackErrorType)) {
        StackDescriptor *ThisStack;   /*  Simplifies references to 's'  */

        *s = (Stack)malloc(sizeof(StackDescriptor));
        ThisStack = (StackDescriptor *)*s;
        ThisStack -> Top = NULL;
        ThisStack -> ElemSize = ElemSize;
        ThisStack -> OnError = (OnError == NULL ? DefaultError : OnError);
}
```

```
void    DeleteStack(Stack *s) {
   void *TopElement;

   while(!StackEmpty(*s)) {
      TopElement = Pop(s);
      free(TopElement);
   }
   free(*s);
}

void    Push(void *NewElem, Stack *s) {
   ListNode *NewNode;
   StackDescriptor *ThisStack = (StackDescriptor *)*s;

   /*  Make a new list node, and check for insufficient memory .
       Call the error function if there is insufficient memory  */
   if ((NewNode = (ListNode *)malloc(sizeof(ListNode))) == NULL)
      ThisStack -> OnError(Overflow);
   else {
      /*  Make a new stack element and check for insufficient memory  */
      NewNode -> Element = (void *)malloc(ThisStack -> ElemSize);
      if (NewNode -> Element == NULL)
         ThisStack -> OnError(Overflow);
      else {
         /*  Insert NewNode at the head of the list  */
         NewNode -> Next = ThisStack -> Top;
         ThisStack -> Top = NewNode;

         /*  Copy NewElem into the new stack element  */
         memmove(NewNode -> Element, NewElem,
                     ThisStack -> ElemSize);
      }
   }
}

void    *Pop(Stack *s) {
   StackDescriptor *ThisStack = ((StackDescriptor *)*s);
   ListNode *ToFree = ThisStack -> Top;

   if (ToFree == NULL)    /*  If empty call OnError  */
      ThisStack -> OnError(Underflow);
   else {
      void *Result = ToFree -> Element;

      ThisStack -> Top = ThisStack -> Top -> Next;
      free(ToFree);
      return(Result);
   }
}
```

```
Bool   StackEmpty(Stack s) {
    return(((StackDescriptor *)s) -> Top == NULL);
}

Bool   StackFull(Stack s) {
    /*  We cannot do anything very useful here; leave error recovery of
        to 'OnError'  */
    return(False);
}

void   *StackElement(unsigned n, Stack s) {
    ListNode *Tracer;
    StackDescriptor *ThisStack = ((StackDescriptor *)s);

    /*  The next loop moves 'n' elements down the stack 's' but stops
        if the list has fewer than 'n' elements.  */

    for (Tracer = ThisStack -> Top; n > 0 && Tracer != NULL; n--)
        Tracer = Tracer -> Next;

    if (Tracer == NULL)
        (ThisStack -> OnError)(Underflow);
    else
        return(Tracer -> Element);
}
```

To use the functions provided here, assume the declarations

```
Stack StructTester;
int  Action;
typedef struct {char ch; float f;} CharFloat;
CharFloat s, *ToFree;
Bool Continue;
```

An illustrative program fragment to demonstrate a stack of **CharFloat** elements is:

```
InitStack(&StructTester, sizeof(CharFloat), NULL);
Continue = True;
while (Continue) {
    scanf("%d", &Action);
    switch (Action) {
        case 0: DeleteStack(&StructTester);
                Continue = False;
                break;
        case 1: scanf(" %c %f", &s.ch, &s.f);
                Push(&s, &StructTester);
                break;
```

```
            case 2: s = *(ToFree = Pop(&StructTester));
                    printf("Popped : ch = <%c> f = %f\n", s.ch, s.f);
                    free(ToFree);
                    break;
        }
    }
```

The calls to these functions are sometimes clumsy because of the need to precede most of the arguments with **&** and the need to free popped elements. They can be simplified by creating macros. For example, for a stack of floating point numbers the macro definitions

```
#define FPush(Value, Stack)    Push(&Value, &Stack)
#define FPop(Stack,f)          {float *fp = (float *) Pop(&Stack); \
                                   f = *fp; free(fp); \
                                }
```

provide a simpler interface. A complete set of macros used in this way can provide a particular instance of a generic stack.

The definition of **FPop** raises an interesting, and non-trivial problem: macro calls cannot be treated as simple statements. Consider the statement:

```
if (some condition)
    FPop(MyStack, x);
else
    exit(0);
```

This will expand to:

```
if (some condition)
    {float * x = (float *) Pop(& MyStack);
        f = * x; free(x);
    };
else
    exit(0);
```

This is not correct C. The semicolon after the **}** will mark the end of the entire **if** statement, not just the first part; the compiler will object to **else**. This is a consequence of the C syntax for the use of the semicolon. In this case the statement should be:

```
if (some condition)
    FPop(MyStack, x)
else
    exit(0);
```

which looks wrong, but is correct.

Some similar problems with the use of macros are discussed in the next chapter and a good study and exposition is given by Koenig [KOEN 89].

Exercise 12.4. Using the technique shown here for implementing a generic package for stacks, make your own package providing an ordered, linked list, a binary tree or a linked list implementation of a queue.

13

File Operations

Input and output operations in C use objects of the type **FILE** which is declared in <stdio.h>. A **FILE** is usually thought of as a disc file or a tape file, but in fact any external device such as a communications channel, a robot arm or a terminal can be treated as a file. Files which are stored on a disc or similar medium are referred to either as text files, which are usually intended to be read by humans, or binary, which are not. (Not all operating systems make this distinction.) C provides a comprehensive set of functions for manipulating files but the effect of these can depend upon the particular type of physical file or device being addressed; it may not make sense, for instance, to rewind a robot arm or to reread data from a terminal.

There are three files which are automatically opened by a C system. These are **stdin** which is a default input file, **stdout** which is a default output file, and **stderr** which is a file to which error messages are written. Whether these are all really operating system files depends upon the system; on microcomputers **stdin** often represents the keyboard and **stdout** and **stderr** the screen, but this is by no means universal.

13.1.   Opening and Closing Files

Reference to files is via variables which are always pointers to a structure of type **FILE**. The internal details of this structure are not defined by the language, and the only way of performing operations on a **FILE** is via a set of functions which have, as one of their parameters, a pointer to a **FILE**. A typical declaration might be

        FILE *Data;

This file can then be opened by

        Data = fopen("SETONE", "r");

This statement will open the file **SETONE** for reading, generate a structure to hold whatever control information is needed, and leave **Data** pointing to it. The nature of the file name given in the first parameter string will depend upon the operating system in use; the example shown is very simple, but on some systems it may be quite complicated and could include some kind of path name, channel number or physical device description. The second parameter is also a string, **"r"** in this case meaning 'read'. The options for this are:

"r" Open an existing file for reading.

"w" Open a file for writing. If the file does not exist then it will be created and if it does exist then its contents will be deleted before writing.

"a" Open an existing file for writing so that new data will be appended to the end of the current file contents.

"r+" Open a file for reading but allow writing. That is, the file can be both read from and written to. However, errors will be handled as if the file were opened for reading.

"w+" The same as **"r+"** except that errors will be appropriate to writing.

"a+" Open a file for appending but allow reading at the same time.

If a file is be opened for binary input or output then a 'b' should be added to the above strings e.g. **"wb"**, **"r+b"** or **"rb+"**. In all cases **fopen** will return a pointer value of **NULL** if the file cannot be opened and so this can be used to test for successful completion of the operation.

The file opened above can be closed with:

```
fclose(Data);
```

File closing is often omitted, but the practice is dangerous, particularly for files which are open for writing. Closing a file releases the space used by the **FILE** structure and ensures, when a file is being written, that the file buffer is emptied. To appreciate why this may be important it is necessary to realize that when a program requests that a character be written to a disc the request is not carried out immediately. Instead the character is placed in an array, called a buffer, which accumulates characters until there are enough to be worth writing. 'Enough', in this sense, usually means the size of a disc sector. If the buffer is not emptied then the file may not include the latest data written. **fclose** ensures that the buffer will be written.

The ANSI standard also includes the function **freopen**, the use of which is illustrated by:

```
freopen("SETTWO", "r", Data);
```

This closes the file already associated with **Data** and opens the file **SETTWO**. It acts in the same way as **fopen** in that it also delivers a pointer to **Data** and delivers **NULL** if the file cannot be opened.

The function **fflush** forces the emptying of output buffers. This is essential if a file is open in one of the 'update' modes ('w+', 'r+' or 'a+') and a change is made from writing to reading; unless **fflush** is called before finishing a sequence of write operations the information remaining in the output buffer will not be written at the correct point in the file. A sequence of such calls could be:

```
fopen("TESTFILE", "w+", Data);
fprintf(Data, "Bonjour");
fflush(Data);
fscanf(Data, &Word);
```

13.2.   Character and String Input and Output

Most of the following functions and macros have been described earlier but are included here for reference purposes.

int fgetc(FILE *inp)
    Delivers the next character from the file **inp**.

int getc(FILE *inp)
    A macro equivalent to **fgetc**.

int getchar(void)
    Equivalent to **getc(stdin)** i.e. delivers the next character from **stdin**.

char *fgets(char *s, int i, FILE *inp)
    Reads up to **i** characters into **s** ending at a newline (the newline character is included in **s**). Returns **s** unless there is an error or end of file, in which case **NULL** is returned.

char *gets(char *s)
    Reads the next line from **stdin** into **s** (without the terminating '**\n**').

Returns **s** unless there is an error or end of file, in which case **NULL** is returned.

int ungetc(int ch, FILE *inp)

Pushes **ch** back so that it will be read by the next read operation on **inp**. Although many implementations allow more, only one character of push back is guaranteed. In other words multiple calls may not work. **EOF** may not be pushed back. The value returned is the character pushed back, unless an error occurs, in which case **EOF** is returned.

int fputc(int ch, FILE *out)

Writes **ch** to **out**. Returns **ch**, unless an error occurs, in which case **EOF** is returned.

int putc(int ch, FILE *out)

Identical in effect to **fputc** but it may be a macro and so its arguments may be evaluated more than once. Therefore beware of side-effects.

int putchar(int ch)

Equivalent to **putc(stdout, ch)**.

int fputs(const char *s, FILE *out)

Writes the string to which **s** points onto the file **out**. The terminating null character is not written. It returns **EOF** if an error occurs and otherwise returns an unspecified, non-negative value.

int puts(const char *s)

Writes the string to which **s** points and a new line to the standard output file **stdout**. It returns **EOF** if an error occurs and otherwise a non-negative value.

13.3. Formatted Input and Output

Many of the functions described in this section have variable argument lists, in other words the number or types of argument are not predetermined. The way to write such functions was discussed in section 3.8. For most of this section it is not necessary to understand all of section 3.8 except for the role of the ellipsis (...), which indicates the variable section of an argument list. (The exceptions in this section are **vprint** and **vfprint**, which require a proper understanding of section 3.8). The use of the ellipsis is illustrated by the prototype for the familiar function **printf**, which is:

    int printf (const char *format, ...)

The first argument is the format string and it is this which is used to give information about how many parameters there are in a particular call and the types they have. The ellipsis denotes the undetermined argument list.

int fprintf (FILE *out, const char *format, ...)

Writes its variable argument list to the file **out** under the control of formatting information held in the string **format**. It returns the number of characters printed unless there is an output error, in which case it returns a negative value.

The format string contains ordinary characters, which are printed directly, and conversion specifications for each argument. The conversion specification causes the corresponding argument to be printed, and specifies the precise style of printing. A conversion specification begins with **%** and ends with a conversion character (**d, i, u, o, x, X, f, e, E, g, G, c, s, p, n** or **%**), but there may be information between them which is used to define the precision of numbers, field widths, details of the format and the length of the argument. These are, in order, *flags*, a *field width*, a *precision* and a *length modifier*. For example, in the specification **%+5ld** the '+' is a flag, '5' is a field width, 'l' is a length modifier and the conversion character is 'd'. There is no precision.

The conversion characters, some of which are synonymous (such as **d** and **i**, or **x** and **X**)   mainly provide information about the type of the corresponding argument.

The flags, with their meanings, are:

+	print a number with a sign, even if it is positive.
-	print the argument on the left of the field.
space	print a space if there is no sign.
0	for numbers, print zeros instead of leading spaces.
#	'alternative form': the effect depends upon the conversion character. For **o** the first digit printed will be zero (e.g 013), for **x** or **X** the value is prefixed by **0x** or **0X** if the argument is not zero, for **e, f, g, E,** and **G** the value has a decimal point and in the case of **G** and **g** trailing zeros are included.

A field width is a number indicating the minimum number of characters to be be used to print a value, such as **%3d**, which means print a decimal number in a field of at least three characters. Notice that this is a *minimum* value; if the item to be printed requires more space than allowed by the field width then more space will be used. If it requires less then it will be padded with spaces on the left, unless a flag has been used to indicate a different action.

The precision, another number, is optional and is separated from the field width by a period (full stop). Its effect depends upon the conversion character. For an **f** conversion it indicates the number of digits to print after the decimal point e.g. **%8.3f** prints a value of type **double** (often as a result of being widened from **float**) in a field of eight characters, with a minus sign if it is negative, and with three digits after the point. With the string conversion character **s** it specifies the *maximum* number of characters to be printed from a given string, e.g. **%4s** will print only the first four characters of its string argument.

Both the field width and the precision may be replaced by ***** in which case the value is taken from the next argument in the argument list, which must be an **int**. An example is shown below.

The length modifiers indicate the lengths of the corresponding arguments and are 'l' for **long** or **unsigned long** arguments, 'h' for **short** or **unsigned short** and 'L' for **long double**.

The conversion characters, their corresponding types, and their effects on printing, are:

d or **i**	int	Print a signed decimal integer.
u	int	Print an unsigned decimal integer.
o	int	Print an octal number (but no leading zero).
x or **X**	int	Print a hexadecimal number (but no leading 0X).
f	double	Print a floating point number.
e or **E**	double	Print in 'scientific' notation, i.e. with an exponent. If no precision has been specified then the default will be 6. For a precision of 0 there will be no decimal point printed.
g or **G**	double	Print a floating point number in a general format. In particular, if the exponent is less than -4 or is equal to, or greater than the specified precision then the effect is the same as **%e**. Otherwise it is the same as **%f**.
c	int	Print a single character.
s	char *	Print a string.
p	void *	Print a pointer. The style used depends upon the implementation.
n	int *	*Put* the number of characters written up to this point by this call of **fprintf** into the corresponding

%
    argument, which will be the address of an integer.
Print a '%'. There is no corresponding argument. For example, **printf(" %d % %", p)** prints the value of **p** followed by a percent sign, e.g. **36%**.

fprintf returns the number of characters printed unless an error occurs, in which case it returns a negative value. Examples of the effects of different conversion specifications are show below for floating point numbers. Assume that a program contains the statements:

```
float x = 123.123456789;
int a = 6, b = 3;
```

The following is a list of possible calls of **fprintf**, each with its effect:

Statement	Output Produced
fprintf(op,"<%f>\n", x);	<123.123459>
fprintf(op,"<%12f>\n", x);	< 123.123459>
fprintf(op,"<%12.2f>\n", x);	< 123.12>
fprintf(op, "<%-12.2f>\n", x);	<123.12 >
fprintf(op,"<%e>\n", x);	<1.231235e+02>
fprintf(op,"<%12.2e>\n", x);	< 1.23e+02>
fprintf(op,"<%*.*f>\n", a, b, x);	<123.123>
fprintf(op,"<%*.2f>\n", a, x);	<123.12>

int printf (const char *format, ...)
Behaves identically to **fprintf** except that output is written to **stdout**.

int fscanf (FILE *inp, const char *format, ...)
Reads values from **inp** into its variable argument list under the control of formatting information held in the string **format**. It returns the number of items read unless the end of **inp** is reached or an error occurs, in which case it returns EOF. The arguments in the variable list must be *pointers* to values; one of the most common errors made by C programmers is to omit **&** before a variable in this list.

The conversion specifications are similar to those of **fprintf**, but without a precision specification. When items are being read, white space characters (space, tab, vertical tab, newline, carriage return and form feed) are ignored, but other characters must match the format string. For example, if the format string is **" %d/%d"** the input must be two integers separated by '/'. If '/' is missing then an error will occur.

After the initial **%**, but before the conversion character, the following optional items are permitted:

* Suppress the assignment of the corresponding argument. This is used to skip over unwanted data items. For example, to read the first and third numbers on a line, but ignore the second the string **"%d%*d%d"** could be used.

num A decimal integer which specifies a maximum field width of an input value. For example, **"%4s%s"** would read the string **hogshead** as the two separate strings 'hogs' and 'head'.

h If the corresponding argument is a pointer to a **short** type (**short int**, or **short unsigned**).

l Indicates that the corresponding argument is a pointer to a **long** type (**long int** or **double**).

L Indicates that the corresponding argument is a **long double**.

The conversion characters, their corresponding argument types and their effects are:

d	int *	Read a (possibly) signed decimal integer.
u	int *	Read an unsigned decimal integer.
o	int *	Read an octal number, possibly with a leading zero.
x or **X**	int *	Read a hexadecimal number, possibly with a leading **0X** or **0x**.
i	int *	Read an integer which will be octal if it starts 0, hexadecimal if it starts **0x** or **0X** and decimal otherwise.
f, e or **g**	float *	Read a floating point number. The type of the argument can be modified by l or L to **long** or **long double** respectively.
c	char *	Read characters from the current position to the number specified by the field width. The default width is one. White space characters are not ignored.
s	char *	Read a string of non-white-space characters.
p	void *	Read a pointer in the same format as that printed by **printf**. The details are implementation dependent.
n	int *	Put the number of characters written by this call of **fscanf** into the corresponding argument.
[. . .]	char *	Read a string up to the first character which does not match one of those enclosed in the square brackets (known as the *scanset*). If the first character in the scanset is] then that is included in the set. See the example below.

[^. . .]	char *	Read a string up to the first character which matches one of those enclosed in the square brackets. See the example below.
%		Expect a % character. No corresponding argument.

The following table shows the effects of various ways of reading strings. **s** is an array of characters.

Statement	Input	Value of Argument
scanf("%s", s);	JS Bach	JS
scanf("%[0123456789]", s);	747b	747
scanf("%[^0123456789]", s);	MI5	MI

int scanf (const char *format, ...)

Equivalent to **fscanf** except that it reads from **stdin**.

int vfprintf(FILE *out, const char *format, va_list args)

Equivalent to **fprintf** except that the argument list is replaced by a **va_list** which must have been initialized by **va_start** (see section 3.8 for an explanation of **va_list** etc.). This is to make it easy for programmers to write functions which imitate **fprintf** in order, for example, to print error messages. An example of its use is shown in the next section.

int vprintf(const char *format, va_list args)

This is equivalent to **vfprintf** but sends its output to **stdout**. The example below shows a function called **Message** with arguments which are identical to those of **printf**. It prints various types of message in a standard style.

```
void Message(char *fmt, ...) {
    va_list args;
    int CharsPrinted;

    va_start(args, fmt);
    printf( "*************************************************\n"
            "*************************************************\n"
            "***                                         **\n"
            "*** ");
    CharsPrinted = vprintf(fmt, args);
    printf( "%*s\n", 45 - CharsPrinted, "***");
    printf( "***                                         **\n"
            "*************************************************\n"
            "*************************************************\n");
    va_end(args);
}
```

With the call

Message("Please insert disc %d", n);

where **n** is an integer variable, this will produce output such as

```
***************************************************
***************************************************
**                                               **
**    Please insert disc 3                       **
**                                               **
***************************************************
***************************************************
```

and the call

Message("Unable to open %s", FileName);

where **FileName** is a string variable, could produce

```
***************************************************
***************************************************
**                                               **
**    Unable to open Accounts                    **
**                                               **
***************************************************
***************************************************
```

13.4.   File Positioning

As has been mentioned, a file is a rather general concept which encompasses any physical or logical device. It is common to need to control the position at which one reads from or writes to a file, but operating systems differ as to which devices or file types can be repositioned. Provided the device is appropriate and the operating system accommodating, the functions described in this section can investigate or adjust the position within a file.

These function are all defined in **<stdio.h>** along with the type **fpos_t** and the constants **SEEK_SET**, **SEEK_CUR** and **SEEK_END**. **fpos_t** is some kind of integer (**long unsigned** for example), and **SEEK_SET**, **SEEK_CUR** and **SEEK_END** are constants used as arguments to the function **fseek** to indicate the beginning of a file, the current position within a file and the end of a file respectively. The precise meaning of an integer of type **fpos_t** is not defined and is left to an implementation; suffice it to say that it represents a unique position within a file. It can be used, in conjunction with the functions here, to allow a reading or writing position to jump about within a file.

The functions are:

void rewind(FILE *Stream)

Positions **Stream** so that the next read or write operation will be at the beginning of the file. If this is not possible then there will be no effect.

long int ftell(FILE *Stream)

Returns the current position within **Stream**, or -1L if an error occurs.

int fseek(FILE *Stream, long int Offset, int Origin)

Sets the file position within **Stream** so that subsequent reading or writing will occur from there. The position is in the form of an **Offset** relative to an **Origin**. The possible values of **Origin** are **SEEK_SET**, **SEEK_CUR** and **SEEK_END**. If an error occurs then a non-zero value is returned; a return value of zero indicates success.

int fgetpos(FILE *Stream, fpos_t *Where)

Puts the current position within **Stream** into the variable **Where**. It can then be stored so that a subsequent call of **fsetpos** can find the same position. A non-zero returned value indicates an error.

int fsetpos(FILE *Stream, const f_pos *Where)

Sets **Stream** at the position **Where**. A non-zero returned value indicates an error.

13.5. File Manipulation Functions

Permanent files are those files which, unless explicit action is taken from within a program, continue to exist after a program ceases execution. They may be deleted by a function call within a program or by an appropriate command to an operating system. Permanent files are automatically created by **fopen**. The other operations on permanent files are deletion and renaming. The corresponding functions are:

int remove(const char *FileName)

Deletes the file, the name of which is contained in **FileName**. If the operation is successful it returns zero, otherwise it returns a non-zero result.

int rename(const char *OldFileName, const char *NewFileName)

Renames a file. If the operation is successful it returns zero, otherwise it returns a non-zero result.

Temporary files are ones which are needed only during the execution of a program and which are automatically deleted when a program ends.

FILE *tmpfile(void)

Creates a temporary file and returns a pointer to it. The file is opened in mode **wb+**. If the file cannot be created then **tmpfile** returns **NULL**.

char *tmpnam(char *Name)

Creates a string (not a file) holding a valid file name that is not the name of any existing file. The maximum number of names that can be created in this way is given by the constant **TMP_MAX**. If **Name** is not **NULL** then the new name will be placed in **Name**, which should be an array of at least **L_tmpnam** characters The name is also returned by the function. If **Name** is **NULL** then **tmpnam** returns a pointer to an internal, static array containing the file name. An example of the use of this function might be two communicating programs running as simultaneous processes. One could use **tmpnam** to create a file of intermediate data, and then pass the name to the other process. The language specification does not say that the file will be automatically deleted when both processes end.

13.6. 'Direct' Input and Output

When reading or writing large data objects it is inefficient to treat them as being made of small, individual components. For instance, a plasma physics simulation program might represent a plasma as an array of structures, the members of each structure denoting the position and velocity of one particle in the simulation. The whole array therefore represents the state of the plasma at a particular time. In order to record the development of the plasma it is necessary to write the whole array to a file at predetermined time intervals. The simulation may involve a million or more particles, and therefore the time taken to write one array to disc is significant. Direct output of a whole array allows an implementation to write the array in the largest chunks possible in a format that makes no sense to humans but is efficient for computers. Direct input and output are many times faster than the other input or output operations for large amounts of data.

The next two functions deliver a result of type **size_t**, which is an implementation defined integer type (**short**, **long** etc.) and is the result type of the **sizeof** operator.

> **size_t fread(void *Data, size_t ObjSize,**
> **size_t NumObjs, FILE *inp)**
>
> Reads from **inp** into the array pointed to by **Data** up to **NumObjs** objects each of size **ObjSize**. It returns the number of objects actually read, which may be fewer than **NumObjs** if the end of file is met.

> **size_t fwrite(const void *Data, size_t ObjSize,**
> **size_t NumObjs, FILE *out)**
>
> Writes to **out** from the array pointed to by **Data** up to **NumObjs** objects each of size **ObjSize**. It returns the number of objects actually written, which may be fewer than **NumObjs** if a write error occurs.

13.7.   Buffering Control

When a program performs input or output operations it causes characters to be sent to, or received from some file or device. Most of the C functions for input and output, such as **getch** or **putch**, create the impression that single characters are the basic units of transaction between a program and the outside world, but this is rarely the case. Every time a program needs to perform an input or output operation it must call some basic operating system function which then causes a physical process, such as writing a sector on a disc, to begin. These *system calls*, with their attendant device operations, are very slow and so to save time all input and output using files, and often also that on terminals, is *buffered*. This means calls to a function such as **putch** do not directly cause a system call to write a character, but instead put the characters to be printed into an array known as a *file buffer* which is output only when necessary.

When output is to a file the size of the buffer will usually correspond to some physical attribute of the device containing the file, such as the size of a disc sector (typically somewhere between a hundred to a few thousand bytes). Output to a terminal may use a buffer corresponding to the maximum length of a line or may actually be unbuffered (one character at a time).

Programmers usually leave decisions about buffering to the system, but occasionally it is necessary to specify some change to the standard actions (for instance to use a larger buffer when writing a tape, or to use single characters for communication with terminals). The C functions provided by standard systems specify three types of buffering: full buffering (the largest buffer size available for the device), line buffering (read or write complete lines) and no buffering at all (read or write single characters).

The header file **stdio.h** contains definitions for two functions **setvbuf** and **setbuf** as well as four constants, **BUFSIZ**, which is the default buffer size, and **_IOFBUF**, **_IOLBUF** and **_IONBUF** which are used as parameters to **setvbuf** to indicate the use of full buffering, line buffering and no buffering respectively. **setvbuf** and **setbuf** can only be called after a file has been opened and before any other operation has taken place on it.

> **int setvbuf(FILE *Stream, char *Buffer, int Mode, size_t Size)**
>
> **Stream** is a pointer to an open file.
>
> If **Buffer** is **NULL setvbuf** will allocate its own buffer space, otherwise it will use the array pointed to by **Buffer**.
>
> **Mode** can be **_IOFBUF**, **_IOLBUF** or **_IONBUF** to indicate the type of buffering.
>
> **Size** is the size of the array **Buffer**.
>
> The return value will be zero unless an error occurs.

> **void setbuf(FILE *Stream, char *Buffer)**
>
> If **Buffer** is **NULL** then buffering will be turned off for **Stream**. Otherwise a call to **setbuf** is equivalent to
>
>   (void) setvbuf(Stream, Buffer, _IOFBUF, BUFSIZ);
>
> Notice that there is no return value; one or other action must occur.

13.8.   Using Strings as Files

Sometimes it is useful to use the facilities of **printf** to construct a string rather than produce output directly. One example would be a program that produces a chart or report with a complicated layout; in such cases it is often convenient to use a two-dimensional array of characters to represent a page or screen of output, to build up the page in this array and then to print the whole page.

Similarly it can be handy to use the facilities of **scanf** to read a string in order to convert parts which contain numbers. For example, if a program has to read data organized in lines such as:

    name = Kernighan, Brian W.
    ISBN = 0-13-110462

it may need to write messages such as

    ERROR IN ISBN: 0-13-110462

To do this it needs first to read a line of text into a string and then read the string as a sequence of numbers. On error the string can be printed with the position of the error.

> **int sprintf(char *Outline, const char *Format, ...)**
> Equivalent to a call to **printf**, but the output is placed in the string **Outline**. A null character is automatically written to the end of **Outline**.

> **int sscanf(const char *Inline, const char *Format, ...)**
> Equivalent to a call of **scanf**, but the input is taken from **Inline**. If the end of **Inline** is reached the effect is the same as reading **EOF** in **scanf**.

> **int vsprintf(char *Outline, const char *Format, va_list Args)**
> is equivalent to **vprintf** with the output going to **Outline**. A null character is automatically written to the end of **Outline**.

13.9.   Handling Errors

Errors which occur during file operations can set indicators which can be tested in order to facilitate error handling. The functions **ferror**, **feof**, **clearerr** and **perror**, all defined in **<stdio.h>**, can test or manipulate these indicators. In addition **<errno.h>** contains a macro **errno** which can be used as an integer expression. It provides an implementation dependent number which gives information about the most recent error.

> **int ferror(FILE *Stream)**
> Returns a non-zero value if an error indicator is set for **Stream**.

> **int feof(FILE *Stream)**
> Returns a non-zero value if the end of file indicator is set for **Stream**.

> **void clearerr(FILE *Stream)**
> Clears any error or end of file indicators for **Stream**.

> **void perror(const char *Message)**
> Uses **errno** to print an appropriate error message on **stderr**. The full output is the string **Message** (if it is not **NULL**), a colon and then a system defined message appropriate to the value of **errno** and finally a new line. e.g.

```
perror("Sorry, an error occurred");
```

might produce the message

```
Sorry, an error occurred: END OF FILE REACHED
```

14

Program Efficiency and
Testing

When discussing efficiency a distinction is often made between speed efficiency and space efficiency. If speed of a program is a concern then one strives to use the fastest operations possible, but if space is a concern then the most compact representation of program and data must be found. However, these two often go hand in hand; usually a reduction in the number of instructions means less space *and* less time. As an example, the machine code generated by a compiler for the statement **i++** is likely to be both smaller and faster than **i = i + 1**.

When trying to speed up a program the most important step is to choose the best algorithm. For instance, when sorting a reasonably large amount of fairly random data, a quicksort written without particular attention to 'tight' coding will be much faster than the tightest implementation of a bubble sort. This chapter will be concerned with both finding better algorithms and implementing them efficiently.

14.1.   Speed of Operations

Improving the efficiency of a program involves finding a way of rewriting it so that its behavior is unchanged but its performance is improved. Before being able to do this it is necessary to have some idea of the 'cost' of various operations. The table on the next page shows representative times, in microseconds, for some of the most common operations as measured on two computers.

The computers used for these measurements were an Apple Macintosh SE, which uses the 16-bit Motorola 68000 processor and a Macintosh II, with a 32-bit Motorola 68020 processor and a Motorola 68881 floating point unit. The choice of these particular machines is not very important as it is the relative speeds which most concern us; in other words, it is more important to know that a floating point operation is slower than an integer operation, and by *roughly* how much, than it is to know the precise time for each operation.

Operation	Time in μs on a 68000	Time in μs on a 68020 with FPU
int + int	3.9	1.6
int * int	10.0	3.2
int / int	24.0	5.0
float + float	750.0	8.0
float * float	800.0	10.0
float / float	1440.0	12.0
double + double	400.0	8.0
double * double	600.0	12.0
double / double	1100.0	12.0
int = int	3.3	1.0
float = float	4.5	0.9
++int	2.6	0.76
int++	2.6	0.76
sqrt(float)	2500	200.0
sin(float)	13300	24.0
a[i]	5.7	1.8
*pi	2.6	0.6
i << 1	2.6	0.9
i << 10	6.2	1.4

For the speed of other operations or accurate values for particular computers, section 14.2 explains how this type of measurement can be made.

From these figures it is clear that floating point operations are slower than integer operations (although floating point hardware makes a big difference) and that division takes longer than multiplication, which in turn takes longer than addition. Subtractions have not been included because the time for a subtraction is usually the same as for addition. The time taken for a shift operation depends on the size of the shift.

Notice in particular that mathematical functions such as **sqrt** and **sin** are *very* slow on computers without dedicated floating point hardware. It appears surprising, at first glance, that operations on **double** values are faster than **float** operations but this effect is caused by implicit type conversions. In the original version of the language, it was specified that in an expression such as **x** = **y** + **z**, where **x**, **y** and **z** are **float** variables, the values in **y** and **z** are first converted to **double** and then the result of the addition converted back to **float** before the assignment. This was intended to improve arithmetic accuracy but is expensive on a machine with an adequate implementation of floating point arithmetic. The new standard does not require the conversion to double, but many current compilers do not take advantage of this relaxation of the rules. The results above show the cost of these conversions. Presumably this difference will disappear on more powerful machines as new compilers become available.

A programmer substituting a faster operation for a slower one is at the mercy of a compiler, and the effect may not always be what is expected; thus, substituting i <<= 1 for i *= 2 will not make any difference if your compiler automatically recognizes situations where shift instructions may be substituted for multiplications. Also, many compilers have an option to request optimization, in which case the compiler may make extensive transformations to your program to make it more efficient. Use of such compilers, where available, is strongly recommended but only after programs have been thoroughly debugged; the transformations carried out by optimizing compilers can involve wholesale movement of sections of a program (for instance, statements can be moved outside loops or expressions simplified) and so can make debugging extremely difficult.

As a final warning, consider again the statement above, i *= 2 and its equivalent i <<= 1. The intention of the first version is obvious, but a reader might take a little time to understand the purpose of the second. Such constructs should only be used when necessary and should be clearly commented. More effort is usually expended maintaining a large program (correcting bugs or adapting to add new or improved facilities) than is spent writing it in the first place, so readability is essential.

14.2. Improving Performance

It is commonly stated that about 90% of a program's execution time is spent in 10% of the code. Whether or not this figure is accurate, it provides a strategy to adopt in improving program speed. It is pointless exerting effort to improve the speed of the 90% of the code that uses only 10% of the time, since it involves nine times more effort to produce one-tenth of the effect; instead work must be concentrated on the crucial 10% once it has been identified. Often the important section is obvious, but sometimes it will require measurements to track it down.

As a case to study we shall use the algorithm known as the Sieve of Eratosthenes, named after its inventor, the Greek mathematician and astronomer who, incidentally, also measured the circumference of the Earth, more than two thousand years ago. This algorithm is used to find prime numbers; that is, numbers that can be divided only by themselves or one without leaving a remainder, the first few being 2, 3, 5, 7, 11, 13, 17, 19. To find the prime numbers up to some maximum N, Eratosthenes used a row of N small pits, each containing a pebble, and he performed the following steps:

After pebble 2, remove every second pebble (i.e. pebbles 4, 6, 8 . . .).
repeat
    Advance up the row until an occupied pit is found and note the
        number of the pit, n (n will be a prime number).
Remove the pebbles from every nth pit after n.
until   n is big enough

After these steps, the numbers of the pits still occupied correspond to the prime numbers less than N. If you are not familiar with this algorithm, take a suitable stretch of fairly level sand and a few pebbles (get a research grant first) and try it. You will realize that removing every second pebble corresponds to removing the even numbers, every third the multiples of three, every fifth the multiples of five, and so on.

It remains to define the meaning of 'n is big enough'. In fact it is sufficient that the final n is the largest integer less than or equal to √N.

Exercise 14.1   Why is it possible to stop when 'n' is the largest integer less than or equal to √N?

In a computer program, Eratosthenes's pits can be replaced by an array of integers with a zero (**FALSE**) representing the absence of a pebble and a one (**TRUE**) its presence. The program below, which will be the basis of discussion for most of this chapter, implements the algorithm. The first loop puts the pebbles in their holes and the nested loops strike out the pebbles corresponding to composite (non-prime) numbers. The loop **for (StrikeOut = 2*LatestPrime)** . . . removes the pebbles which are multiples of **LatestPrime**, i.e. **2*LatestPrime, 3*LatestPrime**, etc. The final loop counts the remaining pebbles. The reason the program only counts the prime numbers and does not print each one is because its purpose is to find a fast way of generating primes; if it were to print all of them then the time taken to print would greatly exceed the time taken to find the numbers.

The statement

```
while (!Sieve[++LatestPrime]);
```

looks a little complicated at first. **Sieve** is the array holding the pebbles and **LatestPrime** is, initially, the prime number that has been found most recently, so that **Sieve[++LatestPrime]** advances **LatestPrime** one element further up the row and gives the contents of the next pit. If this pit is unoccupied then the array element contains **FALSE** and so **!Sieve[++LatestPrime]** delivers **TRUE**. The **while** statement thus moves **LatestPrime** through the elements of **Sieve** until the next occupied pit is found. The index of this pit is the next prime number.

The whole program is:

```
#include <stdio.h>
#include <math.h>

#define   MaxPrime  10000
enum  bool {FALSE, TRUE};

main() {
    int i, LatestPrime, StrikeOut, Primes, Sieve[MaxPrime + 1];

    /*  Fill the pits with pebbles  */
    for (i = 2; i <= MaxPrime; ++i)
        Sieve[i] = TRUE;

    LatestPrime = 2;   /*  The first prime is 2  */
    while (LatestPrime <= sqrt(MaxPrime)) {

        /*  Remove multiples of LatestPrime  */
        for (StrikeOut = 2*LatestPrime;
            StrikeOut <= MaxPrime;
            StrikeOut += LatestPrime
            )
            Sieve[StrikeOut] = FALSE;

        /*  Find the next prime  */
        while (!Sieve[++LatestPrime]);
    }

    /*  Count the remaining pebbles  */
    for (i = 2, Primes = 0; i <= MaxPrime; ++i)
        if (Sieve[i])
            ++Primes;

    printf(  "The number of prime numbers <= %d is %d\n",
        MaxPrime, Primes);
}
```

14.3.   Instrumenting Programs

Looking at the above program one can guess where most time is spent, but such guesses are often unreliable. For such a small program it is possible to analyze the behavior of the program by hand in order to calculate how often each section will be executed and how much time it might take, but this is difficult for large programs. A quantitative approach measures the time used by the most important sections of the program. To do this we can create a tool which provides instruments (sets of functions) which can be placed at significant points in a program to measure performance and give an idea of its dynamic behavior. This is called *instrumenting* a program. The tool used here is very simple. It is a package which implements a set of twenty-one clocks; each can be thought of as a stop-watch which can be started, stopped, resumed and inspected.

The header file for this tool, called **clocks.h**, is:

```
/*  The header file for the clock module   */

#include <stdio.h>

/*  'Res' is a file to which results may be printed.
    'n' is the number of a particular clock.   */

void OnClock(int n);                    /*  Start or resume n          */
void OffClock(int n);                   /*  Interrupt n                */
long unsigned UsesOfClock(int n);       /*  Return uses of n           */
long unsigned TimeOnClock(int n);       /*  Return time on n           */
void PrintClock(int n, FILE *Res);      /*  Print details of  n in Res */
void PrintAllClocks(FILE *Res);         /*  Print all clocks in Res    */
```

OnClock and **OffClock** are used for starting and stopping clocks. **UsesOfClock** returns the number of times a particular clock has been turned on. **TimeOnClock** returns the total length of time a clock has been 'on'. The state of a clock can be printed using **PrintClock** and **PrintAllClocks** prints the state of all clocks. By placing **OnClock** and **OffClock** around sections of a program it is possible to measure the number of times that section is executed and how much time is spent there.

One possible implementation of this package is shown in the file **clocks.c** below. The function call in the macro **PresentTime** is to a standard library function **time** which returns the calendar time. This is not a very sensitive way of measuring time and so the call has been embedded in a macro to make it easy to change. The units of time have also been specified in a **#define** statement in order to facilitate change.

The clocks are represented as an array of structures of type **Timer**. A **Timer** has three members, **Count** which holds the number of times this particular timer has been turned on by **OnClock**, **StartTime**, which holds the time at which **OnClock** was last called, and **ElapsedTime**, which is updated at each call of **OffClock** and holds the total time accumulated when this clock has been 'on'.

```
#include <stdlib.h>
#include <time.h>
#include <stdio.h>
#include "clocks.h"

#define MaxClock       20
#define PresentTime    time(NULL)
```

```
#define TimeUnits          "seconds"

typedef struct {long unsigned Count, ElapsedTime, StartTime;} Timer;

static Timer Clock[MaxClock + 1];
static int MaxClockUsed;        /* static and so initialised to zero */

static void ClockRangeError(void) {
    fprintf(stderr, "A clock has been specified that is either\n"
                    "negative or greater than %d\n", MaxClock);
    exit(0);
}

void OnClock(int n) { /*  Start or resume clock 'n' */
    if (n < 0 || n > MaxClock)
        ClockRangeError();
    else {
        ++Clock[n].Count;
        if (n > MaxClockUsed) MaxClockUsed = n;
        Clock[n].StartTime = PresentTime;
    }
}

void OffClock(int n) { /*  Halt clock 'n' */
    if (n < 0 || n > MaxClock)
        ClockRangeError();
    else {
        Clock[n].ElapsedTime += (PresentTime - Clock[n].StartTime);
    }
}

long unsigned UsesOfClock(int n) {
    /*  Return the number of times clock 'n' has been used */
    if (n < 0 || n > MaxClock)
        ClockRangeError();
    else
        return(Clock[n].Count);
}

long unsigned TimeOnClock(int n) {
    /*  Return the elapsed time on a clock */
    if (n < 0 || n > MaxClock)
        ClockRangeError();
    else
        return(Clock[n].ElapsedTime);
}
```

```
void PrintClock(int n, FILE *Res) {
    /* Print the state of a clock in a specified file */

    if (n < 0 || n > MaxClock)
        ClockRangeError();
    else {
        fprintf(Res, "Clock %d was called %lu times and used "
                     "a total time of %lu " TimeUnits "\n",
                     n, UsesOfClock(n), TimeOnClock(n));
    }
}

void PrintAllClocks(FILE *Res) {
    int i;
    /* Print the details of all clocks in a specified file */

    fprintf(Res, "\n    Clock    Calls    Time\n\n");
    for (i = 0; i <= MaxClockUsed; ++i)
        fprintf(Res,    "%10d%10lu%10lu\n",    i,    UsesOfClock(i),
                     TimeOnClock(i));
}
```

Notice the use of **TimeUnits** in the string in the function **PrintClock**. **TimeUnits** has been defined as a macro with a replacement text in the form of a quoted string. When the pre-processor substitutes this in the string in **PrintClock** the two pairs of adjacent double quotes are removed automatically by the pre-processor. This technique allows macros to be substituted inside strings.

It is important to distinguish between processor time and 'calendar' time; the first is the time which a computer processor has spent obeying your program, the second is the time that has elapsed on the clock on the wall. On a machine such as a small personal computer, which carries out only one task at a time, these two may be the same, but on a multi-tasking machine they can differ radically because the single processor switches constantly between different tasks, allocating small chunks of time to each task in turn. On a typical multi-user computer the calendar time will be much longer than the processor time, and the **PresentTime** macro should be changed to call some other appropriate library function.

Using these functions it is possible to instrument the sieve program; in the version below the principal sections have been instrumented by enclosing each of them within calls to **OnClock** and **OffClock**. The version of the clock package given above measures time in whole seconds. In fact to run the program takes less than one second and so it is necessary to increase its running time artificially so that the measured times of each instrumented section will be an adequate number of whole seconds. This has

been done by repeating the main part of the program inside a loop which is executed
Repetitions times.

```c
#include <stdio.h>
#include <math.h>
#include "clocks.h"

#define     MaxPrime     10000
#define     Repetitions  50
enum        bool         {FALSE, TRUE};

main() {
    int i, LatestPrime, StrikeOut, Primes, Sieve[MaxPrime + 1];
    int j;

    OnClock(1);
    /*  The following 'for' loop is to consume a sufficient amount of
    time to make timings reasonably accurate.  */
    for (j = 1; j <= Repetitions; ++j) {

        OnClock(2);
        for (i = 2; i <= MaxPrime; ++i)
            Sieve[i] = TRUE;
        OffClock(2);
        OnClock(3);
        LatestPrime = 2;
        while (LatestPrime <= sqrt(MaxPrime)) {
            OnClock(4);
            for (StrikeOut = 2*LatestPrime;
                StrikeOut <= MaxPrime;
                StrikeOut += LatestPrime
              ) Sieve[StrikeOut] = FALSE;
            OffClock(4);
            OnClock(5);
            while (!Sieve[++LatestPrime]);
            OffClock(5);
        }
        OffClock(3);
        OnClock(6);
        for (i = 2, Primes = 0; i <= MaxPrime; ++i)
            if (Sieve[i])
                ++Primes;
        OffClock(6);
    }
    printf( "The number of prime numbers <= %d is %d\n",
            MaxPrime, Primes);
    OffClock(1);
    PrintAllClocks(stdout);
}
```

Running this program on a Macintosh SE produced the table shown below. It is clear that there is little point trying to find a better version of the loop enclosed by clock 5 (searching for the next prime); the most likely prospect is the section of program enclosed by clock 3 (striking out multiples).

Clock	Calls	Time
1	1	35
2	50	5
3	50	19
4	1250	14
5	1250	0
6	50	14

The total time was 35 seconds. Dividing by 50 (the number of circuits of the artificial loop) the time needed to calculate 10,000 primes is 0.7 seconds.

On inspecting the **while** loop the most noticeable thing is the call of **sqrt** which is called each time around the loop, and which we know from the instruction timings shown earlier is an expensive operation. By introducing an extra variable and changing this part of the program to read

```
SqrtMaxPrime = sqrt(MaxPrime);
LatestPrime = 2;
while (LatestPrime <= SqrtMaxPrime) { . . .
```

the total time fell to 32 seconds, i.e. 0.64 seconds for one trip round the loop.

Now consider the array **Sieve**. It has been declared as an array of integers and yet it contains only the values 0 or 1. Since a **char** is smaller than an **int** but large enough to hold the values needed, changing this to an array of characters will certainly save space and might have other effects. After changing the declarations at the start of the program to

```
int i, LatestPrime, StrikeOut, Primes, SqrtMaxPrime;
char Sieve[MaxPrime + 1];
```

it was able to count the primes in 0.54 seconds per repetition. This reduction is presumably because the computer used in these measurements has a 16-bit data-bus (it moves data in chunks of sixteen bits) and so can access one integer value in one memory cycle but can access two 8-bit characters in the same time. The reduction on a 32-bit computer could be even more marked but would disappear altogether on an 8-bit machine.

So far a 23% improvement has been made by 'tinkering' with the code, but a more fundamental change can be made to the program. The measurements show clearly that most of the time is being used in the loop which strikes out multiples inside clock 4; a reduction in the work that this loop must do would strongly affect the overall time. Half the elements in **Sieve** correspond to even numbers and are struck out on the first pass through the array. If the program could be modified so that **Sieve** stores only odd numbers then it should be possible to save both space and time. This can be done if element 1 of **Sieve** represents 3, element 2 represents 5 and so on, so that element n of the array will represent the number 2n+1. The next version shows this:

```
#include <stdio.h>
#include <math.h>

#define    MaxPrime 10000
#define    SieveSize (MaxPrime/2 + 1)
enum       bool       {FALSE, TRUE};

main() {
    int i, CurrElem, LatestPrime, StrikeOut, Primes, MaxStep;
    char Sieve[SieveSize];

    for (i = 1; i < SieveSize; ++i)
        Sieve[i] = TRUE;

    MaxStep = sqrt(MaxPrime);
    CurrElem = 1;  LatestPrime = 3;
    while (LatestPrime <= MaxStep) {
        for (StrikeOut = CurrElem + LatestPrime;
                StrikeOut <= SieveSize;
                StrikeOut += LatestPrime
                ) Sieve[StrikeOut] = FALSE;

        while (!Sieve[++CurrElem]);
        LatestPrime = 2*CurrElem + 1;
    }

/*   Primes is initially set to 1 to include two, which is prime but not
     in the sieve   */
    for (i = 1, Primes = 1; i <= SieveSize; ++i)
        if (Sieve[i])
            ++Primes;

    printf(  "The number of prime numbers <= %d is %d\n",
            MaxPrime, Primes);

}
```

With this change the program now needs 0.24 seconds to count one set of prime numbers up to 10,000, compared with 0.7 seconds for the first version. This is a reduction to about one third of the time, and on a 16-bit machine the size of **Sieve** has dropped to one quarter of its original value.

Looking at this version we notice that there are a fairly small number of integer variables; it may be of benefit to declare some of them as register variables. The ones which seem to be used most in loops are **i**, **Start**, **Step**, and **StrikeOut**; declaring these as register variables reduced the time to 0.16 seconds.

The biggest improvement made so far came from modifying the algorithm, tempting us to seek further improvements by again looking for places where the algorithm can be improved. Suppose that the multiples of all primes up to some value n have been removed, then the program above starts to remove pebbles from holes corresponding to multiples of n, starting from the first multiple to be found after n. This starting point is given by the expression **CurrElem + LatestPrime** at the start of the **for** loop in the above program. In fact it is not necessary to start there; if we want to knock out the multiples of a prime n then we need not start before n^2 because they will have already been removed. The reasoning is as follows: any multiple of n less than n^2 must be of the form n x m. But m must be less than n (because n x m < n^2) and so the number n x m will have already been removed (as the nth multiple of m). As an example, when striking out multiples of 7, the first tried in the above program will be 21, which will already have been removed as a multiple of 3. In fact the first multiple of 7 that has not been removed is 49. The first line of the 'striking out' loop can therefore be amended to:

```
for (StrikeOut = (LatestPrime*LatestPrime)/2; . . .
```

Notice the division by 2 because even numbers are not represented; the number 49 is pit 24. With this change the program was able to calculate the primes up to 10,000 in 0.14 seconds. This is not an enormous improvement on the previous version, although the effect is likely to grow when calculating larger primes. The measurements on this version now show that time is spent fairly evenly between the loop which initializes the sieve (clock 2), the main sieve algorithm (clock 3) and the final 'pebble' counting loop (clock 6). It now may be worthwhile to look at improvements in those first and last loops.

The first loop sets each element of **Sieve** to **TRUE** (which has the value 1), but this value is arbitrary. If instead we chose the value zero to represent a pebble, and one the absence of a pebble, then **Sieve** could be declared to be **static** and so automatically set to zeros by the system. Initialization of **static** variables usually takes no execution time as most C compilers put the initial values at the appropriate addresses within the saved, binary image of the program. Therefore these values are put into their variables as part of the process of loading the program. When the program starts execution it has the values already in place.

A modified sieve program that takes advantage of this is shown below, and is the final, fastest version produced. It found and counted the primes less that 10,000 in 0.1 seconds, seven times faster than version one. Attempts to improve further on this, for example by replacing indexing with pointers, did not produce any worthwhile benefit on the computer used for these timings.

```c
#include <stdio.h>
#include <math.h>

#define    MaxPrime     10000
#define    MaxElem      ((MaxPrime + 1)/2 - 1)
#define    SieveSize    (MaxElem + 1)

enum hole  {FULL, EMPTY}

main() {
    int MaxStep, Primes;
    register int  StrikeOut, LatestPrime, i, CurrElem;
    static char Sieve[SieveSize];

    MaxStep = sqrt(MaxPrime);
    CurrElem = 1;  LatestPrime = 3;
    while (LatestPrime <= MaxStep) {
        for (StrikeOut = (LatestPrime*LatestPrime)/2;
            StrikeOut <= MaxElem;
            StrikeOut += LatestPrime
            ) Sieve[StrikeOut] = EMPTY;

        while (Sieve[++CurrElem] == EMPTY);
        LatestPrime = 2*CurrElem + 1;
    }
    for (i = 1, Primes = 1 ; i < SieveSize; ++i)
        if (Sieve[i] == FULL)
            ++Primes;
    printf(  "The number of prime numbers <= %d is %d\n",
            MaxPrime, Primes);
}
```

The moral of this exercise is that after measurements of a program have shown where to concentrate, the largest benefits come from changing the algorithm of that part; the algorithm used is more important than how tightly it is programmed. However, some of the benefits of the earlier changes may disappear on different hardware. For instance, the computer used for these exercises can address single bytes directly; on a word oriented machine it can take longer to refer to a byte than to a whole word. On such a machine it may actually be slower (although it would still save space) to represent **Sieve** as an array of characters.

When measuring a program's speed in this way it is important to realize that the measurements themselves take time; a call to **OnClock** is not free. As an example, suppose you wanted to find the time taken by the statement **x = y**. Obviously it would do no good to write

```
OnClock(0);  x = y;  OffClock(0);
```

because the time taken by the assignment is much less than one second (the unit of measurement for this implementation). Consider:

```
for (i = 1; i < 1000000; ++i) {
    OnClock(0);  x = y;  OffClock(0);
}
```

This is still no good because almost all the time will be spent switching clocks off and on. The next version looks more promising

```
OnClock(0);
for (i = 1; i < 1000000; ++i) x = y;
OffClock(0);
```

but is still no good. Now most of the time will go into the **for** loop; on a typical computer, **x = y** will take two machine instructions and the **for** loop five or six. The next version is likely to give a more reasonable result except with an optimizing compiler:

```
OnClock(0);
for (i = 1; i < 1000000; ++i) {
    x = y;  x = y;  x = y;  x = y;  x = y;  x = y;  x = y;  x = y;  x = y;  x = y;
    x = y;  x = y;  x = y;  x = y;  x = y;  x = y;  x = y;  x = y;  x = y;  x = y;
}
OffClock(0);
```

A good optimizing compiler would recognize that the whole loop can be replaced by a single **x = y** and transform the program back into the original version. This can be very hard to circumvent, and tricks that work will vary from one compiler to another. It will be left to the ingenuity of readers with such compilers to try to find a way around the problem on their particular systems.

14.4.   Other Improvements

If one were to attempt to use the sieve program to find prime numbers on a small computer then the size of the array **Sieve** would become a problem. One character is used for each odd number, and so to find the number of primes less than one million would require half a million characters. Each of those characters only holds the value 0 or 1, and if a character is represented as eight bits, seven-eighths of the storage space is wasted. If economy of space is more important than execution time, then each 'pebble' can be represented as a single bit and an eight-bit character can represent eight pebbles. However it is then necessary to manipulate the individual bits within each character.

To set or test a bit it is necessary to find the array element in which it is located and then to identify the bit within the element. The standard header file **<limits.h>** contains the constant **CHAR_BIT**, which is the number of bits in one character. Using this, the ith bit can be located in element **Sieve[i/CHAR_BIT]** at bit position **i%CHAR_BIT**. A one-bit mask can be made to match the ith bit by shifting 1 left by i places (**1 << i**). Using this mask the required bit can be set to one by using an OR operation (**Element |= (1 << i)**), it can be unset by ANDing with the complement of the mask (**Element &= ~(1 << i)**) and a particular bit can tested by a simple AND (**if (Element & (1 << i)**). (See Appendix 1 for a more detailed discussion of these techniques.)

In the program below these operations are built into the three macros **SetSieveElement**, **UnsetSieveElement** and **IsSetSieveElement**. **UnsetSieveElement** is never used, but is included for the sake of completeness. **MaxElem** has the same meaning as before, but now an element is a bit rather than an array element, and **SieveSize** is the number of array elements needed to hold the required number of bits (the division by two is because even numbers are not represented).

Only one of the bit manipulation macros will be explained as the others all follow the same pattern. To set element i of the sieve it is necessary to set bit **i % CHAR_BIT** of array element **Sieve[i / CHAR_BIT]**. This can be done by ORing the array element with a mask formed by shifting 1 left by **i % CHAR_BIT** places. The final expression is thus (**Sieve[(i)/CHAR_BIT] |= (1 << ((i)%CHAR_BIT)))**), where the extra parentheses around **i** are the usual 'safety net' that should always be enclosed around macro arguments.

The program is:

```
#include <stdio.h>
#include <math.h>
#include <limits.h>

#define   MaxPrime            10000
#define   MaxElem             ((MaxPrime + 1)/2 - 1)
#define   SieveSize           (MaxPrime/(2*CHAR_BIT) + 1)
#define   SetSieveElement(i)  (Sieve[(i)/CHAR_BIT] |= \
                                  (1 << ((i)%CHAR_BIT)))
#define   UnsetSieveElement(i) (Sieve[(i)/CHAR_BIT] &= \
                                  ~(1 << ((i)%CHAR_BIT)))
```

```
#define    IsSetSieveElement(i)    (Sieve[(i)/CHAR_BIT] & \
                                   (1 << ((i)%CHAR_BIT)))

main() {
    register int i, LatestPrime, StrikeOut, CurrElem;
    int Primes, MaxStep;
    static char Sieve[SieveSize];

    MaxStep = sqrt(MaxPrime);
    CurrElem = 1;  LatestPrime = 3;
    while (LatestPrime <= MaxStep) {
        for (StrikeOut = (LatestPrime*LatestPrime)/2;
             StrikeOut <= MaxElem;
             StrikeOut += LatestPrime
            ) SetSieveElement(StrikeOut);

        while (++CurrElem, IsSetSieveElement(CurrElem));
        LatestPrime = 2*CurrElem + 1;
    }

    for (i = 1, Primes = 1; i <= MaxElem; ++i)
        if (!IsSetSieveElement(i))
            ++Primes;

    printf( "The number of prime numbers <= %d is %d\n",
            MaxPrime, Primes);
}
```

Obviously this version of the program will be slower than the earlier versions because of the complicated expressions inside the loops. In fact it took 0.62 seconds, which is still faster than the first, very simple attempt.

Exercise 14.2   The above program can be improved. The final loop, which counts the remaining pebbles, could use the function **BitsIn** from section 9.2. Make this change and measure its effect on performance.

14.5.   Program Testing

Tools such as the clock module can also be used for program testing. When a program is being tested, it is given test data which are intended to show that it behaves according to its specification. Ideal test data would cause a program to follow all possible paths and show that there are no errors on any of them, but this is rarely practicable as the number of paths through any reasonably sized program is huge. It is usually necessary to accept some reduced standard; one commonly adopted is that the test data cause all statements to be executed at least once. This is a minimal, rather than a rigorous requirement but even this level of testing can be difficult to ensure. When statements are buried inside deeply nested conditional statements it is often difficult to be sure that they have been executed.

The clock module counts the invocations of each clock and so can be used to prove that a section of program has been obeyed during a run with a particular set of test data. The fact that a statement has been executed does not prove that it is correct, but one can have no confidence at all in a program which contains important statements which have not been exercised at least once during testing.

Some compilers provide means for making such checks automatically by generating object code which provides instruments for counting executions of sections of the source program. There are also tools which act as pre-processors; they read a C program and generate an equivalent version with the addition of embedded calls to a package such as the clock module. These calls are placed in each section of the program which must be executed sequentially (without branches). For example, a call would appear after an **if** condition, at the start of an **else** block and at the start of each alternative of a switch statement. In the absence of such tools the necessary instrumentation must be inserted by hand, which is a time consuming task but still worth the effort.

Exercise 14.3 The clocks module is more complicated than is necessary for merely counting executions of each of the sections of a program. Write a new module which requires only one action per program section (as opposed to two, **OnClock** and **OffClock**) and which provides a summary of the number of times each section is called during a program execution.

Appendix 1

Number Systems and Operations on Binary Numbers

A1.1.   Conversion between Number Systems

The number system we all use is based on the number ten and is called decimal or denary. The number 169, in this system, is short for $(100 \times 1) + (10 \times 6) + (1 \times 9)$.

We say that 169 here is in *base 10* and we can emphasize that by writing it 169_{10}. The same principle can be applied to other bases and computer programmers often use bases of 8 and 16, while computers use base 2.

To illustrate the octal system (base 8), the number 347_8 (pronounced 'three four seven base eight', **not** 'three hundred and forty seven base eight') is $(64 \times 3) + (8 \times 4) + (1 \times 7)$ or in decimal notation 231. Notice that the octal digit positions represent not units, tens and hundreds but units, eights and sixty-fours $(64 = 8^2)$. In an octal system there are only the eight digits 0, 1, 2, 3, 4, 5, 6 and 7.

The binary system (base 2) only has two digits, 0 and 1, and is used in computers because it is cheap to make electronic circuits which have only two states. The binary number $1101_2 = 8 \times 1 + 4 \times 1 + 2 \times 0 + 1 \times 1 = 13$. When working with binary numbers it is useful to keep a table of powers of two handy. Up to fifteen, these are

$2^0 = 1$	$2^4 = 16$	$2^8 = 256$	$2^{12} = 4096$
$2^1 = 2$	$2^5 = 32$	$2^9 = 512$	$2^{13} = 8192$
$2^2 = 4$	$2^6 = 64$	$2^{10} = 1024$	$2^{14} = 16384$
$2^3 = 8$	$2^7 = 128$	$2^{11} = 2048$	$2^{15} = 32768$

With this table, conversion from binary to decimal is easy. Counting from the right, the digits of a binary number represent $2^0, 2^1, 2^3, 2^4$ and so on. Therefore conversion involves just adding up the powers of two corresponding to the one-bits in the binary number. For example, $10101_2 = 1 + 4 + 16 = 21$.

The reverse operation involves breaking a number down into a sum of powers of two. For instance, $37 = 32 + 4 + 1 = 100101_2$.

Because binary numbers are unwieldy when written, if they have to be read or manipulated by humans they are usually translated into octal (base 8) or hexadecimal (base 16). These bases are chosen because conversion from either to binary is very simple. Each octal digit represents a group of three bits, and each hexadecimal digit represents four bits. Octal to binary translation uses the following table:

$0_8 = 000_2$	$1_8 = 001_2$	$2_8 = 010_2$	$3_8 = 011_2$
$4_8 = 100_2$	$5_8 = 101_2$	$6_8 = 110_2$	$7_8 = 111_2$

To convert an octal number to binary, substitute the appropriate three bits for each octal digit. Thus, $7245_8 = 111\ 010\ 100\ 101_2$. For the reverse process group the binary digits in threes and substitute the corresponding octal digit.

The hexadecimal (base 16) system is nowadays used more often than octal. In this system there are sixteen symbols representing the numbers 0 to 15. The digits 0 to 9 are written in the usual way, and then 10, 11, 12, 13, 14 and 15 are represented by A, B, C, D, E and F respectively. The positions of hexadecimal digits represent successive powers of 16, i.e. units, 16s, 256s etc. As an example, the number $B5_{16} = 11 \times 16 + 5 = 181$. Conversion from hexadecimal to binary uses the following table:

$0_{16} = 0000_2$	$1_{16} = 0001_2$	$2_{16} = 0010_2$	$3_{16} = 0011_2$
$4_{16} = 0100_2$	$5_{16} = 0101_2$	$6_{16} = 0110_2$	$7_{16} = 0111_2$
$8_{16} = 1000_2$	$9_{16} = 1001_2$	$A_{16} = 1010_2$	$B_{16} = 1011_2$
$C_{16} = 1100_2$	$D_{16} = 1101_2$	$E_{16} = 1110_2$	$F_{16} = 1111_2$

To convert a hexadecimal number to binary substitute the appropriate four bits for each hexadecimal digit. Thus the hexadecimal number $A68B_{16} = 1010\ 0110\ 1000\ 1011_2$. For the reverse process group binary digits in fours and substitute the equivalent hexadecimal digit.

A1.2. Negative Numbers

If a number is declared as **unsigned**, there is no need to represent negative values. In this case the largest possible value has ones in all bit positions. For example, on a sixteen bit computer the largest unsigned value is $1111\ 1111\ 1111\ 1111_2$ which is 65535_{10}. However, for a signed integer value the same bit pattern would (on most machines) represent -1.

The left-most bit of a signed value is called the *sign-bit*, with zero indicating positive and one indicating negative. However, a number cannot be made negative just by reversing the sign bit. Computers use what is known as one's-complement or two's-complement notations.

In one's-complement notation the negative of a number is formed by reversing all its bits, so that +17 is represented as 0000 0000 0001 0001 and reversing all the bits gives us -17, which is 1111 1111 1110 1110. In this notation the largest positive value on a 16-bit machine is the bit pattern 0111 1111 1111 (32767 in decimal), and the most negative value is 1000 000 000 000 (-32767 in decimal). Few computers use one's-complement notation to represent integers because it has two representations for zero, namely 0000 0000 0000 0000 and 1111 1111 1111 1111. Instead two's-complement is favored.

In two's-complement notation the negative of a number is formed by reversing all the bits and then then adding one to the result. The table below shows some values on a sixteen bit computer

32767	0111 1111 1111 1111
2	0000 0000 0000 0010
1	0000 0000 0000 0001
0	0000 0000 0000 0000
-1	1111 1111 1111 1111
-2	1111 1111 1111 1110
-32767	1000 0000 0000 0001
-32768	1000 0000 0000 0000

Notice that the most negative value has a larger absolute magnitude than the most positive value. Notice also that overflowing (trying to produce a value out of the range of integers) will, unless detected by the system, produce a result of the wrong sign. For example, adding 1 to 32767 will produce 1000 0000 0000 0000, which is -32768. If your C system does not detect such errors automatically, and many do not, then the error can be very hard to find by hand.

A1.3.   Bitwise Operations

The bitwise operations on whole integers are AND, INCLUSIVE OR, EXCLUSIVE OR and COMPLEMENT (otherwise known as NOT). In C these operations can be invoked by using the operators &, |, ^ and ~ respectively. The operands are usually unsigned **char**, **int** or **long int**, although signed values can be used.

The following truth table illustrates the operations on individual bits **a** and **b**.

a	b	a & b	a | b	a ^ b	~a
0	0	0	0	0	1
0	1	0	1	1	1
1	0	0	1	1	0
1	1	1	1	0	0

The bitwise AND operation between two operands produces a resulting bit pattern which has a one-bit only at the positions where *both* operands have one-bits. A bitwise INCLUSIVE OR operation produces a pattern with a one-bit where *either* operand has a one bit. A bitwise EXCLUSIVE OR operation produces a pattern with a one-bit where *either* operand has a one bit, but *not both*. A COMPLEMENT operation reverses the value of each bit.

Assuming **v1** and **v2** are eight-bit quantities, the example below illustrates these operations.

```
       v1   =   0101 1101
       v2   =   1101 0111
    v1 & v2  =   0101 0101

    v1 | v2  =   1101 1111
    v1 ^ v2  =   1000 1010
     ~ v1   =   1010 0010
```

A1.4. Shift Operations

Shift operations on bit patterns are classified as logical, arithmetic and rotational, but C does not provide all these. Consider the bit pattern

```
0101 1101
```

A logical shift moves the whole pattern, with the bits moving off one end being discarded and zeros being added at the other end. A logical left shift of three places on the above pattern produces

```
1110 1000
```

The shift operations of C (<< and >>) produce logical shifts if the left operand has an unsigned type (**unsigned int**, **unsigned long int** etc.).

In a logical shift the whole group of bits being moved are treated as an unsigned quantity. Arithmetic shifts, on the other hand, consider the left-most bit to be a sign bit. Different computers implement arithmetic shifts in different ways, but a common approach is to move all the bits except the sign bit, on a left shift moving in zeros from the right, and on a right shift copying the sign bit into the positions vacated on the left. For example, if the sixteen-bit word

$$1111\ 1111\ 1111\ 1100$$

which represents the value -4, is shifted right arithmetically by one position the result will be

$$1111\ 1111\ 1111\ 1110$$

which is -2. A left arithmetic shift by one position is equivalent to multiplying by 2, and a right shift produces division by 2. For negative numbers the result can vary between implementations and is not specified by the C language.

In some implementations of C the operators << and >> provide arithmetic shifts if the left operand is a signed type, but this is not guaranteed by the ANSI standard. However, it is guaranteed that in a shift expression of the form $v << n$, where v is a signed, positive value, the result will equal v times 2^n, provided overflow does not occur. Similarly the expression $v >> n$ produces v divided by 2^n. In all such expressions the action is not defined if n is negative. In general you can only be sure of your result if v is unsigned, or signed but positive, and if n is not negative.

A rotational shift of a bit pattern causes bits lost at one end to reappear at the other. For example, if the pattern

$$1101\ 1011\ 0011\ 1110$$

is rotated right by five places the result is

$$1111\ 0110\ 1101\ 1001$$

Unfortunately C does not provide rotational shift operators; if needed the effect must be achieved rather clumsily by combining logical shifts and bitwise operations.

Appendix 2

Solutions to Selected Exercises

An alternative version of a function to compare two lists:

```
ListsAreEqual(ListNode *List1, ListNode *List2) {
    return( (List1 == List2)
        ||  (((List1 != NULL) && (List2 != NULL))
            &&    ((List1 -> Value) == (List2 -> Value))
            && ListsAreEqual(List1 -> Next, List2 -> Next)
            )
        );
}
```

Exercise 8.1

A tree structure can be printed by using a pre-order traversal e.g.

```
void SubPrintTree(TreeNode *t, int Level) {
    int Space;
    for (Space = 1; Space <= Level; ++Space)
        printf("   ");
    if (t == NULL )
        printf("- - -\n");
    else{
        printf("%s\n", t -> Value);
        SubPrintTree(t -> Left, Level + 1);
        SubPrintTree(t -> Right, Level + 1);
    }
}
```

```
void PrintTree(TreeNode *t) {
    SubPrintTree(t, 0);
}
```

The extra function **SubPrintTree** is a subordinate function called by **PrintTree**, in order that the depth of a node can be passed as a parameter.

Exercise 12.1

A program to recognize correct bracket sequences:

```
#include "Astack.h"
#include <stdio.h>
main() {
    Stack Brackets;
    char ch, Left;
    int Error = 0;

    InitStack(&Brackets, 50);
    while (ch = getchar(), ch != '\n' && Error == 0) {
        if (ch == '(' || ch == '[' || ch == '<' || ch == '{')
            Push(ch, &Brackets);
        else if (ch == ')' || ch == ']' || ch == '>' || ch == '}') {
            if (StackEmpty(Brackets))
                Error = 1;
            else {
                Left = Pop(&Brackets);
                if (!(ch == ')' && Left == '(' || ch == ']' && Left == '[' ||
                    ch == '>' && Left == '<' || ch == '}' && Left == '{'))
                    Error = 2;
            }
        }
        else
            Error = 3;
    }
    if (Error == 0 && !StackEmpty(Brackets))
        Error = 4;

    switch (Error) {
        case 0:printf("The sentence was correct\n");     break;
        case 1:printf("Too many right brackets\n");      break;
        case 2:printf("Bracket mismatch\n");             break;
        case 3:printf("Incorrect character\n");          break;
        case 4:printf("Too few right brackets\n");       break;
    }

}
```

Appendix 3

The Standard Library

The ANSI standard requires that certain header files be available to define standard macros, constants, types and functions. In order to use something declared in a header file it should be included in a program with a **#include** statement before using any of its contents. The most important header files and their contents are given below.

< assert.h >
This defines only one macro, **assert** which is used to test programs. It is defined as follows:

> void assert(int expression)
>> If **expression** gives a zero result then the program will abort after producing a message in the style

>> Assertion failed: **expression**, file **filename**, line **line number**

>> If the constant **NDEBUG** is defined then the macro will be ignored. For a full description of the use of the **assert** macro see section 11.8.

< ctype.h >
The functions or macros defined in **<ctype.h>** are all used to test characters or to change the case of letters. They are described in section 5.1. The character testing functions are:

isalnum(c)	c is alphabetic or a digit
isalpha(c)	c is alphabetic
isascii(c)	c has a value in the range 0…127
iscntrl(c)	c is a control character
isdigit(c)	c is a digit

219

isgraph(c)	c is a printable character other than space
isprint(c)	c is a printable character including space
ispunct(c)	c is printable but not a letter, digit or space
isspace(c)	c is 'white space' (space, tab, vertical tab, newline, return, formfeed.)
isxdigit(c)	c is a hexadecimal digit (0...9, A...F, a...f)

The letter-case changing functions are:

tolower(c)	converts c to lower case if it is an upper case letter.
toupper(c)	converts c to upper case if it is a lower case letter.

\<errno.h\>

Many of the file manipulation functions detect error conditions such as attempting to read beyond the end of a file. **\<errno.h\>** contains the definition of a variable called **errno** which holds a number corresponding to the most recent error. The actual value that **errno** will hold for a particular error depends upon the implementation.

The file also contains the constants **EDOM** and **ERANGE**, which are, respectively, the values used to indicate a domain error (an argument to a function outside the acceptable range) and a value returned from a function outside the possible range of a **double** value.

\<float.h\>

This header contains constants which relate to the representation of floating point numbers such as the accuracy or maximum value. In the lists below, which give the most important of the constants, where a value is given, it represents the smallest permissible value for a constant under the ANSI standard.

FLT_DIG	6	The number of decimal digits of precision of floating point numbers
FLT_EPSILON	1e-5	The smallest value v where $1.0 + v > 1.0$
FLT_MAX	1e+37	The largest floating point value
FLT_MIN	1e-37	The smallest normalized floating point value
FLT_RADIX	2	The radix of the exponent
DBL_DIG	10	The number of decimal digits of precision of double precision numbers
DBL_EPSILON	1e-9	The smallest value v where $1.0 + v > 1.0$
DBL_MAX	1e+37	The largest **double** value
DBL_MIN	1e-37	The smallest normalized **double** value

<limits.h>

This header provides constants giving information about the representation of integer types. Where a value is given, it represents the smallest permissible value for a constant under the ANSI standard. The constants are:

CHAR_BIT	8	The number of bits in a **char**
CHAR_MAX		The maximum value of a **char**
CHAR_MIN	0 or SCHAR_MAN	The minimum value of a **char**
SCHAR_MAX	127	The maximum value of a **signed char**
SCHAR_MIN	-127	The minimum value of a **signed char**
UCHAR_MAX	255U	The maximum value of an **unsigned char**

<math.h>

This header provides prototypes for the following mathematical functions. The trigonometric functions (all with arguments in radians):

```
double sin(double x);
double cos(double x);
double tan(double x);
```

The inverse trigonometric functions giving a result in radians:

```
double asin(double  x);
double acos(double  x);
double atan(double  x);
```

The hyperbolic functions:

```
double sinh(double  x)
double cosh(double  x);
double tanh(double  x);
```

and some general mathematical functions:

double exp(double x);	The exponential function e^x.
double log(double x);	The natural logarithm of **x**.
double log10(double x);	The logarithm to base ten of **x**.
double pow(double x, double y);	x^y where **x** and **y** are both of type **float**.
double ceil(double x);	The smallest whole number greater than **x** (note that the result is **double**).
double floor(double x);	The largest whole number smaller than **x**.

double sqrt(double x);	The square root of **x**.
double fabs(double (x);	The absolute (i.e. positive) value of **x** where **x** is **float**.
int abs(int i);	The absolute (i.e. positive) value of **i**.
double fmod(double x, double y);	The remainder of **x/y**.

\<setjmp.h\>

Sometimes it is difficult to return from deeply nested function calls when some exceptional condition, such as error being detected, occurs. A **goto** statement cannot be used because such a statement must be in the same function as the label to which it jumps. **\<setjmp.h\>** provides a suitable mechanism for escaping from a function. It defines a type **jmp_buf** which is used to declare an array to hold environment information. The function (or macro) **setjmp** saves the current environment in a variable of type **jmp_buf** and establishes a destination to which a subsequent call of **longjmp** will return. The return value of **setjmp** is zero when it is called directly.

A call of **longjmp** does not return to the statement following the call, but to the statement following a **setjmp** call. The following program illustrates the mechanism.

```c
#include <setjmp.h>
#include <stdio.h>

jmp_buf environment;

int ReadIntInRange(int low, int high) {
    int i;
    scanf("%d", &i);
    if (i < low)
        longjmp(environment, 1);
    else if (i > high)
        longjmp(environment, 2);
    else
        return(i);
}

int main() {
    int i;
    switch (setjmp(environment)) {
    case 0: /* Return here on a direct call of setjmp */
            i = ReadIntInRange(1, 5);
            printf("Returned value is %d\n", i);
            break;
    case 1: printf("Value too low\n");  break;
    case 2:printf("Value too high\n");  break;
    }
}
```

The call to **setjmp** in the **switch** statement returns the value zero and saves the necessary information in **environment**. The calls to **longjump** from the function **ReadIntInRange** specify the environment to which to return and the value to be returned by **setjmp**.

The prototypes for **setjmp** and **longjmp** are:

```
int setjmp(jmp_buf environment);

void longjmp(jmp_buf environment, int ReturnValue);
```

A direct call of **setjmp** returns zero. A call of **setjmp** via **longjmp** causes **setjmp** to return **ReturnValue** except in the special case when **ReturnValue** is zero, when it returns an undefined, non-zero value.

<signal.h>

Certain types of program need to respond to events which may be generated either externally or internally. In some languages, Ada being the best known example, such events are called *exceptions*. An external event might be an interrupt from a peripheral, and an internally generated event could be the detection of an error condition (overflow or violation of memory limits for example).

The header **<signal.h>** declares two functions, **raise** and **signal** respectively to raise an exception and to respond to one. It also provides some constants to indicate the type of an exception and three pointers to functions, **SIG_DFL**, **SIG_IGN**, and **SIG_ERR**. The defined constants are all integers and their interpretations are:

SIGABRT	A call of **abort**, or a similar abnormal termination
SIGFPE	A floating point error such as overflow
SIGILL	An illegal instruction
SIGINT	An external interrupt
SIGSEGV	Illegal memory reference e.g. reference above memory limit
SIGTERM	This program has been requested to terminate

Implementations may add other constants to this list.

The three function pointers, which are intended to be used as parameters to **signal**, are **SIG_DFL**, which is the default, implementation-defined action, **SIG_IGN** meaning that the signal should be ignored, and **SIG_ERR**, which is the return value from **signal** if an error occurs.

The definition of **signal** is:

```
void (*signal(int sig, void (*func)(int))) (int);
```

where **sig** is one of the constants defined above, or some other, implementation,or user defined, constant, and **func** is a function to be called corresponding to the signal **sig**.

<stdarg.h>

This header gives facilities for implementing functions with a variable number of arguments. It is described in detail in section 3.8 and defines the type **va_list** and the macros:

```
void va_start(va_list ap, param);
void va_end(va_list ap);
type va_arg(va_list ap, type);
```

The **va_list ap** is initialised by a call to **va_start** with **param** being the last fixed function parameter. Successive calls of **va_arg** return the subsequent arguments from the variable part of the parameter list. **va_end** is called when the complete list has been processed.

<stddef.h>

This header defines a number of system dependent types. These are

```
wchar_t
size_t
ptrdiff_t
```

In some implementations there is an extended character set which cannot be represented by the type **char**. The type **wchar_t** is used to represent such characters. **size_t** is the result type of **size_of**, and **ptrdiff_t** is an integer type able to hold the signed difference of two pointer values.

<stdio.h>

The functions defined by this header are listed in Chapter 13.

<stdlib.h>

This header contains definitions of many general purpose functions. They are:

double atof(const char *s)

Converts the string **s** to a floating point value.

int atoi(const char *s)

Converts the string **s** to an integer value.

long atol(const char *s)

Converts the string **s** to a long integer value.

double strtod(const char *s, char ** suffix)

Converts the initial section of s to a double, floating point value. It ignores leading white space characters. **suffix** will be left pointing to the portion of s after the converted text, if there is any, unless **suffix** is **NULL**. If the result would overflow then the returned value will be **HUGE_VAL**, with the correct sign. If the result would underflow then zero is returned. In either case **errno** is set to **ERANGE**.

long strtol(const char *s, char **suffix, int base);

Converts the initial section of **s** to a long integer value. It ignores leading white space characters. **suffix** will be left pointing to the portion of s after the converted text, if there is any, unless **suffix** is **NULL**. If the result would overflow then the returned value will be **LONG_MAX** or **LONG_MIN**, depending upon the sign. In this case **errno** is set to **ERANGE**. If **base** is between 2 and 36 the contents of **s** will be treated as being a number in that base. The letters a - z and A - Z stand for the digits after 9 when **base** is greater than 10. If **base** is 0 then the contents of **s** are treated as being in base 8, 10 or 16, according to whether the number starts with 0, a non-zero digit or 0x, respectively.

unsigned long stroul(const char *s, char **suffix, int base);

Identical to **strtol** except that the result is an unsigned long integer. If overflow occurs the result is **ULONG_MAX**.

void * malloc(size_t size);

Generates space on the heap for **size** bytes and returns a pointer to it. If the space cannot be generated then the result will be **NULL**. The space generated will not be initialized.

void * calloc(size_t number, size_t size);

Generates space on the heap for **number** objects each of **size** bytes and returns a pointer to it. If the space cannot be generated then the result will be **NULL**. The space generated will be initialized to zero.

void * realloc(void *obj, size_t size);

Changes the size of the space pointed to by **obj** to **size** bytes. The contents of the space will be unchanged, unless the new object is smaller than the old, in which case the last part will be lost. If the new object is larger than the original the extra space will not be initialized. If the reallocation succeeds the result is a pointer to the new space, and if it fails it is **NULL**.

void free(void *obj);

> Releases the space pointed to by **obj**, which must have been created by a previous call of **malloc**, **calloc** or **realloc**.

void abort(void);

> Causes the program to terminate abnormally. The action will depend upon the system, but normally an error message would be produced.

void exit(int status);

> Terminates the program normally. Open files will be closed and any functions registered with **atexit** will be called in reverse order of registration. A zero value of **status** is normally taken to be a signal to the operating system that the program has executed successfully. The effect of other values depends upon the system.

int atexit(void (*func) (void));

> Registers **func** so that it will be called before the termination of the program. It returns zero if the registration is successful and a non-zero value otherwise.

int system(const char *command);

> Passes **command** to the operating system for execution. Not all systems have a command processor. This can be determined by passing **NULL** as the value of **command** in which case a return value of zero indicates that there is no command processor.

int rand(void);

> Returns an integer randomly selected from the range 0 to **MAX_RAND**. The smallest permissible value of **MAX_RAND** is 32767.

void srand(unsigned int seed);

> Sets the seed used for generating random numbers returned by **rand**. It is important to realize that numbers generated by **rand** are pseudo-random. This means that the sequence is not truly random, although it will satisfy certain tests of randomness. In particular, for an initial value of a seed the sequence of numbers produced by **rand** will be the same. Changing the seed makes **rand** produce a different, but nevertheless determined, sequence. The initial, default seed is 1.

int abs(int n);

> Returns the absolute value (positive value) of **n**.

long labs(long n);

    Returns the absolute value (positive value) of the long integer **n**.

div_t div(int numerator, int denominator);

    The type **div_t** is a structure having two integer members **quot** and **rem**. The function **div** divides **numerator** by **denominator** and the result of the function, of type **div_t**, will have the quotient in its **quot** member and the remainder in the **rem** member.

ldiv_t ldiv(long numerator, long denominator);

    The same as **div**, except that the arguments are long integers, and the members of an **ldiv_t** are long integers.

void qsort(void *array, size_t NoElements, size_t size,
                    int (*compare)(const void *, const void *));

    See section 10.3.

void bsearch(const void *key, const void *array, size_t NoElements, size_t size,
                    int (*compare)(const void *, const void *));

    See section 10.3.

<string.h>

This header defines functions for manipulating strings and for copying arrays. It also defines the constant **NULL** and the type **size_t**. Many of the functions are discussed in detail in section 5.2. The array copying functions are:

void *memcpy(void *a1, const void *a2, size_t n);

    Copies **n** characters from **a2** to **a1**. It returns a pointer to **a1**. The arrays **a1** and **a2** must not overlap.

void *memmove(void *a1, const void a2, size_t n);

    Identical to **memcpy** except that **a1** and **a2** may overlap.

char *strcpy(char *s1, const char *s2);

    Copies the string pointed by **s2** to **s1**, including the terminating '\0'. It returns a pointer to **s1.**

char *strncpy(char *s1, const char *s2, size_t n);

    Copies up to **n** characters from **s2** to **s1**. If **s2** contains fewer than **n** characters then the remainder of **s1** will be filled with '\0'.

The concatenation functions are:

char *strcat(char *s1, const char *s2);
> Concatenates a copy of **s2** onto the end of **s1** and returns **s1**. The first character of **s2** replaces the character '\0' at the end of **s1**.

char *strncat(char *s1, const char *s2, size_t n);
> Concatenates up to **n** characters from **s2** onto **s1** and returns a pointer to **s1**.

The functions for comparing arrays and strings are:

int strcmp(const char *s1, const char *s2);
> Compares **s1** with **s2** and returns a negative number if **s1** < **s2**, zero if **s1** = **s2** and a positive number if **s1** > **s2**.

int strncmp(const char *s1, const char *s2, size_t n);
> Compares up to **n** characters of **s1** with **s2** and returns a negative number if **s1** < **s2**, zero if **s1** = **s2** and a positive number if **s1** > **s2**.

int memcmp(const void *a1, const void *a2, size_t n);
> Compares up to **n** characters of **a1** with **a2**. The return value is the same as for **strcmp**.

The string search functions are:

void *memchr(const void *s, int uc, size_t n);
> Returns a pointer to the first occurrence of **uc**, treated as an **unsigned char**, within **s**. If **uc** does not occur within the first **n** characters of **s** then the return value will be **NULL**.

char *strchr(const char *s, int c);
> Returns a pointer to the first occurrence of **c**, treated as a char, within **s**. If **c** does not occur within the first **n** characters of **s** then the return value will be **NULL**.

char *strpbrk(const char *s1, const char s2);
> Returns a pointer to the first occurrence of any character from **s2** in the string **s1**. If none of the characters in **s2** occur in **s1** then the return value will be **NULL**.

char *strrchr(const char *s, int c);
> Returns a pointer to the last occurrence of **c**, treated as a char, within **s**. If **c** does not occur in **s** then the return value will be **NULL**.

size_t strspn(const char *s1, const char *s2);

> Returns the length of the substring at the beginning of **s1** which consists entirely of characters from **s2**.

size_t strcspn(const char *s1, const char *s2);

> Returns the length of the substring at the beginning of **s1** which does not consist of characters from **s2**.

char *strstr(const char *s1, const char *s2);

> Returns a pointer to the first occurrence of **s2** within **s1**, or **NULL** if it is not present.

char *strtok(char *s1, const char *s2);

> Breaks **s1** into tokens which are identified by being delimited by characters from **s2**. **strtok** must be called once for each token. The first call specifies the string **s1** to be analyzed and if subsequent calls have a **NULL** first parameter then **strtok** will continue to work on the same string. For example, if the variable **text** points to the string:

> > Three be the things I shall never attain:
> >   envy, content and sufficient champagne.

> and **delims** contains ', :.' (comma, space, colon and period) the call

> > s = strtok(text, delims);

> will leave **s** pointing to **'Three'** and replace the space after the first word with the null character. Then a call

> > s = strtok(NULL, delims);

> sets **s** to point to **'be'** and its following space to null. This can be continued until **text** is exhausted, when **strtok** returns **NULL**.

The remaining functions are:

void *memset(void *a, int uc, size_t n);

> Copies **uc** (as an unsigned char) into each of the first **n** characters of **a**.

char *strerror(int n);

> Returns a pointer to an error message corresponding to error **n**.

size_t strlen(const char *s);

    Returns the length of the string **s**.

<time.h>

This header defines types, macros and functions for manipulating time. The types **clock_t** and **time_t** are arithmetic types representing times. There is also a structure **struct tm**, used to hold components of the calendar time and which has the following members (at least), all of which have type **int**:

tm_sec	seconds after the minute (0...59)
tm_min	minutes after the hour (0...59)
tm_hour	hours since midnight (0...23)
tm_mday	day of the month (1...31)
tm_mon	months since January (0...11)
tm_year	years since 1900
tm_wday	days since Sunday (0...6)
tm_yday	days since January 1st (0...365)
tm_isdst	Daylight Saving flag

tm_isdt is positive when daylight saving time is in effect, is zero when not, and negative if the information is not available. The functions are given below.

clock_t clock(void);

    Returns the processor time used by the program since execution started or -1 if it not available. The units are such that dividing by the constant **CLK_TCK** gives a time in seconds.

double difftime(time_t time1, time_t time2);

    Returns the difference, in seconds, of the two times **time1** and **time2**.

time_t mktime(struct tm *TimePtr);

    Converts the local time represented by **TimePtr** into a **time_t**.

time_t time(time_t *TimePtr);

    Returns the current time, or -1 if it not available. It is not specified how a time is encoded as a **time_t**.

char *asctime(const struct tm *TimePtr);

    Converts the time represented by **TimePtr** to a string in the style:

        Sun Nov 18 11:25:30 1990\n\0

char *ctime(const time_t *TimePtr);
>   The same as **asctime** but its parameter is a **time_t**.

struct tm *gmtime(const time_t *TimePtr);
>   Converts **TimePtr** to Coordinated Universal Time (UTC), also known as Greenwich Mean Time, and returns the converted value.

struct tm *localtime(const time_t *TimePtr);
>   Converts the **TimePtr** value **time_t** to a **struct_tm**.

size_t strftime(char *s, size_t MaxSize, const char *format, const struct tm *TimePtr);
>   Formats and converts **TimePtr** into a string **s**. **MaxSize** is the maximum number of characters to be placed in **s**, and **format** is a string, in a style similar to a **printf** format, and is described below. The returned value is the number of characters placed in **s**, excluding the terminating '\0', unless that tries to exceed **MaxSize**, in which case it is zero. Characters in the format string, as with **printf**, are converted directly into **s**, unless they are conversion sequences; these are:

%a	The abbreviated weekday name.
%A	The full weekday name.
%b	The abbreviated month name.
%B	The full month name.
%c	The appropriate representation of date and time.
%d	The day of the month in the range 01...31.
%H	The hour on a 24 hour clock in the range 00...23.
%I	The hour on a 12 hour clock in the range 01...12
%j	The day of the year in the range 001...366.
%m	The month as a decimal number in the range 01...12.
%M	The minute as a decimal number in the range 00...59.
%p	The local version of AM or PM.
%S	The second as a decimal number in the range 00...59.
%U	The week number, 1st Sunday starts week 1, in the range 00...53
%w	The week day, Sunday being 0, in the range 0...6.
%W	The week number, 1st Monday starts week 1, in the range 00...53
%x	The local date representation.
%X	The local time representation.
%y	The year without the century, in the range 00...99.
%Y	The year with the century.
%Z	The name of the time zone, or no characters if not available.
%%	%

Appendix 4

Standard Operators

Below are all the operators grouped by class; **l** represents a left operand, **r** a right operand and **m** a middle operand.

Postfix monadic operators:

l++	Post-increment. **l** is incremented by one but the value delivered by the operator is the original value of **l**. Thus, after **b = 27; a = b++;** the value of **b** would be 28 and **a** would be 27.
l--	Post-decrement. Like **++** but **l** is decremented. In this case **b = 27; a = b--;** would leave **b** equal to 26 and **a** equal to 27.
(...)	Function arguments **sin(x)** presents the argument **x** to the function **sin**.
[...]	Array subscript. **table[j]** selects the jth element from the array **table**.
.	Select a member from a structure, e.g. **Mercury.Diameter** selects the member **Diameter** from the structure **Mercury**.
->	Select a member from a pointer to a structure, e.g. **Turn->Right** selects the member **Right** from the structure pointed to by the pointer variable **Turn**.

Prefix monadic operators:

+	Monadic plus. **+i** yields **i** without change.
-	Monadic minus. **p = -q;** copies the negative of the value of **q** into **p**.
++r	Pre-increment. **b = 27; a = ++b;** would leave **b** equal to 28 and **a** equal to 28.

--r	Pre-decrement.
	b = 27; a = --b; leaves **b** equal to 26 and **a** equal to 26.
!	Logical negation. **while (!FALSE) ...** is equivalent to
	while (TRUE) ....
~	Bitwise complement
	word = ~000377; would leave **word** with the value 0177400 on a 16-bit machine. Note that the values are in octal because of the leading zero.
&	Address of a variable. e.g. **p = &q;** puts the address of **q** into **p.**
*	Indirection. **q = *p;** would put into **q** the contents of the location pointed by **p.**
sizeof	Number of bytes needed to store an object. **sizeof(int)** gives the number bytes required for an **int**.
(type)	A cast to convert operand type. **x = sin((float)i);** converts an integer variable **i** to floating point before passing it to the **sin** function.

Diadic operators all associate left-right and are grouped below in descending order of priority. They have a lower priority than the monadic operators.

* / %	Multiplication, division and modulus. If both operands of / are integer, then the division will be integer division but if either operand is of type **float** then floating point division is used.
+ -	Addition and subtraction.
>> <<	Right shift and left shift. The result of **0377 >> 2** is 077, that is, the bit pattern of 0377 shifted right by two places. See Chapter 9 for more information.
< <= > >=	Less than, less than or equal, greater than, greater than or equal.
== !=	Equal, not equal.
&	Bitwise and. See Chapter 9 for more details.
^	Bitwise exclusive or. See Chapter 9 for more details.
|	Bitwise inclusive or. See Chapter 9 for more details.
&&	Logical and.
||	Logical or.

Triadic condition operator ? : is the only operator which takes three operands. The style in which it used is **left ? mid : right**. If **left** is non-zero (representing TRUE) then the operator delivers the value of **mid** and otherwise it delivers **right**.

Assignment operators all have equal priority and associate right-left. They each change the value of the left-hand operand which must be a variable; the right-hand operand is an expression. Each operator also yields a value, which is the value assigned to the left operand, e.g. **q = 27; p = 2*(q += 3);** will leave **q** holding the value 30 and **p** with the value 60. Some of the operators manipulate bit patterns; see Appendix 1 for an explanation of binary numbers. The assignment operators are:

= Assign the value of the right operand to the left operand. **a = 27;** puts the value 27 into **a**.

+= Add the right operand to the left operand. **p = 4; p += 2;** leaves **p** holding the value 6 and is short for **p = p + 2**.

-= Subtract the right operand from the left operand. **p = 4; p -= 2;** leaves **p** holding the value 2.

*= Multiply the left operand by the right operand. **p = 4; p *= 2;** leaves **p** holding the value 8.

/= Divide the left operand by the right operand. **p = 4; p /= 2;** leaves **p** holding the value 2.

%= Replace the left operand by the remainder of the left operand divided by the right operand. **p = 5; p %= 2;** leaves **p** holding the value 1.

<<= Shift the bit pattern of the left operand by **r** bit positions to the left where **r** is the value of the right operand. For example, **Pattern <<= 5;**

>>= Shift the bit pattern of the left operand by **r** bit positions to the right where **r** is the value of the right operand. For example, **Pattern >>= 5;**

&= Form the bitwise and of the left and right operands and replace the left operand with the result. For example, **ch &= 0177** leaves the seven least significant bits of **ch** unchanged but sets the rest to zero.

|= Form the bitwise inclusive or of the left and right operands and replace the left operand with the result. For example, **ch |= 0200** forces bit eight of **ch** to be a one.

^= Form the bitwise exclusive or of the left and right operands and replace the left operand with the result. For example, **ch ^= 0177** will reverse the last seven bits of **ch**; in other words, the one-bits become zeros and the zero-bits change to ones.

Sequence operator , (comma) has the lowest priority. It associates left-right and its purpose is to ensure that the left operand will be evaluated before the right operand. The result it yields is the value of its right-hand operand. For example:

p = (total = 1 + 2 + 3,   square = total*total)*2;

would leave 6 in **total**, 36 in **square** and 72 in **p**. It as the same effect as:

total = 1 + 2 + 3;
square = total*total;
p = square*2;

Bibliography

BOYE 77   'A Fast String Searching Algorithm'
               Boyer, Robert S. and Moore, J. Strother
               Communications of the A.C.M.
               Vol. 20   p. 762   Oct. 1977

KER 78   *The C Programming Language*
               Kernighan, B.W. and Ritchie, D.M.
               Prentice Hall 1978

KOEN 89   *C Traps and Pitfalls*
               Andrew Koenig
               Addison-Wesley 1989

STRO 86   *The C++ Programming Language*
               Stroustrup, B.
               Addison-Wesley 1986

TAN 81   *Computer Networks*
               Andrew S. Tannenbaum
               Prentice Hall 1981

Index